Pick of
PUNCH

'Giles!'   'Amanda!'

Pick of PUNCH

Edited by David Thomas

1990

A PUNCH BOOK
Published in association with **GRAFTON BOOKS**

'Tragic case — three years ago he forgot his PIN number'

Grafton Books
A Division of the Collins Publishing Group
8 Grafton Street, London W1X 3LA

Published by Grafton Books 1990

Copyright © Punch Publications 1990

A CIP catalogue record for this book is available from the British Library

ISBN 0-246-13652-9

Designed by Chris J. Bailey

Printed in Great Britain by
William Collins Sons & Co. Ltd, Westerhill, Glasgow

CONTENTS

'But have you thought what it might do to the environment?'

'A Harvey Wallbanger for me and a Harvey Doppelgänger for him.'

'Gee, I dunno – those clouds look threatening'

'Oh dear, I had a feeling the cat might contest.'

HAROLD:REX:INTERFEC-TVS:EST

ET FVGA:VERTERVNT ANGLI WILLIAM EST ET OMNIA VICTOR QVOD FEMINA AMAT

MILK TRAY

M.PICKLES 85

Apologies to Goya

'I think you've had enough there, sir.'

'*Good Lord, Robinson! I never realised you were a freemason.*'

'This is serious – even Shit Creek's up shit creek'

chapter 1

IN WHICH MR PUNCH

PRESENTS A MAGNIFICENT ARRAY OF

HIS REGULAR COLUMNISTS

I spent years of my life trying to be fashionable. God only knows why. It didn't do any good. It's not as if it improved one's attractiveness to women – nothing short of serious elective surgery could do that – nor did it in any way help my job prospects. But as time went by and my waist spread out, I gradually gave up on keeping abreast of the latest trends and settled down to the life of a contented bourgeois paterfamilias.

To my amazement, however, I now discover that I have inadvertently regained what we ageing punks used to call 'street credibility'. For it turns out that contented bourgeois dads – and contented bourgeoise mums too, come to that – have become the latest thing, *le dernier cri*, the veritable cat's miaow. Grainy snaps of happy family groups have replaced semi-clad Swedish blondes as the image most likely to sell almost any commodity that comes to mind.

What's quite clear, however, is that none of the people who are putting together these advertisements and features can actually have children themselves. If they did, they would know that few of the idyllic scenes they picture in their moody photo spreads could actually exist in the real, parental world.

For example, a recent edition of *GQ* magazine – less a periodical, more of a paper posing pouch – ran a fashion feature with the headline, 'Quality Time'. This declared that, 'After a hard week's work, it's time to swap power dressing for the latest casual looks.' Just to ensure we got the point, there was another slogan, this time in capital letters: GEARING UP FOR THE WEEKEND WITH 48 HOURS OF STYLE.

This seemed to me to be the first major error. For most working men, a truer line would be, GEARING DOWN FOR THE WEEKEND WITH 48 HOURS SLUMPED COMATOSE IN FRONT OF THE TELLY. That, however, is not the world of the *GQ* man. For, as the next few pages slip shinily by, we discover that his universe is one of unadulterated fashion consciousness.

Friday night sees Our Hero casually dressed in £795s' worth of

The world according to MR

Cerruti suit, as he nips out for a *diner à deux* with Mrs Hero. Fair enough, although I must say I favour a pair of jeans and a take-away pizza. By Saturday morning he's helping out in the kitchen clad in Paul Smith cardigan, £89 and Nicole Farhi's plum silk shirt £125. At this point his little blonde daughter makes her first appearance, along with the next major Lifestyle Inaccuracy. The daughter's face is completely cereal-free. So is her lilac sweat shirt (Agnes B £27). Nor is our hero wiping milk up off the floor.

But it may be that Little Miss Hero does choose to amuse herself in a true-to-life manner by pouring cereal all over her dad's plum silk shirt once the camera-man's back is turned. Because by the next shot he's buying flowers dressed in a £342 checked jacket and a depressingly cheap £42 sweatshirt. Actually, it's a fascinating shopping expedition all round, because he hits the vegetable market in a beige mac and as he examines his daughter's brand-new yellow bike (pity it's about 14 sizes too big for the little tot) he's très dapper in brown linen and white cotton drill. (Forget the prices – just take it from me, we're talking a tailor's bill the size of the National Debt.)

None of this, however, really strains the credulity of those of us who know the true joys of family life. No, the bit that does that is when Mr and Mrs are pictured with the tag-line GET IT TOGETHER – MELLOWING OUT IN THE AFTERNOON. There they are, stretched out on their bed, a big grin on his face, a look of contented exhaustion on hers. You wish. Parents, however, know better. Saturday afternoons in our household are spent with Mrs Punch upstairs desperately trying to get some kip to repair the ravages of the week, while I try to entertain the nipper by building Lego castles *and* keep one eye on the rugby.

At this point in the *GQ* narrative, however, the daughter disappears from the scene completely, enabling our happy couple to get up late on Sunday morning and share orange juice and croissants. The feature ends with the words RECHARGED, REFRESHED AND READY FOR THE WEEK AHEAD. This is the reverse of the truth. The kids are all-too present for every waking minute of the weekend, and some of the sleeping ones as well. I go to work to escape the utter exhaustion of staying at home.

I was ruminating on this fact just last Sunday. We were staying with some friends who have fled the rat race for an idyllic existence in a Suffolk village. (Well, they think it's idyllic, but those of us who regard a decent Indian takeaway, an accessible video rental joint and 24-hour hot water as the minimal requirements for a civilised life would tend to disagree.) There were four children aged under three confined within the cottage. Their cries echoed through the building like the agonised yelps of inmates in some grisly Romanian asylum.

As they set about destroying the kitchen (they worked in pairs; two crawled off on a ground-level search-and-destroy mission, the others wreaked their havoc at table level), I realised that I was looking at the best part of half-a-million pounds' worth of kindergarten, school and university fees. And that's in today's money. If we stopped to consider what the cost of private education was going to be, allowing for 15 years of inflation, we'd pack the little beggars off to the nearest comp and let ILEA do its worst.

That, of course, is why the notion of the child-as-fashion-accessory is so misguided and so insulting to those of us who are living parenthood for real. We can't afford the stuff that the advertisers are trying to sell us because we're all skint. We can't lie around in bed because the kids come first. And we wouldn't have it any other way because to us children are not accessories, but the most important things in our lives. That's not very trendy. But it happens to be the truth. ■

> **Grainy snaps of happy family groups have replaced semi-clad Swedish blondes as the image likely to sell any commodity**

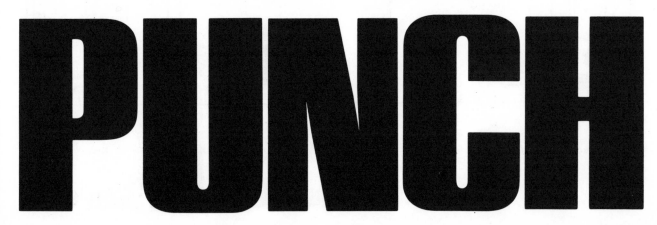

'Beats me why they never ask themselves how many of us
will be around in 1997...'

'I wouldn't allow headscarves either...'

'Perhaps you could persuade Mrs Thatcher to give up her
single party dictatorship...'

'My sentence, as night follows day, is subject to appeal...'

sideswipes

Wimpy Burgers have reinstated two women after sacking them for being too old for their image. They said that at least they make the burgers look fresh.

The noun 'le cricket' can now be found in French dictionaries. 'Le racist mercenary' is likely to follow.

'When I think of all the men I could have divorced.'

Frank Bruno will referee the next Mike Tyson fight. This is to ensure that no knock-down is counted beyond ten.

Guttersnipe

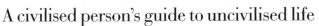

A civilised person's guide to uncivilised life

IT HAS RECENTLY emerged that Mr Nicu Ceausescu, the son of the deposed dictator of Romania, had used the Olympic gold-medal-winning gymnast, Miss Nadia Comaneci, as a 'sex slave'. According to authoritative reports, 'the fiend tore out her fingernails to satisfy his perverted lust.' Guttersnipe, however, believes that Mr Ceausescu may be misunderstood: far from being a 'fiend', he may simply be a manicurist *manqué*.

Mr William Shatner, the actor who played Captain Kirk in innumerable episodes and films of *Star Trek* is being sued by two mistresses for jilting them. One wants £3 million while the other wants £5 million. The discrepancy between these two figures might be explained by the fact that he went more boldly with the latter than the former.

Mr Joseph Bugner, the pugilist, has recently admitted that he used to 'beat up' his first wife. 'I treated her like a dog,' he averred. Guttersnipe forbears to doubt Mr Bugner's veracity but anyone who ever saw him box would have no fears for his spouse.

The marriage of the 'actor' Mr Chris Quinten (see below) and Miss Leeza Gibbons, an American television interviewer, is reported to be at an end after 15 months. Mr Quinten has admitted to a 'pal' that he has been 'a bad boy'. In an editorial, the *Daily Star* opined. 'He may have been popular but his acting talent made the cat in *Coronation Street*'s opening titles look like Laurence Olivier.' Like Laurence Olivier? What, deceased?

Meanwhile, the tenacious *Sunday Sport* has managed to locate President Gorbachev's half-sister. 'The 42-stone sag bag stunned Reds by announcing herself as the secret love-child of Gorby's dad. "I've kept my silence for years – now it's Glasnost and time to tell the truth," belched the 48-year-old gutbucket.' Such authoritative reporting is sure to act as a beacon for a nation currently hastening towards its very own free press.

Finally, in the week that Mr Nelson Mandela took his first steps in fulfilling his destiny, it was reported that Mr Jeremy Beadle, the television 'personality', claims to have invented the word 'bonking' as a synonym for copulation, and that Miss Anneka Rice, also a television 'personality', summoned her husband from 'hundreds of miles away' because 'the bubbly blonde had just realised the time was right for her to conceive'.

Who, pray, is ... Chris Quinten?

Guttersnipe's dictionary of national biography

Mr Chris Quinten is a British thespian who formerly portrayed the garage mechanic, Brian Tilsley, in independent television's continuing drama series *Coronation Street*. His role ended when his character was stabbed to death outside a nightclub. Mr Quinten, who has a reputation as a ladies' man, has referred to himself, or rather his manhood, as the 'Dick of Death'. He is said to be returning home, so perhaps Mr Kenneth Branagh should look to his laurels. ■   **MITCHELL SYMONS**

'Look out, it's the advertising gangs. That's Bartle, Bogle and Hegarty and the other two are Ogilvy and Mather!'

'We'd better start on the sandwiches without him.'

sideswipes

As with MP John Browne, Kenneth Clarke has also failed to declare an interest – in the NHS.

'Would it be breaking sanctions if she accepted a reverse-charge call from Mr Mandela?'

A burglar has broken into the World Snooker Association headquarters. He stole the result of the next Francisco-Griffiths match.

'Yes, but I'm sure you've got interests you haven't declared.'

Life isn't so bad for . . .

This week . . .
SOPHIE MIRMAN:

So Sock Shop is £16 million in the red, so Sock stock has been suspended, so analysts want you to sack your husband, but don't worry Sophie, at least:

1) *You don't owe money to John Browne, MP*
2) *You don't own Perrier*
3) *You don't sell Free Nelson Mandela T-shirts*
4) *You're not an ambulance driver*
5) *You'll be able to open a branch in Carey Street*
6) *You never have to hunt for socks in the morning*
7) *. . . or darn old ones*
8) *You can write your life story:* Everything You Ever Wanted to Know About Socks, But Were Afraid to Ask
9) *Nobody's burning socks in Bradford, but most of all . . .*
10) *You're not doing jury service at the Guinness trial*

Guttersnipe

A civilised person's guide to uncivilised life

NEW INTELLIGENCE emerged last week as to the possible drawbacks of regular athletic exercise. The High Court was told that the celebrated Olympienne Miss Tessa Sanderson had shared a bed with a married man. But the gallery was relieved to learn that fatigue ensured no indiscretion took place which might cause Miss Sanderson's companion to regret his marriage vows.

No stranger to the marriage vow is one of our foremost comic players, Mr James 'Jim' Davidson, who was wed for the fourth time. 'I love Tracie,' he reported. 'And this time it's for keeps.' We wish Mr Davidson well, but would politely remind him that even King Henry VIII, a noted enthusiast for the wedding ceremony, was 13 years older than our young friend on the occasion of *his* fourth wedding.

Mr Davidson may also appreciate some timely advice from the most eminent member of the Yellow Press. Under the expert tutelage of Mr 'Kelvin' MacKenzie, *The Sun* advised its public on 'How to put a sparkle back into your sex life, folks' with 'Your Complete Guide To Better Loving'. Miss Sanderson, of course, does not need the advice of the good Mr MacKenzie. She knows when to leave well enough alone.

Mr William Treacher, an actor often seen as Arthur Fowler (see below) in that most dramatic portrait of Cockney life, *EastEnders*, has revealed an intense dislike of Mr Fowler's immediate family. 'I'd have dumped a family like that years ago. They make me sick', he declared.

Illness brings your correspondent neatly around to the subject of Signor Paolo Magri, an Italian gourmand, who well earned his title as the World Spaghetti-Eating Champion when he sucked down a pound *avoirdupois* of pasta in 42 seconds with his hands tied behind his back. Given the addition of a suitable speech impediment, he could now be in a position to challenge for the Deputy Leadership of the Labour Party.

Finally, in the week that the diplomatic salons of Europe were agog with talk of Prussian unity, it was reported that Mr Garfield 'Gary' Glitter, a strolling minstrel, is to play His Holiness the Pope in an Australian musical, that Miss Samantha Fox, the model and chanteuse, has been on holiday with 'a crippled pal' whom she 'treats like a brother' and that Mr Robin Williams, America's foremost humorous actor, is to be considered for the part of Mr Lech Walesa in a cinematic biography. Whatever next? Can Miss 'Bo' Derek be preparing to take on the mantle of Mother Teresa?

Who, pray, is . . . Arthur Fowler?

Guttersnipe's dictionary of national biography

Mr Arthur Fowler is a street trader who lives in Albert Square, London E20. He is married to Pauline Fowler (née Beale) and their offspring include Michelle, who herself had a child as a result of an affair with Mr Dennis Watts, a publican who was subsequently shot. He has discovered a corpse, endured prolonged periods of unemployment, stolen money, suffered a 'nervous breakdown' and taken part in a television quiz-show. Mr Fowler does not exist. ∎

MITCHELL SYMONS

THE EURODOLLAR

NO. 0001   WEAK ENDING RADIO 4, 11:00 | PRICE: ONE ECU | EUROPE'S FIRST ESPERANTO NEWSPAPER

MAN OF THE YEAR

The Eurodollar honours a giant among East European leaders
PAGE 99

SPOT THE ECU

How you can help the extinction of an endangered species
PAGE 15% VAT

MAN NOT IN THE EYE

Why Private Eye won't be saying anything rude about the Eurodollar
COURT 1

Euro leaders grapple unification issues

With its launch issue already short of news, *The Eurodollar* is desperate to find a European story ● Robert Maxwell reports

THE summit meeting this week produced full agreement among the group's leaders, with the exception of Mrs Thatcher (Europe West).

The meeting seemed set for deadlock until the timely intervention of the charismatic owner of *The Eurodollar*

stepped in with his announcement of 'booze, birds and bingo for all'.

Statesmen from all nations were said to be 'delighted' with Mr Maxwell's new paper. "At last we have a common voice in Europe," said all those who could speak English.

Irishman arrested on suspicion

SELF-CONFESSED Irish entertainer Mr Terry Wogan has been detained by police following allegations that he had plotted to 'publicly humiliate' Mr Tom King by inviting him on his show. It is believed that the notorious left-wing organisation the 'BBC' was also involved.

Mr Wogan is well known for exposing his talents before a live audience in pursuance of his naked ambition.

Mr King said that "Obviously this is all *sub judice*, so I can't tell you just how guilty he is."

Swiss traditionalists beat brawling ballotbox bimbos

THE Swiss parliament at Appenzell Innerhoden (pictured left) have voted decisively for a return to the times when men were men and women were still amoeba.

Rejecting worldwide criticism, spokesburgher N. E. Anderthal said: 'Ngghg.' Women will be allowed to join the Swiss Army but will not be given their own penknives.

Snooker - another European victory

IN AN astonishing and historic final, Steve Hendry (Europe North-West) has finally ousted reigning champion Stephen Davis (Europe West) from the

coveted title Sports Lack of Personality of the Year.

Wearing his distinctive black bow tie and snug-fitting waistcoat, the cheeky 14-year-old

told *The Eurodollar* in an exclusive interview: "Quite frankly I'm speechless. Words fail me. And you can quote me on that." He later described the

match as "Indescribable".

Davis, however, was less than complimentary about the final. "It was a frame-up," he commented.

sideswipes

'No Mr Mandela, the ambulance dispute isn't over yet.'

Former soccer star Danny Blanchflower denies reports that he has lost his memory — he says he can even remember when England last scored a goal.

Troops have been sent in to break the week-long dancers dispute at Covent Garden. The Special Ballet Corps will perform a specially-written work, Swan Light.

'I don't think we've done a family tree for an egg before.'

The New Breed

The first creature crawls from the ocean onto dry land.

Pants! I need pants!

8-15

Joe Spooner

PLAINCLOTHES FIREMAN

Sidney Harris

HELP RETRAIN STUPID PEOPLE

Ken Krimstein
7-6

Richard Orlin
7-24

'Sell 10,000 shares at 46¼ and have an anchovy pizza delivered to Exit 42.'

BALTIC BREAKDOWN – YOUR GUIDE TO THIS MONTH'S REVOLTING REPUBLICS:

Lithuania — First stop for Gorby on his mini-tour. Immortalised by Louis Jordan in the song, 'Lith-you-is or Lithuania My Baby?'

Azerbaijan — Best known of all the Soviet republics, mainly because Kate Adie has a holiday home here

Biriani — Up and coming hotspot on the Black Sea

Moldavia — Up and coming fungus on the loaf Gorbachev left in the bread-bin when he went to Lithuania

Estonia — Smallest of the republics and strangely twinned with Dorking. Famed for its black tea shops

Meantophonya — Last stop for Gorby on his tour. It was here that he remembered he hadn't rung Raisa

'How do I know you're not my Labour MP?'

'Looks like a bad case of mad cow disease.'

WELCOME TO THE WEST

Batten the hatches

Dive! Dive! Dive! OOFY PROSSER thinks the markets are going down fast

W hy, when I look about me at the markets, at the men who make the markets, at the men who move the markets and at the men who merely follow the markets, am I reminded of a 1940s cartoon? You know the scene; it's been played over and over again. Bugs, Daffy, Mickey, Droopy, Wile E Cayote, Tom or Jerry are running ahead furiously when they suddenly realise that they have gone over the edge of the cliff. Until that moment, they had been managing perfectly even though they are supported only by thin air. Looking down they see the ground hundreds of feet below them, but they don't fall immediately. By making their little legs move even faster, they get a few moments respite before Wwwwhhhhheeeeeeeee and down they go, muttering something like 'Boy, am I dumb!'

The investors who collectively make up the stock market are at exactly the stage when, with legs flailing madly, they should be putting their hands to their mouths and going 'Duh' very loudly. Having spent the first two weeks of the year running up to and beyond the edge of the cliff and a week or so trying to clutch at thin air, they are beginning to realise what idiots they have been (unlike *Punch* readers, who were given plenty of warnings here). Not only are interest rates not going down, but there is talk of mortgage rates having to rise again, the balloon of inflation is being pumped up once more and a brace of Maggie's Men, businessmen once fêted and lauded as the answer to an iron maiden's prayers, are on the brink of disaster.

There is always a delay between my writing this and you reading it, and a lot can happen in the market in just a few days. However, if things have steadied, I would suggest that all that has happened is that the market has managed to grab desperately at a tree on the way down. It won't be long before it realises its shoe-lace is undone and, with its usual degree of common sense, takes both hands off the branch in order to do it up again.

It's hard to know just where the bottom is, and even harder to prophesy whether the cliff falls vertically to the ground or whether it begins to slope as it approaches it so that the fall might not prove fatal. I wouldn't be surprised to see the 2,200 level on the Footsie broken soon. In fact I wouldn't be too astounded if 2,000 was not achievable before too long.

Wherever the bottom is, climbing back up to the top again is going to take an awfully long time.

YESTERDAY'S MEN?

YOU DON'T need to go very far back to find newspaper after newspaper and magazine after magazine full of profiles of such successful and highly-regarded businessmen as Jimmy Gulliver, the man who lost out in the contest to acquire Distillers, or John Ashcroft of Coloroll, the Guardian's Young(!) Businessman of the Year in 1987. Not now. Both men have tripped up badly and their problems are likely to be only the tip of a particularly large and cumbersome iceberg.

Those cautious souls who expressed qualms about companies borrowing heavily to finance takeovers, buy-outs and the like were dismissed as being killjoys. Whatever joy there was has been short-lived. Coloroll, once the darling of the market, has laid off 600, has debts of £140m and is looking for help from its bankers. Gulliver's Lowndes Queensway is to get an emergency transfusion of £68m and is laying off 1,000. If Lowndes goes down, that will hit Coloroll even harder.

These aren't the only ones in difficulty and they won't be the last. Magnets is in the proverbial, up to the top of its wellies, as is MFI. In fact, there must be scores of businesses, particularly in the retail sector, which are suffering a double whammie: the rise in interest rates is making it more difficult to service loans while, at

the same time, the decline in consumer spending as a result of those higher interest rates is making it still more difficult to service the loans. It begins to look as if the worst sufferers from higher interest rates are not going to be consumers at all, but the entrepreneurs who have broken bread with the great lady at Number Ten so often over the past decade.

At times it seems that most of those whose companies aren't collapsing under them are instead playing host to the DTI or SFO or popping the boxing shorts on for a bout versus Regina in the red corner. What strange times we live in.

PRINCESS TRUMP 2

it's evolution, things get bigger..

YACHT STUFF

NOW SEEMS a peculiar time for that most modest of men, Donald Trump (the property zillionaire who suffers from the misfortune of knowing that, in parts of Britain, his name means 'fart') to be thinking of selling his boat, the reticently named *Trump Princess*. For it has to be said that yachts are pretty much a buyer's market at the moment, particularly with Bondie and other busted Australians trying to get rid of their playthings as well.

It isn't all that long ago that Trump bought the boat from Khashoggi (who now has problems of his own) for £30 odd million that he had lying around. At the time he claimed that 'it's simply one of the most wonderful and incredible jewels of the world and I feel that America really should have these things. I want America to own the most beautiful things.' Maybe he does, but the *Trump Princess* is soon to be flaunting its assets at potential buyers in Singapore, Hong Kong and Japan, where round-eyes are a little thin on the ground.

Perhaps Trump can't stand his wife's idea of interior design. All the rooms are named after precious stones or metals, such as the Sapphire Room, the Lapis Lazuli room and the Diamond Suite (the Trump's own boudoir). All that onyx, marcasite and marble must get a bit wearying after a while, even if you are bombing along at 18 knots in a 300-foot boat armed with helicopter pad, disco, cinema, swimming-pool and operating theatre, the last presumably equipped for emergency plastic surgery should anyone on board show signs of developing any unsightly wrinkles or sags.

We musn't weep too much for Trump. His new boat, which at 420 feet is longer even than HMQ's yacht, will be ready in a couple of years' time. It's name? *Trump Princess 2*. ∎

ILLUSTRATIONS BY STEVE WAY

CALL-IN FEE

BALMORAL International Hotels, run by Peter Tyrie, want to get their hands on Norfolk Capital Group and are trying to persuade Norfolk's shareholders to accept their offer. Their methods of persuasion seem a little bizarre. Putting an advert in the newspapers giving a phone number for Norfolk shareholders to ring to hear the Balmoral point of view is nothing new. But this is the first time I have come across a case where shareholders have to pay 38 pence a minute (or 25 pence off-peak) in order to be persuaded of the virtues of a take-over bid. If nothing else puts me off Balmoral, this sort of parsimony certainly would.

AT THE THIRD STROKE, IT WILL BE EXACTLY TIME TO SELL YOUR SHARES

SPY INTEREST

THERE ARE times, I admit, when I have been more than a little rude to that fine body of men who make up the nation's bankers. I have occasionally cavilled at the bank's charges, inefficiencies, mismanagement, rudeness and other minor trivial irritations. But as an employer myself, I think Lloyds' management showed a great deal of initiative in trying to test the competence of its staff by pretending to be customers. To the fury of the Banking Insurance and Finance Union, Lloyds rang up banks with fake queries, sent stooges into queues to see what sort of service was on offer and posted letters purporting to come from the public.

I can understand the Union's anger. Why, if employers went about doing things like this they might actually begin to understand why it is that the public is so cheesed off, fed up to the back teeth with slow, rude and plain bad staff who view customers as a nuisance to be tolerated at best and ignored and abused at worst. With the bank in danger of discovering the truth, no wonder the Union called Lloyds' methods 'underhand and outrageous'.

What perplexes me is that Lloyds has now backed down and suspended its checks. What could be more popular with the public than the idea that they might be thought by the bank staff to be a potential management spy? Think what improvement in service there would be. From now on, one must assume that Lloyds, like the other banks, will resort to letting its staff police itself, with the inevitable result.

They should not be so craven. Employers the length and breadth of the land, whatever their business, should set up narking departments, sending their chaps and chappesses out into shops, restaurants, garages, banks, hotels and the like to find what it is really like to be a consumer in Britain today. What a depressing picture they would find.

SECRET ORDERS

COUNTERFOIL INTELLIGENCE

Office politics

JULIA LANGDON reports on the battle for workspace in Westminster

If you invite guests to the House of Commons they are usually delighted in principle and horrified in practice. 'You work here?' they cry in alarm, after a brief inspection of the Press Gallery. 'In here! Like this!' If they are those sort of people they start talking about the Office, Shops and Railway Premises Act. If they are Americans they usually faint.

And that's just the Press Gallery. Actually it doesn't seem quite that bad when you work there but I suspect that is because, like living in New York, it's amazing what you can put up with once you're used to it. I rather like it. The offices remind me of what newspapers used to be like before new technology, in the good old days of 1986, when journalists still used to talk to each other.

But our Victorian conditions are nothing compared to those inflicted on MPs. At least most of our offices have windows, and even those who are not so blessed are allowed to glimpse daylight from time to time. The same is not true of the rooms allocated to many MPs. There are dozens of them in the Palace which are windowless, airless boxes, rather resembling interrogation

rooms favoured by repressive regimes before they move their clients on to the torture chamber. On second thoughts, many of them probably represent torture chambers and they are certainly the kind of places that would drive anyone barmy in double-quick time. (As regular readers will know, of course, many MPs are barmy before they get here so it could be argued that this scarcely matters. On the other hand it is not surprising that anyone ends up barking after a relatively short occupation of such a hell hole.)

The Labour MP Austin Mitchell described the House of Commons the other day as 'the legislative slum of this world's Parliaments' and he certainly had a point. These windowless cells are found in little warrens all over the Palace and offer something of the density of occupation and the squalor of the better parts of the Neapolitan back streets. They would be worse if everyone used them: in fact many MPs are quite rightly scared for their sanity and their health if they stay too long and merely scuttle in and out to collect their messages. Others can't bear to sit at their desks because they can't bear the person, or people, with whom they have to share. (You have to be a very big cheese indeed to get an office entirely to yourself.)

And these are the lucky ones. They are the people who actually have a desk in the Palace itself. Some people wait years for the privilege and lose their seat before they get in from the rain. In the meantime they are accommodated in one of the parliamentary outbuildings which are to be found dotted all over Westminster, within an eight-minute running range. That is the length of time allowed for an MP to reach the division lobbies after the bells starts ringing for a vote. It is extremely inconvenient to have an office outside the building if there are frequent votes in the course of an evening: you either spend the time trotting to and fro – or give up and go to the bar. Needless to say, it's considerably worse when it's raining.

The Victorian conditions of the Press Gallery are nothing compared to those inflicted on MPs

There are a multitude of other inconveniences in this very superior slum. The marvels of a Victorian central-heating system mean that it is too hot in winter and the areas that are air-conditioned are too cold in summer. There are constant rumours circulating among the press that an outbreak of Legionnaires' Disease is inevitable. The loos are few and far between – particularly the Ladies' – although if you can find them they are clean and sanitary and compare favourably to some other Legislative slums

I've seen. (In this regard I would particularly recommend going out of your way to avoid the facilities in the Prime Minister's office in Dar es Salaam.) There is a post office and a barber and a souvenir shop and you can buy any number of coffee sets and coasters and keyrings, but you can't buy a pair of tights.

It is the office accommodation, however, which most troubles MPs and, not least, the fact that such secretarial and research staff as they are able to afford are usually located at some distance from them – which could be half a mile away, even within the main building. Many MPs only ever speak to their secretaries on the telephone – unless, that is, they also happen to be their wives.

There is an excited expectation therefore about the prospect of a new parliamentary office building which may considerably improve conditions. It is currently under construction across the road from Big Ben although it still appears to be some years off completion. No one really believes, however, that it will make all that much difference. Things won't change until MPs pay themselves a professional salary and oblige themselves all to work full-time. And that will probably never happen. ∎

WITH A TRYST

A great deal of high-minded criticism is levelled at the practice of parliamentary lobby journalism. This happened again recently when it was disclosed that the Health Secretary, Kenneth Clarke, had held a meeting with Sunday lobby correspondents. It is, however, entirely understandable that from time to time Ministers may want to talk privately and I cannot for the life of me see how this causes so much controversy.

But this particular incident did cause me some personal discomfort. One of my colleagues on a daily newspaper rang to inquire about this alleged meeting with Mr Clarke and I was obliged to pretend that I didn't know what he was talking about. Half an hour later the Secretary of State was interviewed on the radio about the meeting and mentioned my presence. My colleague rang back: 'How would you like me to spell your name?' he inquired genially.

CHAUFFEUR, SO GOOD

It has been claimed – and officially denied – that Mr Clarke's own Government driver is paid a handsome salary well beyond the dreams of avarice, or ambulance drivers anyway.

If this were true, it would be thoroughly deserved. The drivers in the Government car service are too often overlooked. They occupy one of the most powerful jobs in Britain. They are privy to more secrets than anyone could imagine. They learn more than the rest of us have forgotten. It is they who know first when there is going to be a reshuffle (they have to drive the victims) and it is they who learn from their colleagues a great deal more about what is going on in other departments than people in desks are ever prepared to vouchsafe. The price of their silence for any Minister would be above most things.

There are a couple of drawbacks, of course. If a Minister's in a hurry you get the speeding ticket. And if some terrorist organisation plants a car-bomb, you're in the hot seat, as it were.

On the bore path

Ferguson Gillespie
on the potential
cause of the next war

When my startled guests, choking on their claret, ask me *why* I think there will be a major war within ten years, I do not give them any of the obvious answers. As I lean across the table (eyes glinting, flecks of foam at the corners of my mouth), I do not say:

'*Mes copains*: but it is as plain as the nose on your face (and plain is the only word to describe that sorry protuberance). First, you have the Russian Empire crumbling. Second, you have a plethora of enfeebled petty states emerging, from the Baltic to the Balkans. And third, you have Rhinelander and Saxon, Bavarian and Brandenburger united once again. You ask me why there will be war. I say: look at your history books.'

No, I do not say that. Nor do I say, drawing pensively on my cigar and exhaling as I declaim: 'The fact is, gentlemen, there has been, since the time of the Prophet, a fundamental conflict between Christendom and Islam. The difference is this time Johnny Arab is crusading in our direction. And, to crown it all, we are providing him with his armour and sword, by gad.'

None of these lines are currently featured in my rich and varied repertoire. In fact, the reason I anticipate imminent international conflict is altogether simpler. War is inevitable, so I tell my hushed audience, *because we are all so bloody bored.*

IT IS NOT just the tedium of the traffic jams, the sight of the fat, sweaty middle-managers picking their noses in the rear-view mirrors of the Ford Sierras in front of us. Nor is it just the booming inanity of Mr Simon Bates's voice as it emanates from van after van, Portakabin after Portakabin, hole after hole in the street, day after day. Nor is it even the tax forms, the bills, the bank statements and the irksome telephone calls to people called Sharon in Milton Keynes.

For these mere irritants are as nothing compared with the mind-numbing, stultifying boredom induced by our supposed pleasures and comforts. To begin with, there's food. Your mouth is almost certainly full of the stuff as you read this piece. If not, there are bits of it between your teeth, and the promise of a fresh intake within the hour. Croissants from the freezer for breakfast, with coffee made in some preposterous continental percolator. For lunch, either a 'granary bap' sodden with mayonnaise or, if you have an expense account, an orgy of parma ham, poached salmon and sorbet. And then home for your dinner – a multi-coloured confection of the latest novelties from the open-all-hours, drive-in Sainsbury's, washed down with two – three? four? – glasses of Chianti.

Then there is that staple indulgence of our times: clothing. Be honest; how many wardrobes do you possess, stuffed to bursting-point with garments which you never, ever wear, simply because on the way home from the shops you convinced yourself that they did not flatter your figure or 'fit in' with your 'image'? Not to mention the rows of dainty shoes you have amassed like a leather Luftwaffe in your secret bedroom hangar.

Your belly is full, your body partially encased in fabric and hide. What now? A video perhaps? Of a film you have already seen several times, containing familiar and comforting scenes of smut and carnage. And then – why not? – a mindless drive. Yes, that truly represents the acme of human enjoyment: a mindless couple of laps round the ring road, to the accompaniment of some bland, plodding dirge.

NOW, I AM an old hand who does not need to be told that the way of life I describe here represents, all things considered, the pinnacle of human achievement. This (north-) western way minimises misery; and is the dream of the vast majority of eastern and southern mankind. But there is no getting away from the fact that it palls. Consumption, when it becomes too easy, simply becomes a bore. At this point, the testosterone begins to rise among the males of the species, who begin to dread, if only subliminally, the idea of living a wholly unremarkable, cushy life.

'What did you buy in the Lawson boom, Grandad?' – I predict that the next world war will be caused by nothing more complex than fear of this one deadly question. ■

'They really go for his over-the-garden-fence approach.'

'I hate to tell you but I've still got the headache.'

'He was very proud of his toupee.'

'He invented the automatic flush.'

Batting on

FRANK KEATING previews the English cricket tour of the West Indies

I have been with the England cricket team in the Caribbean on their last three tours as they have prepared and patched their armour in readiness for another Test series against the merciless West Indians. Fat lot of good my presence did them, so I am giving it a miss this time.

The opening one-day international is in Port-of-Spain on, ominously, St Valentine's Day. That's where we played the first Test which got the whole thing off to a calamitous start in 1981, and I remember going in the team bus every day from the Hilton, across the Savannah to the Queen's Park Oval – and always past the Roxy cinema which that week was showing something called *Phantasm*, and the place was plastered with lurid posters proclaiming, 'If this trip doesn't scare you, man, then you're already dead and buried!' The message was not lost on the team. It was to prove horribly spot-on.

Mind you, England lost only two Tests out of four on that tour, so in retrospect, and mindful of what was to come through the rest of the 1980s, it wasn't a bad effort to escape with two honourable draws in that series. England's best bat in 1981, by far, was Graham Gooch, who averaged almost 60 in the four Tests against what most scholars still reckon the best of all the West Indian attacks in history – Holding, Roberts, Croft, and Garner in their ferocious prime, with the apprentice, Marshall, as third change.

Now, nine years older, Gooch is back as captain. England cannot have had a more lugubrious, cares-of-the-world general since Len Hutton, as it happens the last opening bat to have to lead from the front and be first over the top. One reason – dotty, I agree – that there is a feeling somewhere in the bones of English cricket that this winter we might at last have the lads giving as good as they get in the Caribbean. I feel it too, though I am not actually taking any bets till well after Valentine's Day.

What a coup for Gooch if he could bring it off. Just to give Viv Richard's lot a ruddy good game every time would be triumph enough, wouldn't it? A nice little bonus, too, for Geoffrey Boycott, who was called up to coach the batsmen in the arts and sciences of playing fast bowling. Not only the tyros, Hussain and Bailey, admitted that the cussed old Tyke's know-how was invaluable, but Gooch himself was big man enough to thank Boycott for spotting, and eradicating, some basic flaws that had unconsciously been taken on board his own technique.

In the Barbados Test match nine years ago, Gooch was Boycott's junior opening partner. Gooch made a valiant 116 out of an England total of 224. Geoffrey made one of Test cricket's most famous ducks. I will never forget it. Bridgetown's rickety, crickety stadium was full to every corrugated rooftop, and the jabbering din only died into an expectant quiet as Boycott took guard and Michael Holding paced out his menacing run. He was almost using the sight-screen at the pavilion end as a catapulting starting-block.

First ball snortingly tore a strip off the knuckle of Boycott's left-hand batting glove and dropped just in front of third slip as the batsman wrung his hand in pain. The second was shorter and even more spiteful, and Boycott jack-knifed his forehead out of the way with a millimetre between his life and a coroner's verdict of misadventure due to the whiplash effect.

Next ball was off a fuller length, but no less wicked, and it licked back cruelly to splatter the inside of Geoffrey's unguarded left thigh. The infinitely courageous Englishman stuck to his middle-stump scratch-mark, and the fourth ball had him in all sorts of ungainly contortions as he endeavoured to keep down the missile again with his already wounded left hand; the thing squirmed away to gully. The fifth delivery again had you fearing for the stubbornly gallant knight's life as it reared angrily at his throat like a buzzsaw looking to at least peel his Adam's Apple. Still Boycott stood his ground.

As if the hateful half-dozen had been orchestrated into one gigantic, discordant crescendo, the sixth and last ball of the over was a snaking yorker which fiercely ripped Boycott's off-stump out of the ground and had it spearing fully 20 yards as if, for a moment we thought, it would impale itself in the very heart of the wicket-keeper, Murray. It missed him by a whisker.

The vast throng was silent, stunned, for a split-second. Boycott jerked round to watch the flight of the stump then, as the great, crazed noise erupted all around his ears, his mouth gaped and he tottered in his crease as if he'd seen the very Devil himself. Then, agonised and tremulous, he walked away, tearing his batting gloves off with his nervously juddering teeth. By the time he got to the pavilion step he was erect again; beaten this time, sure, but already determined on his counter.

The old warrior showered quickly then, his head wrapped in a pale green towel, sat quietly in the corner of the dressing-room ▶

◄ pondering not so much his humiliation (for that, precisely, is what it had seemed to everyone watching in awe of Holding's quite brilliant brutality), but his possible answer to it.

In the second innings, Boycott made a solitary single (a nick through the slips) before the rampantly sleek assassin, Holding, pranged him amidships again; this time, snaffled in the gully off another unplayable fizzer. It seemed really possible that the old boy who had first played for England almost 20 years before was through, *sans* eye, *sans* bottle.

Oh, us of little faith. What Boycott had made sure of was keeping a copy of the BBC tele-recording of that Holding over. Night after night, he had the BBC TV news reporter on the tour, a fellow Yorkie, Michael Blakey, play it through on the Steenbeck. I went with Geoff a couple of times to those late-night dark-room sessions. The loop was only four or five minutes long. He would watch it again and again and again, occasionally telling Blakey's operator to stop the machine so as to study the freeze-frame at a particular point in the over. He'd pore over the fuzzy monochrome, stop-start, rewind, or fast-forward to the last *coup de grace*. Finally, just before the next Test began in Antigua two weeks later, Boycott seemed to announce himself satisfied that he'd seen enough.

The team unashamedly blubbed their eyes out as they stood for a minute's silence

In Antigua, on a broken pitch, Boycott saved the match and England's bacon with an unbeaten century. A smiling Holding shook the rum Yorkshire emperor's hand as he led the opposition's rueful applause at the pavilion gate at the end of the game.

That famous duck of Boycott's in Barbados had been so mercilessly and cruelly executed by Holding that I still reckon it contrived somehow to the utter tragedy that was to come that evening. The England team had been skittled out by close of play. The bus that took the team back to the hotel was full only of stunned silence: the feeling was that they had not only let themselves down but, even worse, their beloved coach, Ken Barrington, who had sat all afternoon at the pavilion window, chain-smoking and worrying as his grim-faced batsmen came regularly back and forth. Gatting 2, Gower 17, Butcher 17, Botham 26, Willey 19, Bairstow 0, Emburey 0, Jackman 7, Dilley 0, Extras 8.

Only the press stayed up late that night. Ken and his wife, Ann, who had arrived for a holiday a few days before, went out for an early supper. They were back about nine. In their bedroom, Ken flopped into an armchair and Ann pottered for a minute or two in the bathroom. When she came out, Ken didn't answer her. He was unconscious. Ann ran into the corridor to shout for their next-door neighbour, the team's physio, Bernard Thomas. He saw at once that Kenny was dead.

Next morning, the team unashamedly blubbed their eyes out as they stood to attention before play started for a minute's silence to their friend and coach and confessor. The death of Ken Barrington ruined the tour even more cataclysmically than being thrown out of Guyana at the end of the notorious 'Jackman Affair' ever did.

Only Graham Gooch, of that mortified band of young men,

remains in the England colours this winter. If he had one, I always reckoned Gooch was Barrington's favourite: two of a kind, he admired hugely the deadpan stubborness at the crease, the technical resolution, and the four-square honesty of the Essex man. Win or lose this series, I know Gooch will be invoking the spirit of his beloved mentor a great deal this next couple of months in the Caribbean.

And even grinning in affection as he tells tales of some of the onliest Barrington's endearing malapropisms when the chips were down.

Like the time there had been a minor riot during the first Test at Trinidad. Kenny had asked the local police to send some reinforcements to mingle in the crowd next day. 'That's it,' he said, 'we want a load more plain-clothes protectives!' Another time he praised Emburey for a caught-and-bowled off Richards – 'John, you really caught 'im in two-man's land!' When anything, like local practice wickets or generally scatty organisation, got his goat, he would say with cheery exasperation, 'I dunno, talk about Gymkhana's Army!' He meant of course, Fred Karno's. Opposition bowling, he would sometimes dismiss as 'pretty inosculous'; heavy rain would be coming down, not like stair-rods, but 'pea pods'; and if he slept well it would be 'yeah, like a baby lark'.

One of the last ever tasks of this good and kindly man was to chide his team of young bloods and yobs and ask them, please, to desist from referring rudely to the hordes of mostly retired, middle-class British holidaymakers (another army of them will be packing their khaki shorts and sunhats this week) out for a three-week package to watch the cricket. The team call them WINKS – as in 'Wankers Incorporated', and the game would be to send them up rotten whenever possible once they had emerged blinking (sorry, winking) from the tropical airport out of an English winter. Like, say, one is hobbling about the team's favourite bar on a walking-stick and cadging autographs. 'Ooh, look, a Wink on a stick!' and the team would be convulsed. Or another perhaps has been too readily introducing himself to the rum ie, a 'tiddly Wink'. Another might look a bit camp in his beach shirt – nudge, nudge, 'a sod is as good as a Wink'.

One of the best was Dusty Miller's on that 1981 tour. An old boy and his wife, Penelope, had finally got the message that the team was more than slightly bored by his advice on how to stand firm against Holding, Roberts and co., and he had been led away from the bar by his wife for a stroll alongside the beach before supper. They looked, as they ambled, a perfect picture in the golden fiery sunset. What a lovely shot, said one of the players, romantically. 'More,' said Dusty, quick as a flash, 'like a pen and Wink drawing!'

Fair's fair, it really is about time the Winks had something to cheer about on their package hols. Wouldn't it be something if Gooch's lot could really bring home the bacon this time. I feel it in my bones. For Boycott's sake, for one thing, and for Kenny Barrington's blessed memory. It would, in his own words, 'be a brilliant performance in anyone's cup of tea!' ■

chapter

2

FROM BISHOPS TO BOTHAM

CLIFF RICHARD
Once thoroughly wholesome, Cliff Richard – nearly 50 – now goes in for leather jeans and throbbing synthesisers, all the better to belt out such raunchy sermons as 'Devil Woman'. Accustomed to leading a large flock, his pastoral mission has been sorely tried by sexual insinuations. Christ alone knows if these are true. Mr Richard has saved the souls of Wendy Craig and Van Morrison. He is the author of *You, Me and Jesus* (1983), and *Jesus, Me and You* (1985). Mr Richard at three-score-and-ten will still be annointing himself with Oil . . . of Ulay.

JOHN SELWYN GUMMER
The Tory Party at prayer, Mr Gummer has attacked the clergy for meddling in politics despite his own enthusiasm for meddling in the church. Son of an Anglican canon, his sister-in-law is a Methodist minister. A member of the Church of England Synod, last year Mr Gummer was able to bring a specialist knowledge of loaves and fishes to the post of Secretary of State for Agriculture, Fisheries and Food. A contributor to *Faith in Politics* (1987) and *To Church with Enthusiasm* (1969), Mr Gummer would surely be Mrs Thatcher's favourite for the job.

The men for

A new Archbishop of Canterbury need not believe in God, but must be toug

NOBODY IN their wildest dreams could describe mild-mannered cleric Dr Robert Runcie as turbulent in the Thomas à Beckett mould, but with the announcement that he is to resign as Archbishop of Canterbury in January, the Prime Minister is at last rid of her mildly-irritating priest.

When Mrs Thatcher wanted dancing in the streets after the Falklands War and whoops of 'We Thumped The Argies', Runcie wrung his hands in the pulpit of St Paul's and asked us all to remember the Argentine dead. When Mrs Thatcher was on her knees praying for a thunderbolt to give Arthur Scargill a short, sharp shock, Dr Runcie was criticising her handling of the miners' strike. And just to ensure he was struck off the No. 10 Christmas card list, last October the Archbishop attacked the emergence in Britain of a Pharisee society of intolerance and self-interest. Always the diplomat.

So it is more than likely that the next Archbishop – whose job is in the gift of the Prime Minister – will be more Father Tebbit than Mother Teresa. Even belief in God may not be a necessity. And the current crop of contenders – bishops to a man – leaves much to be desired. For a start they keep going on about the inner cities. And one of the 11 men mentioned in *The Times* as frontrunners for the job, the Bishop of Chelmsford, is a caravanning enthusiast. 'You'll never guess who had the plot next to me on that site in Torquay – the Archbishop of Canterbury. Ever so considerate, he was.' Don't see it, somehow.

No. What Mrs Thatcher wants is somebody who won't want to

JAMES ANDERTON
The Greater Manchester Chief Constable has the beard of an Old Testament prophet and friends in very high places: the former Methodist lay preacher claimed he was 'moved by the spirit of God' to make his 1986 Aids speech accusing homosexuals of 'swirling around in a human cesspit of their own making.' He once told Terry Waite he was Chief Constable because it was God's Will. A past president of the Christian Police Assocation, Anderton is half fire, half brimstone – the Future of Divine Law Enforcement.

PAUL JOHNSON
Mr Johnson is a venerable Catholic whose middle name is Bede. But, having undergone a Pauline conversion on the Road to Thatcherism, this should not stand in his way. Delivers regular sermons in the *Daily Mail* asking why oh why has the country abandoned traditional values, ie his own. The author of definitive histories of both the Christians and the Jews, Mr Johnson could be Archbishop or Chief Rabbi. He would be the first Archbishop to have won the *Yorkshire Post* Award for a biography of Pope John XXIII.

the Ministry

n whingers and scroungers. *Punch* lines up the right-thinking candidates

dabble in politics, someone who won't criticise Conservative policy on the inner cities. What she wants is a Conservative. Unfortunately, Conservative bishops are in rather short supply.

So an imaginative Prime Minister like Mrs Thatcher must cast her net wider. Where should she look for a candidate with sound views and the proper clerical background? No further than the Department of Agriculture, Fisheries and Food. John Selwyn Gummer, thou shalt be a fisher of men. Gummer is the son of a Church of England canon and himself a conservative member of the Synod who has attacked the clergy for meddling in politics. Indeed if many Tories had their way the clergy would be banned from dabbling in religion, confining themselves to visiting sick old ladies.

The next candidate, the author A N Wilson, wanted to become a nun in early life, because he liked the clothes. A love of purple robes and flowing cloth would be an advantage for applicants, but the Rev Wilson would probably be too busy writing purple prose to attend to his duties.

There are born-again Christians galore to choose from in the world of showbusiness. The singer Donna Summer, the actress Charlene Tilton (Lucy Ewing from *Dallas*) will make fine candidates once the ordination of women is rushed through the Synod over the Bishop of London's dead body. Cliff Richard, whose outlook is evangelical and whose age is apocryphal, could bring in more converts to the Church of England's decreasing flock. But Mr Richard is no politician: what the Prime Minister really needs

The men
least likely...

Ms Winterson's devout Baptist upbringing – doing the Lord's work in Morecambe – is recounted in her confessional *Oranges Are Not the Only Fruit* whose chapter headings are taken directly from a truly Good Book. As a woman with practical and enlightened views on homosexuality, Ms Winterson would be the ideal candidate from the liberal wing of the church. Already exorcised, so a candidate for safe secularity, she recently dealt the dealth blow to *Ritz* by prostrating herself across its pages – full frontal before the Lord.

CHARLES MOORE
Charles 'Bobby' Moore could be just the skipper the C of E needs. He shares with John Habgood, Archbishop of York, an Eton and Cambridge education, but unlike Ebor, Mr Moore can be relied upon to support both God and the Tory party. Has steered clear of religion in his *Express* column – a sign of pre-election discretion? Or is he just saving it up for his ascension to that other great doctrinal calling, the editorship of *The Daily Telegraph*?

A N WILSON
Mr Wilson's earliest ambition was to become a nun: he fancied their clothes. Embracing both Marxism and Catholicism (tendencies moderated by marriage), he worked in Thornton's theological bookshop, and later told a Capital Radio interviewer that he had not read *Gay News* since his year at St. Stephen's theological college. Co-author of *The Church in Crisis*, as an undergraduate Wilson – struck by divine inspiration – entered for the Ellerton Theological Prize and won ...largely because no-one else knew it existed.

BRIAN REDHEAD
Faced with Bishop Brian's Christian socialism and distinct lack of humility, Mrs Thatcher may be tempted to revive burning at the stake. Alas, Mr Redhead will have to confine his sermons to the radio, where he has presented a series of religious broadcasts – *The Christian Centuries, The Good Book,* and *Pillars of Islam.* As a Geordie, however, he would hit it off with Newcastle-born Basil Hume, Archbishop of Westminster.

BISHOP OF DURHAM
Mr Jenkins was blamed for the thunderbolt that struck York Minster after he said within the hearing of the Lord that he didn't believe in the bodily resurrection or the Virgin Birth. Tories distrust both academics and clergymen, so as a former professor of theology, David Jenkins fails on both counts. He also has links with the left-wing World Council of Churches, probably doesn't like Poll Tax, and plays bridge with the devil.

is somebody who knows how to stand up for himself. Paul Johnson is that man.

Unfortunately for the Anglican church, Mr. Johnson is a Catholic. But he sets a fine example of religious enthusiasm. He preaches regular sermons from his pulpits in the *Daily Mail* and *The Spectator,* and has the extra zeal of a convert to Thatcherism, having been a former editor of the *New Statesman.* But Mr Johnson will turn down the job. He wants to be Pope.

With Mr Johnson out of the running, the way is clear for the saintly Charles Moore, devotee of the works of Thomas Cranmer and youthful editor of *The Spectator.* He has the appearance of a country clergyman, ambitious to become Rural Dean. But he has a strong power base. He was in the forefront of the Young Fogey movement, a central feature of which was an obsessive interest in Church of England affairs. Charles Moore and John Selwyn Gummer were possibly the only people in England who would have listened to Radio 4's *The Week In Synod.* Mr Moore also has an evangelising pen. With the Reverend A N Other and Christopher Hawtree, he wrote an attack on the Anglican establishment, *The Church In Crisis.* But is it possible to combine being Top Anglican with the editorship of *The Daily Telegraph,* for which St Charles has been destined virtually from conception?

This leaves one candidate: a man of stature, a man who can walk with Kings but keep the common touch, a man whose regular broadcasts have touched the nation with their simple message of faith. Your country needs you, Rabbi Lionel Blue. ■

'…but I thought somebody was doing something about that bloody hole.'

Salman Rushdie, master of disguise

They seek him here, they seek him there, they seek poor Salman everywhere. But wherever they look, they just can't find the Ayatollah's favourite author.

This is partly because he lives under round-the-clock police protection. And it also has something to do with the fact that he's almost certainly been disguised. But how? STEVEN GOODALL played plastic surgeon with a picture of Salman Rushdie. JOHN ARROW describes the results.

1. The Author from Ipanema

For months now, playground comedians have asked the question; what's blonde and busty and lives in Rio? The answer, of course, is Salman Rushdie. But what if the jokers are right? Modern surgeons could turn the swarthy, balding wordsmith into a luscious beach bunny quicker than you can say 'gender reassignment'. Into the operating theatre goes a death-threatened Indian gentleman. Out comes the subcontinent's answer to Jan Morris. If one of the Women's Pages starts a column by Renee Rushdie, you'll know that life has imitated art.

2. Hell's Rushdie

What could be more of a contrast with the bookish environs that have provided our hero's natural environment than the chicks'n'choppers world of the notorious Hells Angels? With his head shaved and his colours on his back, our newly butched-up bike boy would be more than a match for any murderous mullah. And if Salman didn't get you, you can bet your life his mates would.

3. Matt Gosside

At last! We've finally found that elusive third member for Bross. With his short-cropped hairstyle, Salman would set teenage hearts a-flutter from Torquay to Teheran. But what if he should bump into Cat Stevens at a rockbiz party? Now Yussuf Islam, the former feline, has stated his support for the elimination of Rushdie. Whatever you do, Sally-babe, don't take tea with the tillerman.

4. Into the Clone Zone

No one has ever cast any aspersions against Salman's heterosexuality. Twice-married and red-blooded, he's the very last person one would expect to find cruising the gay bars of San Francisco. So what better place could there be for him to hide out? Unless, of course, he goes to…

5. Souks and Bizarres

Oh, the mysterious ladies of Araby, their almond eyes fluttering as they fight for goat meat in the Food Halls of Harrods. What secret do they hide behind the mask? Why, what else but the amazing truth that they are none other than Salman Rushdie, the famous Satanic Versifier. ■

THE FIRST ANNUAL
INTERNATIONAL PUNCH PRO-CELEBRITY

EGO THON

A transatlantic search for the richest, brashest, most self-publicising, overexposed tycoon in the world.

YOU COULD CALL it the Kane Complex – that passionate desire that comes over certain captains of industry to let the world know of their success. No film star or pop personality can ever hope to equal the resources or determination that a really top-ranking tycoon can put behind the business of self-promotion. They couldn't, for example, afford the ocean-going yachts that are the *sine qua non* of any major mogul. Nor do they have much chance to label corporations, skyscrapers or the aforementioned gin-palaces with their own names. There is no Sting Corp, no Sting Plaza, no *HMS Sting*.

Orson Welles based *Citizen Kane* on William Randolph Hearst, creator of the extraordinary San Simeon estate in California, lover of movie stars, and proprietor of newspapers and magazines. But who would be his model today?

Certainly not Rupert Murdoch. He may buy newspapers, shut out unions, launch satellites and generally act as though he owns the world (perhaps he does). But he does not appear to suffer overmuch from vanity. There is no Murdoch Building in London, Sydney or New York. His company does not bear his name. He is rarely photographed next to world leaders, nor does he carry out foolish publicity stunts.

Not like Malcolm Forbes. He never forgot where his money came from – his magazine was called *Forbes*. He rode around the world in hot air balloons and motorcycles. Liz Taylor was photographed riding pillion. He spent $2 million on a party in Morocco, to which he invited three jets full of plutocratic American socialites and half the world's press. His jet was christened Capitalist Tool. But Forbes didn't get to the Egothon final because, as we shall discover, there's another American even more flagrant than he is. And also, poor man, he died.

Aussie ex-billionaire Alan Bond is another man who failed to make the cut. He's done his bit. He's bought breweries, television stations and Van Goghs with equal abandon. He's been the money behind Australia's successful assault on the America's Cup. He's had his pictures in the papers almost as often as his fellow countryperson Kylie Minogue. But the recent collapse of his business, which gave way under a mountain of debt, disqualified him from further progress in this competition. We can but apologise to our Aussie readers.

The same condition of entry – a vastly successful business – disqualified Sir Clive Sinclair, despite his recent high-profile brush with a Mensa member half his age. Similarly, the fact of his recent imprisonment proved an insuperable handicap to that otherwise champion ego, Adnan Kashoggi. Nor was yachtdom in itself enough to put Peter de Savary into the latter stages of the event. A word of commendation in passing, however, for his sterling attempt to make the grade; no one could fault the energy he brought to the hyping of his not-quite-victorious America's Cup bids, his purchase of Land's End, his transformation of Littlecote from country house to junior theme-park, or his many development projects around the British Isles.

Praise too for Sir Terence Conran, guru of good taste. If this award were open to a team, there can be no doubt that the combined efforts of Sir Terence, his cooking wife Caroline, his writing (just about) ex-wife Shirley, his designing sons Jasper and

Sebastian and his restauranting brother-in-law Antonio Carlucci would prove irresistible. Next year, perhaps.

As good Europeans, we must look to the Continent for inspiration. It cannot be long before names like Agnelli (the man behind Fiat) and Berlusconi (the man behind terrible Italian TV) become as well known in this country as they are in their own. And it is in the heartland of Central Europe that we find the roots of our first contestant in the finals of the Egothon, Robert Maxwell.

What a man. At the Forbes party mentioned previously, Maxwell arrived in the robes of an Oriental pasha. A few weeks later he turned up to another event in the uniform of a British Army captain (Capt. Bob was once both slim and heroic; he won the MC for gallantry in action). These diverse outfits typify this man of many parts. A longstanding friend to communist dictators the whole world over (what will he do now that they've all been kicked out?); an enthusiastic supporter and purchaser of football clubs; a familiar face to readers of newspapers he owns and in whose pages he has been known – ever so occasionally – to appear; a proprietor of global corporations; a familiar litigant in the libel courts; a lifelong socialist who is still a council house tenant; a billionaire who was famously described as 'unfit to run a public company' … he bestrides the world like a corpulent colossus of communications.

He certainly dwarfs the slim figure of Richard Branson. Yet the mild-mannered former public schoolboy makes up in publicity what he lacks in pounds. Unlike Maxwell, Branson does not use his own name for that of his companies. But the fact that the airline, record labels, nightclubs, books and films are all called Virgin does not in any way prevent Branson from ensuring that his bearded features are as familiar to the public as those of any of the stars whose records he sells.

Branson adores driving motorboats across the Atlantic, but one suspects that he would pedalo across the pond if there were a record to be broken and a film crew to be kept busy. His recent attempt to balloon across the Pacific was preceded by detailed accounts of the moments at which he and co-pilot Per Lindstrand would be mere moments from death, but fell flat when his balloon turned out to be as limp as one of his corporate condoms. Not that this, of course, prevented even his failure to take off from becoming front-page news.

Familiar faces though Maxwell and Branson may be to British eyes, Americans have a champion ego of their own. His name is Donald Trump. Not content with sticking his name on every other building in New York, he runs casinos, stages boxing matches, writes bestselling books, insults fellow-mogul Leona Helmsley in public, embarks on a headline-heavy marital spat with his much-publicised wife Ivana, fights with tenants and even plays himself in a TV miniseries (Judith Krantz's *I'll Take Manhattan*). To Americans, it would be inconceivable that anyone could be more blatantly self-obsessed than Mr Trump.

The contest will be decided over 18 rounds. Scoring has been structured on as even and scientific basis as possible and each contestant has been investigated with an equal degree of intensity and thoroughness. The result will be both honest and objective. So, without further ado, let battle commence… TURN FOR RESULTS ▶

ROBERT

DONALD

RICHARD

EGO THON

Sir Clive Sinclair: just not vain enough

Ivana Trump: can you feel divorce?

Rupert Murdoch: may be next year

Contestant No. 1
Donald Trump

DYNASTIC NEPOTISM	Promoted his wife Ivana to manager/interior decorator of the Trump Castle. She was then installed as manager of the (Trump-owned) Plaza, only to lose her job on commencing her divorce case. 6 points (-3 for subsequent retraction)
NAME FETISHISM	The Trump Organisation, Trump Castle, Trump Plaza, Trump Air, Trump Tower, The Trump Princess, the Tour de Trump. 10 points
MERCENARY SAMARITANISM	Saved Central Park skating-rink and zoo from a bureaucratic death by disrepair … but solicited gushing publicity and praise by installing a repeating taped message on the rink's muzak track extolling his own good deed. 5 points plus 4 bonus publicity points.
PATRONAGE OF THE COURTS	Sued a small company called 'Trump real estate', which had been around since he was in nappies, for using *his* trademarked name. He lost. He tried again against an established business card company called Trump Cards. Same result. Loopiest of all he sued architect Philip Birnbaum for 'self-plagiarism' after deciding Birnbaum's design for a building Trump planned to erect across the street from Trump Plaza, looked too much like the Birnbaum-designed Trump Plaza. 5 points, plus 8 point bonus for total lack of logic.
HENRY KISSINGER 'DELUSIONS OF INTERNATIONAL STATESMANSHIP' HALLUCINATION SYNDROME	Had arranged to meet Mikhail Gorbachev at Trump Tower when the Soviet leader visited New York City … but ended up shaking hands with an impostor. 0 points
OVER CONSPICUOUS CONSUMPTION (STAGGERINGLY RICH MEN'S PLAYTHINGS)	The Trump Princess (a luxury yacht complete with gold-fringed toilet fixtures, and a bullet-proof sun-deck; Trump is planning to sell it in favour of a larger model), Trump limited edition Cadillac (complete with built-in fax machines…) and of course Trump Tower, Trump Air, Ivana Trump… 10 points
REWRITING HISTORY	The Trump Organization's official pre-divorce line about Mrs Ivana Trump said she was a former Olympic skiier, former top fashion model, and licensed interior designer. She wasn't an Olympic team-member, she was a very minor model and she has never had a licence. 10 points
OUTRAGEOUS MARITAL SCANDALS	Currently involved in the world's number one celebrity divorce case. His friendships with actress Catherine Oxenberg and model Marla Maples were the talk of New York long before they hit the tabloid front pages. So, too, were Ivana's despairing attempts to have herself surgically perfected to the point where her husband would look at her again. She's fighting for his money. He's changed the office locks. This one will run and run. 10 points
PHOTO OPPORTUNISM (Accompanying the rich and famous in public)	More an ambition than a reality. 1 point

Contestant No. 2
Robert Maxwell

Contestant No. 3
Richard Branson

Robert Maxwell	Richard Branson
5 of the 7 Maxwell children are employed by Maxwell-owned companies. 8 points	Kids still a bit young… 0 points
Maxwell Communications, Maxwell House (New York), Maxwell House (Marylebone Road, W1), Maxwell House (Queen Street), Maxwell House coffee brand, no relation. 6 points	For 'Virgin' read 'Branson' throughout: Virgin-Atlantic Airways, Virgin Records (Films, Books, Games, ditto), Virgin Megastores, the Virgin Challenger, ad nauseum… 8 points
Bailed out the Commonwealth games … though in 1988 the deficit was still £3.8 million. 6 points plus 4 bonus publicity points for headline 'MIRROR SAVES THE GAMES'.	He styled himself the figurehead of Mrs T's UK 2000 campaign … but one year later positive results were hard to find. 3 points and 3 bonus publicity points for 'yoof' consciousness.
A regular plaintiff, most famously against *Private Eye* and his unofficial biographer, Tom Bower. 8 points plus 6 point bonus for fine displays of emotion in court.	More sued against than suing with writs from Sting and Mike Oldfield. 0 points
His official biography, *Maxwell*, has him pictured with no less than 20 past, present or future heads of state. 10 points	Shows an unfortunate predilection to be photographed with the young and trendy rather than the high and mighty. 0 points but 5 bonus points for being Margaret Thatcher's Minister of Silly Walks.
Ocean-going yacht, the *Ghislaine* has mirrors on the ceiling above … the dining-room table. Also, Strand House, 'designed as a miniature Xanadu filled with priceless *objets d'art* and garish gold-plated modern appliances … less a home than a testament of wealth where taste was not allowed to interfere with the spectacle' – *Maxwell the Outsider*, Tom Bower. 9 points	Balloons, speedboats, planes, trains and automobiles, not to mention a private island. 10 points plus 10 point bonus for element of danger.
Official biographer/loyal employee Joe Haines portrays Maxwell as 'the man who singlehandedly won the war, established peace between Russia and China, climbed Everest without oxygen, and wrote *Bonfire of the Vanities*' – Peter Hillmore in *The Observer*'s Pendennis column. 7 points	Still too busy trying to make history (or the *Guinness Book of Records*). No doubt he will rewrite it when the time comes. 0 points
Amidst all the controversy and publicity surrounding Robert Maxwell, there has never been the faintest whiff of scandal attached to his marriage. 0 points	Lived with his current wife for many years before marrying her, breeding children in the process. Their union may have been informal, but it has always been entirely respectable. 1 point
Loves doing it, *Mirror* readers less happy about having to see it in print. 10 points	For an old hippy, remarkably happy to be seen with a Tory PM. ·5 points

EGO THON

Peter de Savary: an also-ran

Minxy Marla Maples:
Mr Trump topped
her poll in bed

	DONALD TRUMP cont.
POWER PURCHASING	Buying the Plaza Hotel in NY City, favourite stopover for the almost-as-rich-as-Trump and famous. 7 points
BOND VILLAIN-LIKE EMPIRE	**'Goldfinger':** Casinos, hotels, airlines, real estate, sports promotion. 7 points
HEROISM IN SPORT **(by association)**	Once owned the ill-fated USFL Generals, currently best friends with Mike Tyson, sponsored the 'Tour de Trump', negotiating to keep the US Open in Flushing, New York. 7 points
ETHICAL PURITY	Hardly Mother Teresa, but as yet beyond suspicion 5 points
'CAT-WHO-ATE-THE-CONGLOMERATE' GRIN	Smug. 7 points
EGO-AFFIRMING **(biographies/autobiographies)**	*Art of the Deal*: by Trump and journalist Tony Schwartz 10 points…plus 5 for appearing on bestseller lists.
PARTY ANIMALISM	'Rookie of the year' award from *SPY* Magazine in their annual Ironman Nightlife decathalon. 9 points
FANCY DRESS FETISHISM	Always sensibly besuited. 0 points
ICARUS COMPLEX	Approximately one month after he put his Trump Shuttle into service, one of his planes crash landed. The only serious casualty was Trump's ego. 4 points
LEADERSHIP FANTASIES	Regularly buys full-page ads in newspapers to expound his candidate-like views. Recently said, 'I'm not running for president, but if I did…I'd win'. Score 10
OGREISM	Evicted thousands after real estate purchases. His wife Ivana gutted the staff of the Plaza within 30 days of her arrival. Trump advertised Trump Air helicopter service to East Hampton … before telling East Hampton. 10 points

THE WINNER

AND NOW FOLKS HERE'S
1990's MR EGO…

ROBERT MAXWELL

ROBERT MAXWELL cont.	RICHARD BRANSON cont.
Generously assisted former PM Harold Wilson in his search for lordly accommodation in Oxford. (NB also Joe Haines, who originally loudly opposed the Maxwell takeover of the *Mirror*, but was so thoroughly mollified with the job of Mirror Group Political Editor that he ended up writing the slobbering *Maxwell* biography.) 9 points	Often 'lends' his 'private island paradise' in the Caribbean to members of the Royal family. 8 points. Plus 8 bonus publicity points for giving Fergie a koala stuffed with condoms.
'Blofeld': Newspapers, textbooks, publishing, football teams, television, communications. 6 points	**'Drax'**: Airlines, record company, television, radio, nightclubs, condoms, clothing, publishing, retail. 10 points
Rescued Oxford United from bankruptcy, made himself chairman of Derby County and attempted to buy Watford FC. And don't forget those Commonwealth Games. 10 points	Self-styled record breaker/adventurer 8 points plus 10 bonus points for actually engaging in a physical activity.
Maxwell was declared unfit to run a public company. Minus 5 for ego damage	Virgin Records USA was recently alleged to have dealt with a Mafia payola-linked record promoter. Minus 5 points for ego dent, but 5 bonus points for cachet of Mafia connection.
Very Smug. 8 points	Quite extraordinarily smug. 10 points
Maxwell, by Joe Haines 8 points plus 7 for audacious one-word title and serialisation in own paper, but lost 5 points for not selling as well as unofficial and less flattering versions.	*Richard Branson, The Inside Story*, by Mick Brown 5 points — 5 for containing occasional (if gentle) criticism. 3 bonus points for a recently released updated edition.
40th wedding anniversary was arguably The Party of the Eighties. In terms of opulence, comparisons were made to *The Great Gatsby*, said Tom Bower. 8 points	During a party held at his quiet Virgin mansion he had one of his Virgin 747's buzz the party, much to the terror of surrounding residents. 10 points
A pasha, an officer, a fat man in a baseball cap. 10 points	This is a man who wears a flying helmet in the bath. 10 points
The Chinook Helicopter that crashed in November 1986, killing 45 people, belonged to the Captain. 10 points	The Virgin Atlantic Flyer, and its recent successor, have been plagued with disaster. Is Richard Branson sailing too close to the sun? 5 points
Told his wife when he married her that he was going to become PM. 5 points for failing (as yet) to keep his promise, in true prime-ministerial style.	A recent poll found Richard Branson to be the number one choice for the next PM 10 points
Fired his own son for failing to meet him at the airport. Apocryphal legend has it that Maxwell once fired a man he found smoking in the Mirror building, giving him a week's salary in cash and telling him to 'clear off'. The man was a bike messenger on a temporary visit to the building. Recently in dispute with the NUJ over sackings at his Pergamon book publishers. 10 points	Mr Nice Guy. But how long can it last? 0 points

Yes the winner on points is The Bouncing Czech himself — Robert Maxwell with a walloping 160 EGO points. A distant second was the undisputed North American Ego Champ Donald Trump with 147.

Richard Branson was a dismal third with 139 points. A sure sign of an underdeveloped Ego, but we are certain that with enough time and isolation from society this young man will develop an Ego to be reckoned with for the 1991 Ego-Thon. See you then, egomaniacs of the world. ■

Harold Pintochet, man about-town

Given that Harold Pinter is such a witty writer, and that his job involves inventing fictional characters, it's odd that he seems to suffer Total Sense of Humour Failure when confronted with other people's creations.

Harper's and Queen magazine recently reported a dinner party at which Tory adman Tim Bell commented that General Pinochet appeared to be introducing democracy to Chile (fair enough, since he allowed elections in which he was defeated). 'Pinochet the murderer!' exclaimed the cheery Pinter. As a tease Bell then invented an American banker, Jack Robinson, and proceeded to recount various 'facts' about Chile that Robinson had given him. After a while he confessed that he'd made the whole lot up. At this point, says Bell, 'Pinter was furious, really mad at me and demanded I stand up at the dining table and apologise to everyone, which I did, at which juncture Antonia Pinter decided to go home, saying that she couldn't take me any more.'

Respect for the other man's point-of-view is a key Pinter trademark. That's why he said Lord Dacre (formerly Hugh Trevor-Roper) was 'aligning himself with the forces of barbarism' when he made a comment about the Rushdie affair with which Pinter disagreed, which, in turn, is why Dacre refused to appear with Pinter on a Sky TV chat show.

Pinter's deep personal commitment to free speech was further demonstrated at the first night party for Simon Gray's play *Melon*. On meeting diminutive hackette Jane Kelly he inquired, 'Who do you work for?' When she replied *The Mail On Sunday*, he shouted, 'F...ing *Daily Mail*,' several times and insisted that she leave forthwith.

His unwavering readiness to fight for individual freedom was also displayed at a gathering of the absurd 20th of June Group of overprivileged lefties. The meeting was held at The River Café, a *très chic* London eaterie run by architect Richard Rogers and his wife. As the meal began, Pinter noticed a shady character waiting by the door. His suspicions were aroused, so he went over to the man and asked, 'Are you a journalist?' The man confessed that he was. Pinter immediately shouted at him to leave, which he did. A few moments later, the man reappeared. Once again, Pinter had him ejected. At this point the man went to a call-box, phoned the restaurant and explained something to the manager; vis, that he was waiting for his girlfriend, had booked a table and was rather hoping to be allowed to eat his dinner without being thrown out by a paranoid playwright. Finally, the man was allowed to eat in peace, but Pinter's evening was ruined. He spent the rest of the occasion complaining that the air-conditioning was too noisy and left the restaurant dejected.

Sometimes one is better off being slung out of a Pinter *soirée* than staying. Radical revellers who attended the party in honour of Nicaraguan leader Daniel Ortega, held at the Pinters' million-pound home in Campden Hill Square, had to listen as Ortega rambled on for an eternity in Spanish. When eventually he finished, his interpreter went on for just as long in English. Finally the partygoers were let loose on the food and booze only to discover that the Pinters had made a gesture of solidarity with their guest of honour; they had decided not to serve their usual lavish helping of caviare. Truly, it's a tough life trying to build the New Jerusalem. ■

HUSBAND
Wild world

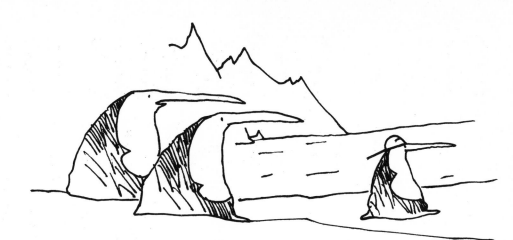

'He certainly keeps up with the trends.'

'Yes, we sell lead free petrol – you pay for the petrol and the lead's free.'

'I honestly think you'll be pleasantly surprised by the north, Jenkins.'

'I wouldn't go overboard on the jockey idea, Manson.'

IT'S A GAME OF TWO SYLLABLES, JOHN

Steve, Dave, Paul, John, Gary, Brian, Nigel, Kevin, Ian, Alan and Andy. No, not a team of builders from Basildon, but the results of an in-depth *Punch* survey. These are the eleven most common names amongst the lads who slip on a jock-strap, slap on the Deep Heat and kick an inflated bladder around of a Saturday afternoon in the First Division.

Is it a daft haircut, the uncanny ability to make inane comments when interviewed, or perhaps a natural flair for the game that makes a professional footballer? Strangely enough it is none of these. It's a name of two syllables, John. Or if at all possible, one. Athletes can be called Sebastian. England cricketers can get away with Robin or even Timothy. But footballers need a name that's short and sharp. Why?

Two reasons above all. In the first place, it's got to be something that can be shouted out in the six-yard box. Trev, Kev, Nev, even – theoretically – Bev; all these can be grafted on to the end of a warning or command. 'Man on, Trev!' 'On the 'ead, Kev!' – these are the mating calls of the footballing pro. And the second reason? Simple – no footballer can reasonably be expected to remember beyond the third syllable of any word, and names are no exception.

This mania for brevity applies to footballers, irrespective of their social position. Even if you head for Windsor to see the legendary Old Etonians, FA Cup winners in 1879 and 1882, you won't hear cries of 'Awfully sorry to trouble you, but could you kick it to the far post, Tristram?' or 'Pop it on my head please, Rupert'; rather 'Line ball, Andy,' or 'Stay with him, John.' As the table below demonstrates, short is sweet.

Simple names are also vital to the chants and abuse of scansion-minded fans. Take that classic song of the early Eighties, 'He's fat, he's round, he bounces on the ground, Sammy Lee, Sammy Lee.' It just wouldn't have been the same if he'd been christened Peregrine.

It seems, then, that mastery of the banana kick whilst still in nappies, or years of training at Bisham Abbey, count for very little if your parents shoot for the wrong name at the font. But then again, football isn't the only sport with rules about names. When did you ever hear of an England cricketer called Kevin? ■

If you want to be a professional footballer, you've got to have a name that's short, simple and irrefutably laddish. ANDREW CONRAD investigates

The Boy Platsy and *(below)* Arsenal's Augustus Caesar. Gus, surely

First there was Trev (Brooking), then there was Trev (Francis) and then there was, er, Kev (Keegan)

11 COMMONEST NAMES IN THE FIRST DIVISION

1 Steve
2 Dave
3 Paul
4 John
5=Gary
  Brian
7=Nigel
  Kevin
  Ian
  Alan
11 Andy

ON THE HEAD, GARY
Mr Lineker and his team of namesakes

1 Gary Walsh
2 Gary Gillespie
3 Gary Stevens
4 Gary Mabbutt
5 Gary Pallister
6 Gary Micklewhite
7 Gary Crosby
8 Garry Parker
9 Gary Thompson
10 Gary Lineker
11 Gary Bannister

TORY UNUNITED
A footballer's trophy Cabinet

Sergei (Maggie) BALTACHA (Ipswich)
Pat HEARD (Rotherham)
Gary PARKINSON (Middlesbrough)
Jason GUMMER (Everton)
Wayne CLARKE (Everton)
Des WALKER (Nottingham Forest)
Graham BAKER (Southampton)
Dean KING (Blackpool)

And those old Downing Street stars…

Wayne HESELTINE (Manchester Utd)
Adrian HEATH (Aston Villa)

Kevin WILSON (Chelsea)
Nigel CALLAGHAN (Aston Villa)

A RIGHT BUNCH OF HOMONYMS…
Not quite as well known as their soundalikes

Jimmy Carter (Millwall) – the man they all call 'El Pres'
Tony Hancock (Stockport County) – only gives 30 minutes
Paul Smith (Torquay Utd) – the best-dressed team in the league
David Puttnam (Leicester City) – from Killing Fields to playing fields

QUITE REMARKABLE, DAVID
A completely ridiculous crew

Craig Shakespeare (Sheffield Wednesday) – *Comedy of Errors*
Augustus Caesar (Arsenal) – man on, Gus
Jeremy Goss (Norwich) – the musical one of the family
Ian Stringfellow (Mansfield Town) – plays extremely wide
Peter Haddock (Leeds Utd) – chip it, Pete
Neil Parsley (Leeds Utd) – cover him, Neil
Perry Digweed (Brighton) – always pulling them out of the net
Dean Greygoose (Crewe) – a little flyer
Darren Mountain (Scunthorpe) – the big lad at the back
John Thomas (Crewe) – sticks it in

BORN WITH A SILVER STUD IN THEIR MOUTH
A suspiciously upper-class quartet

Matthew Le Tissier (Southampton)
Graeme Le Saux (Chelsea)
Peter Rhoades-Brown (Oxford Utd)
Justin Edinburgh (Southend Utd)

ENGLAND '89 v OLD ETONIANS '89
An in-depth syllabic analysis

ENGLAND
Peter
Stuart
Gary
Des
Terry
David
Brian
Peter
John
Gary
Chris

TOTAL SYLLABLE COUNT…19

OLD ETONIANS
Christy
Nick
Scott
James
Andy
John
Jim
Paddy
George
Nick
Chris

TOTAL SYLLABLE COUNT…14

AND THE TELLY BOYS
The rules apply to them, too

John Motson
Barry Davies
Brian Moore
Gerry Sinstadt
Gary Newbon
Jim Rosenthal
Des Lynam
No job there for Christopher Martin-Jenkins

A MESSAGE TO YOU, RUUDI
Do the Name Rules apply to foreign players? Absolutely, Brian. From Barnsley to Buenos Aires, footballers all have the same names, as this exclusive table shows

Foreign Player	Nickname	English Name	English Nickname
Franz Beckenbauer	Der Kaiser	Frank	The Boy Becksy
Diego Maradona	Little Bull*	God	The Boy Godsy
Gerd Muller	Der Bomber	Gerry	The Boy Gezza
Johan Cruyff	Not Known	John	The Boy Cruffy
Edson Nascimento	Pele	Eddy	The Boy Nasher
Paolo Rossi	Not Known	Paul	The Boy Rozzer
Michel Platini	Not Known	Micky	The Boy Platsy
Emilio Butragueno	The Vulture	Mel	The Boy Butch
Ruud Gullit	Bob Marley	Rod	The Boy Guzzer
Ramon Quiroga**	El Loco	Ray	The Boy Roger
Karl-Heinz Rummenigge	Rum	Carl	The Boy Niggsy

NOTE: We rang a number of sources to ascertain nicknames. Another one given for Maradona was 'Pelusa', or Little Pele. The Sun's sports desk suggested 'That f***ing Argentinian cheat'. Sounds fine to us.

**NOTE: This Peruvian goalie was not, admittedly, one of the all-time greats due to his penalty box allergy. But he had a memorable and entirely appropriate nickname.*

Where did the GO-GO GIRLS GO?

For almost a decade five girls with fairies' names and very few dance steps found their way into our hearts, limbs and living-rooms during the three-minute dance spot on *Top Of The Pops*. They put modern dance on the map and paved the way for early morning exercise and celebrity work-out books. If they hadn't existed we might never have witnessed camp, cross-eyed Wayne Sleep or 'Mad Lizzie' Webb opening her legs on TVam. Pop stars knew them as real pros. The public knew them as Pan's People. MICHAEL COLLINS retraces their steps

The word 'boutique', the colour purple, the phrase 'go-go dancer': all these were sacred talismans to Sixties children, and Pan's People were the personification of all three. When founder-member Flick Colby discovered Dee Dee, Babs and Ruth at the Covent Garden Dance Centre in 1966 she could hardly have foreseen the effect these girls would have over the youth – nay, the *lives* – of those of us who were raised in the latter part of that decade and the first half of the drearisome Seventies.

TV dancing had, of course, existed before Pan's People. But the Tiller Girls were all bare bums and American tan tights. Frank & Peggy Spencer's formation team was barely alive. And Peter Gordeno perspired too much for prime-time TV.

A crimper by name and a hoofer by stature, Flick knew – long before Debbie Allen – that fame *costs*. And foreign television was where Pan's People started paying. Unable to get bookings in Britain, the girls were forced to find work in Amsterdam – presumably as dancers – before returning home and eventually getting their slot on *Top Of The Pops*.

The programme's producer required them to dance to the records of American artists who couldn't appear (crippled crooners), and British acts who refused to appear (radical rock stars). Pan's People were seen at their best when interpreting the ballads of the day but gradually tackled anything: the experimental music of The Carpenters, all those raunchy hits with 'Run' in the title, even the heavy, rootsy dub of 'Johnny Reggae'.

FLICK
Choreographer
Flick soon stepped out of the spotlight and into a Miss Bluebelle role as choreographer. Her eclectic dance sequences drew on such diverse sources as tap, jazz, folk and occupational therapy; Merce Cunningham, Martha Graham and Helen Keller were thought to be her major influences. Not every *homage* worked: limited space and strangulated camera angles meant that the Hollywood-style synchronised swimming routines owed more to the 'Okey Cokey than to Busby Berkeley. The girls danced to a deadline. Flick conjured up the choreography in a single day and gave the girls three for rehearsal, occasionally in an empty rugby club. This location inspired one of their most characteristic movements: The Scrum. Colourful costumes were also an important ingredient in the troupe's appeal.

"I guess every typist who makes the disco scene thinks she'd like to join us," Flick once said. And it was true. Throughout Great Britain teenagers applied Biba blusher, copied the girls' clothes and emulated their movements. Meanwhile extremists on the right described the girls

as 'too rude' while those on the left considered them 'exploitative'. (Ardent feminists once threw bottles at the stage during a Pan's People performance in Bath.) Nevertheless, at the height of their career they were among the most sought-after contemporary pin-ups in the country and had an audience of more than ten million viewers each week.

BABS
TRAINING: Arts Educational Trust Stage School
The most memorable member of the dance group was the long-standing, long-legged blonde, Babs Lord. Babs had a very posh accent

a. falling off the stage.

> Their eclectic dance sequences drew on such diverse sources as tap, jazz, folk and occupational therapy; Martha Graham and Helen Keller were thought to be major influences. The synchronised swimming routines owed more to the 'Okey Cokey than to Busby Berkeley

and the grace of an usherette. In a previous, poorer lifetime she would have been exposed as a Barbara and relegated to the aisle of an ABC, dishing out strawberry Mivvis to the beat of Pearl & Dean.

As it was, she clocked up several hundred Pan's People appearances before finally breaking away and becoming Mrs Robert Powell in 1976, thereafter restricting any *step-together-step-point* practices to the confines of her kitchen. Babs' final routine was at the Cambridge Hotel, Camberley, where she gyrated to Curtis Mayfield's 'Move on up'. She wore a black sequinned number with thigh-length split and feather trim.

b. tripping up.

DEE DEE
TRAINING: Elmhurst Dance School
As with Beatlemania, every punter had their favourite Pan's Person. Diplomat's daughter Dee Dee – a diminutive for Patricia – Wilde, was undoubtedly the most popular. This flaming redhead once revealed how a teenage boy had begged for a lock of her hair. Oddly enough I was that boy. (Now a receding redhead, aged 28, I would be grateful for a lock of anyone's hair.) Not all her admirers were so obsessed, however. Some were satisfied with an autograph; others hoped for hand relief. Despite this idolisation Dee Dee reached 29 and decided to quit. Cries of 'stay' from fans and 'bitch' from the other dancers did not prevent her from seeking an alternative career, firstly as a rich Greek's fiancée and then as something in the insurance business. (See 'Pan's People II'.)

c. stubbing a toe.

▶

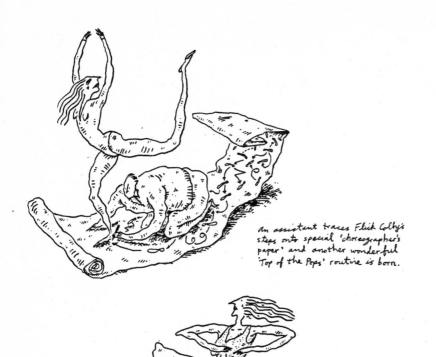

an assistant traces Flick Colby's steps onto special 'choreographer's paper' and another wonderful 'Top of the Pops' routine is born.

Following budget cuts at the BBC Flick's assistant is replaced by a state-of-the-art pair of choreographer's painting shoes.

RUTH
TRAINING: Ballet Rambert

"We get quite a lot of letters from people who want to borrow our costumes," Pan's Person Ruth Pearson told Norma Matheson in the 1975 *TOTP* annual. Most of these notes were written by men of the cloth or members of the Metropolitan Police, which surprised raven-haired Ruth from Surrey. After all, what possible use could these men have for soiled boob tubes or five well-worn gussets that weren't even warm? Fan mail for the girls flooded in daily, usually from the forces. Dissatisfied naval officers posed a recurrent question: How do I become a Pan's Person? The answer to this was supplied in the aforementioned annual: "It's about as easy as becoming the first woman Prime Minister". Four years later Margaret Hilda was at Number Ten and Ruth, like the rest of us, was no longer dancing.

LOUISE
TRAINING: Corona Stage School

The lot of the TV dancer is not a lucky one. High kicks and fixed smiles are replaced in later life by the excruciating pain of being either arthritic or Lionel Blair. Original member Louise Clarke recognised the pitfalls early on. "You can go on dancing for as long as you can," she observed with prescience. For philosopher Louise the end came in the high-waist, halter-neck summer of 1974. Love blossomed and Yorkshire beckoned – she got married. One of

---

The choreography of Flick Colby

Step 1
THE SCRUM
– huddle in a group during the intro to a song then fight your way to the camera for the opening phrase.

Step II
SOLO SPOT
– rush expectantly to front of stage then dart off in another direction as if you've been offered a job on the other channel.

Step III
MAYPOLE
– dance in a circle, waving imaginary scarves, occasionally smashing into the girl in front.

Step IV
CHEERLEADER
– stand in a line, stage right, thrust hands out and up as the camera is focussed on an empty centre stage.

Step V
BREASTSTROKE
– bring knee up to cleavage, flick head back and hope that there is an agent in the audience.

Step VI
DO THE SAPPHO
– twirl alone at the corner of the rostrum until another dancer approaches and begins massaging your neck.

Step VII
THE TOTAL AMNESIA
– improvise madly and grin like a moonie as the other girls remember the steps and smugly finish the sequence.

the last singles that she helped push down the charts was 'I know what I like (in your wardrobe)' by Genesis. The dance routine may well have contributed to Pete Gabriel's decision to leave the band.

SUE
TRAINING: Arts Educational Trust Stage School
By the time eighteen-year-old Sue Mehenick replaced Louise, the dance troupe's CV consisted of a BBC2 *In Concert* profile, guest spots on the Glen Campbell show and appearances at Tiffany's discothèques up and down the country – all achieved without the aid of an Arts Council grant. They could have been massive but for some reason they chose not to be. They turned down chat shows, seldom gave interviews and organised themselves as a collective, with each member assigned an individual task. Sue arranged costumes, Babs read fan mail, Cherry fixed travel, Ruth covered admin and Dee Dee dealt with publicity. Unlike the others, Sue later went on to celluloid stardom by doing the bump in the nightclub scene of *The Stud*.

CHERRY
TRAINING: Bush Davies School
In 1973 Cherry Gillespie succeeded Andy (Andrea Rutherford) who had become known as the Pete Best of Pan's People. Cherry stepped into her shoes and found that the glamorous life of the dancer was marred by verrucas and the sound of Flick's voice. "Okay … sustain that … let it grow … build and smile … for God's sake Cherry, *smile*," screamed the choreographer as she put the girls through their paces. Cherry survived these setbacks and is still in show-business today. She has starred in *A Chorus Line*, works out at the Hogarth club and may well be available for pantomime.

RUBY FLIPPER
Pan's People were dropped from *TOTP* in April 1976 because a 'new look' was needed. Flick – still under contract – recruited Ruth as manager and came up with Ruby Flipper (a creative combination of the two girls' names). Cherry and Sue remained in the line-up as two new girls and three boys were brought in. Whereas Pan's People relied on more classical dance steps such as the plié and the pirouette, Ruby Flipper pouted at the camera and squatted on each other's faces. After several shows they were sacked. Inevitably, four scantily-clad white girls fondling a flaccid thong-clad black man tended to look like an out-take from *Mandingo – the muscle-bound musical*.

PAN'S PEOPLE II
Dee Dee returned to the dance world in the late Seventies, with the Pan's People name. She began auditioning new dancers, stipulating that they must be 5ft 5in tall and talented. She

did, however, make an exception when enlisting sixteen-year-old Sarah Brightman from Berkhamstead. Sarah, of course, went on to lose her heart to a starship trooper and her cherry to an ugly composer. Dee Dee and the company toured Thailand, got banned in Bahrain and were auctioned off at Sotheby's in 1980. (An anonymous bidder paid £5,000 to charity for the girls' services on New Year's Eve.)

HOT GOSSIP
Anyone who remembers Him & Us or the Teri Scoble Dancers on Granada's *Get It Together* will know that these were but a pale imitation of Pan's People. Hot Gossip was the only other dance team to come close to equalling the popularity of Flick Colby and Co. As Auntie Beeb mourned the passing of the *Black and White Minstrels*, the multi-coloured 'naughty bits' of Hot Gossip popped up and out on ITV, but they very soon went down and in again. Mary Whitehouse has never forgiven the group for turning the reverse missionary position into a dance step. Music lovers have never forgiven them for giving trooper's trouper Sarah Brightman her second big break.

DEATH OF THE TV DANCER
After the all-girl Legs & Co and the ill-fated *ZOO*, the dance slot was finally axed from *TOTP*. The audience grew louder and the advent of the video promo ultimately killed off the TV dancer. Nowadays, male and female backing dancers can be seen on stage, underneath Stephanie Lawrence in a summer season, but they lack the personality and appeal of Dee Dee, Babs, Ruth and the rest. Pan's People was an idea that had had its day. They – not the Young Generation – taught a discordant nation how to hustle and guided us through Sixties stax, Seventies soul, glam rock, reggae and ska – first time around. Alas, all that remains of them in the 'vogueing' Eighties is some faded footage in the vaults of Television Centre. The girls are now too old for a comeback and too content for a revival, so all we can do is look back, have a laugh and let sleeping dancers lie. ∎

Babs.

Sue.

Cherry.

Dee Dee.

Louise.

Ruth.

?

The unseen, mystery 'Pan's Person' – Flick Colby.

Dance steps for the 'Scrum':

Just not cricket

MICHAEL COLLINS catches Ian Botham live on stage

According to the writer Umberto Eco 'every sports act is a waste of energy,' and any 'sports chatter is therefore a glorification of waste'. These sentiments weren't in evidence at the Queen Elizabeth Hall on London's South Bank for the 27th date of the tour of **An Evening With Ian Botham**. Folk that are fans of team sports, and subsequently communal showers, apparently go a bundle on the England cricketer turned sports 'personality' Ian Botham. Mr Botham's celebrity was confirmed when he was the subject of a *This Is Your Life* episode. Certainly, his achievements are remarkable. He has starred in a series of commercials for Dansk alcohol-free lager. He has won great acclaim for his captaincy of a team on BBC's *A Question of Sport*. And, apparently, he has also squeezed in a brief spell as captain of the England cricket team. But Mr Botham (or 'Beefy' or 'Guy the Gorilla' or 'Botty' as he is affectionately known to his chums and fans alike) has never stuck to just playing the game.

In his guise of all-round entertainer, 'the world's greatest all-rounder' added to his unorthodox image by using the phrase 'stark bollock naked' on a stage usually reserved for Dvořák recitals. This also fired the imaginations of the Women's Institute ladies present in their blouses modelled on festooned blinds. Mr Botham is the nearest they'll get to a bit of rough. The chances of these women getting Mr Botham into bed are a lot slimmer than they are themselves. They do the next best thing – tuck themselves in with a copy of Kathy Botham's autobiography *Living with a Legend*, or pay out £8.50 for a ticket to his one-man show. Their corpulent companions, the Billy Bunteresque ex-public schoolboys in the front row, know that the nearest they will get to *being* Ian Botham is the nickname of Beefy. These lads are the 'sport chatterers' who rarely participate, but frequently discuss their team at a test match. In the same manner of Mr Botham's

idol, Mrs Thatcher, announcing the birth of her grandchild, they continually use the statutory 'we'.

For them Mr Botham is the archetypal *Lad's Own* hero. Both ladies man and country lad, Mr Botham has the body mass of a stud bull and the highlighted hairstyle of a simpleton. For his London stage debut he wore the uniform favoured by Barratt househusbands on a Bank Holiday – powder-blue polo shirt and baggy jumbo-cord hipsters. This introduced a casual tone to the evening and made the audience feel that they were in the snug of a country pub and not a *Scandinavian-moderne* concert hall.

The production opened with a 30-minute film of Mr Botham's greatest triumphs. This featured his TV debut as a choirboy at the age of nine in BBC's *Songs of Praise* – a suitable primer for a career where dropped balls are the kiss of death. The second act consisted of Mr Botham actually appearing on stage. His friend, David English (the author of the boot-sale bestseller *The Bunbury Tales*), supplied him with feed lines and pulled audience questions from a ballot box. For example, 'What fist did you hit Chappel with?' 'Right.' Or, 'How many times have you got Viv Richards out?' 'Not nearly enough.'

Mr Botham's mastery of microphone technique improved with the intimacy of questions – no doubt supplied by the Billy Bunter brigade. 'Did Gatting really tonk the barmaid?' You could almost hear the cheap seats thinking, sod the batting averages, let's hear about the legovers-before-wicket. 'I don't believe the stories,' replied Mr Botham, 'because I know that nothing goes into Gatt's room after 10.30 unless he can eat it.' This didn't exactly constitute a denial. Mr Botham then launched into a more matey mode and began discoursing about his contemporaries as if they were characters in an Enid Blyton book. The adoring audience became privy to locker-room anecdotes and tales of derring-do starring

> To the ex-public schoolboys in the front row Mr Botham is the archetypal *Lad's Own* hero

the cricket world's very own Famous Five: Rosie, Lambie, Hendo, Hoggy and Fletch.

How we laughed about that time in Karachi when Botty and Arkle (Derek Randall) got the 'runs' – no cricket pun intended. How we roared about the sewage problem in the Pakistan hotel – ''ere comes a lumpy one, lads'. Gatts emerged as a red meat man who likes some slap and tickle with his ham and pickle. 'I stepped over the service trays outside Mike Gatting's suite,' teased Mr Botham. Later he put his mate straight by defending Mr Gatting's decision to play in South Africa: 'the Government ridicules players for going to South Africa, while still trading there'. Mr Botham is a passionate extoller of the view that sportsmen break down more barriers than politicians ever do.

'Do you fancy politics?' asked David English. 'What, Foreign Secretary?' joked Mr Botham. 'We'd be at war with Pakistan within eight days.' A question was read out from a bespectacled woman in row B called Laura. 'Should girls be encouraged to play cricket?' it asked, at once striking a blow for the cricketing wives who stay home ringing out the Pampers while reading about their old man's exploits in the papers. Laura got herself a free programme and a kiss from Mr Botham. 'Sport,' he said in earnest, 'is all about timing and co-ordination, not physical strength. Certainly girls should be encouraged. I'd definitely be willing to play rugby with them.'

There are those who dismiss cricket as a posh version of rounders and don't know a Gooch from a googly. Sport, for them, is a last resort like sex. It is something you do to kill a couple of hours (minutes even) on a Saturday afternoon. Anyone who makes a career out of what should essentially remain a hobby can count themselves lucky. Which, for the moment, Mr Botham can. In five years time, however, when his innings is up, these entertaining lectures might well prove to be his only source of income. Already, Mr Botham is booked for a tour of the Far East.

To raise money for charity Mr Botham once followed in the footsteps of Hannibal the Great. Now as he cashes in on the Oriental cabaret circuit he will be following in the footsteps of such notables as Mr Max Bygraves and Mr Shakin' Stevens. ∎

'Happy birthday son. You owe me £278.'

'You mean you rang me to tell me that water rates and Telecom profits are both up?'

'Do you take Czechs?'

'Thatcher's resignation? It doesn't go that far into the future.'

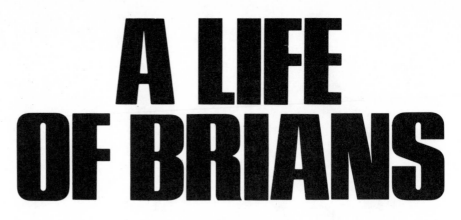

A LIFE OF BRIANS

Sports commentators have a tough job. There's no other word for it, remarkably difficult. Ironically, that's what makes it so easy – in every sense of the word. So what are your thoughts, BILL MATTHEWS…

ARMED ONLY with fact-sheets, helped only by a producer blaring in their ears, the men behind the mikes have to improvise their way through many a sporting event. They have to give out information, opinions and history, while identifying the players. And, if possible, they have to add tension, atmosphere and excitement. The thrill of live television is that anything can go wrong, and when it does, it's not usually on the pitch, the court or the track, but inside the commentator's head.

Yet David Coleman or Murray Walker lose no popularity through their gaffes. In fact, they would lose popularity without them. Many of Britain's commentators have become so well known that watching certain sports would be unthinkable without them. Motor racing without Murray Walker? Boxing without Harry Carpenter? Like love and marriage, you can't have one without the other.

Curiously, with one exception, all commentators in this category are from the BBC. Perhaps it is because ITV gave up on sport, apart from football and athletics, when they axed *World Of Sport* in 1986. But even in those sports that ITV covers just as frequently as the

BBC, Alan Parry is no David Coleman, Reg Gutteridge no Harry Carpenter (as Frank Bruno confirmed when he asked Reg, 'Where's Harry? I want to talk to Harry'), and a hundred people must have heard of Peter O'Sullevan for every one who's heard of Graham Goode.

The exception is ITV's football commentator, Brian Moore, if only because he's the only man alive today who was already bald when Bobby Charlton wasn't. Sky TV is of course making some headway with Tony 'Goodnight, Charlie!' Grieg. Perhaps significantly (but probably not), the only BBC commentator whose position is not unassailable is football's John Motson (his is unassailable only in Mrs Thatcher's meaning of the word) and it is also significant (or not) that of those listed here, he is the youngest.

For the BBC's commentary team is growing old together (though I don't mean in each other's houses). Out of those we've covered, four are in their 60s, one in his 70s and one in his 80s. Only one is under 59. They have become so established, that it is impossible for their understudies to stamp their personalities (where applicable) on their sport. Is there life after Dan Maskell?

THE PUNCH GUIDE TO SPORTS COMMENTATORS

HARRY CARPENTER

SPORT: Boxing   **AGE:** 63

CAREER RECORD: Had his debut in 1949, but didn't win a regular place in the team until 1962, since when Harry has cheered on (completely impartially, of course) 15 British World Champions, plus Barry McGuigan. He also serves as linkman for tennis and golf, but has achieved an odd kind of fame as the butt of Frank Bruno's sparkling wit – know what I mean? – and thus become familiar to millions who wouldn't know a boxing glove if it hit them. Recently voted the finest sports commentator by a New York jury.

CHARACTERISTICS: Tends to pick a winner in Round One and stick to him, despite knockdowns, knockouts, the arrival of the ambulance etc. Unashamedly jingoistic ('He's hurt Tyson – go on, Frank!'). At his best when being morally indignant at bad decisions, as at the Olympics in '84 (pro-USA) and '88 (anti-USA).

PRETENDERS: Desmond Lynam is the official number two, when he's not too busy being handsome (how can anyone with a moustache be handsome?).

TRIVIAL FACT: Mike Tyson once asked Harry for his autograph.

TYPICAL SENTENCE: (at every fight) 'Well, I've never seen anything like this in all my years of boxing.'

WHAT HE DID SAY: 'They've given it all tonight but there's a little left to give yet.'

DAN MASKELL

SPORT: Tennis   **AGE:** 81

CAREER RECORD: The Dilys Powell of tennis. Has attended 65 successive Wimbledon tournaments, and from 1929 to 1955 was head coach there. He began TV commentary in 1951 and, while times and the game have changed, his commentary style has suited every era perfectly. There is no question of his retirement from Wimbledon; he simply wouldn't want to be anywhere else.

CHARACTERISTICS: His enthusiasm about the game is boundless, and infectious. The amount of times 'we won't see a better cross-court backhand pass than that' is also boundless. He accentuates the positive, eliminates the negative; doesn't go for Mr Inbetween.

PRETENDERS: Gerald Williams (ugh!), John Barrett (who?), Bill Threlfall (I thought he was John Barrett). In the early Eighties, Dan used to be crowded out in the commentary box by all the British players who'd lost in Round One.

TRIVIAL FACT: He won the British Professional Championships 16 times – when all the top players were amateurs, and only they were allowed to compete at Wimbledon.

TYPICAL SENTENCE: 'Ooh I say . . . in all my years of tennis . . . that peach of a volley by the Swede completely foxed his opponent . . . Mark Cox.'

WHAT HE DID SAY: 'You could see he was going to play a disguised lob there.'

RICHIE BENAUD

SPORT: Cricket   **AGE:** 59

CAREER RECORD: After being arguably the best captain in Australia's history, he could have had any job he liked in the cricketing media. Having made a successful transition to Australian TV, he made his BBC debut on the radio in 1960 and on TV in 1964, since when he has never known a winter in either Australia or Britain, never seen a robin nuzzling a stray twig on a snowy lawn. He has commentated on 16 series between the two traditional enemies.

CHARACTERISTICS: Tact when an umpire is wrong ('that must have been close'), understatement ('not a bad shot for six'), the pregnant pause (after Tony Lewis hands over to him, he'll wait ten minutes before replying, 'Thank you, Tony') and the squint (when being interviewed, he appears to stare straight at the camera, but he is actually looking at the interviewer).

PRETENDERS: Jack Bannister (too smug), Tony Lewis (too Welsh), Tom Graveney (too rural).

TRIVIAL FACT: In the early Sixties, he was offered a safe seat in the Australian Parliament, but chose to be a commentator.

TYPICAL SENTENCE: 'We pick up play with England on 56 for seven, Hughes to Gooch [off-drive], no point chasing that one.'

WHAT HE DID SAY: 'That slow motion replay doesn't show how fast the ball was travelling.'

JOHN MOTSON

SPORT: Football   **AGE:** 44

CAREER RECORD: Quite clearly here, Motson began TV commentary in 1971, having moved from *Sport on 2*, and oh! I think, here, yes, it must be, that his takeover of the FA Cup Final in 1977 was a clear indication that he was here to stay. But Motson quite literally faced disaster when ITV took over exclusive rights to the League, leaving the BBC with the FA Cup and Motson trying to convince us that Billingham Synthonia vs Rochdale is more important than Arsenal vs Liverpool.

CHARACTERISTICS: Statistically obsessed (in fact, this is the 26th time in his career he's been called that), wise after the event ('That's a free kick, surely' when it's already being taken), and adept at sheer unadulterated waffle (no room to illustrate).

PRETENDERS: Barry Davies (much better), Tony Gubba (help!).

TRIVIAL FACT: On commentary days, he always goes to the toilet exactly half an hour before kick-off.

TYPICAL SENTENCE: 'And you have to say this, Jimmy Hill, the big Bulgarian is probably the danger here perhaps Trevor Brooking and interestingly it's the 17th time at Wembley that the first shot of an international has landed in Block G of the stands in fact Bobby Charlton. . . *(to be continued)*

WHAT HE DID SAY: 'Nine minutes to go. That speaks for itself.'

MURRAY WALKER

SPORT: Motor Racing
AGE: 66

CAREER RECORD: Started out in 1949, in time to see the inception of the World Motor Racing Championships the next year. Spent 29 years as an understudy – first in motorcycling to his father Graham until 1962, then in motor racing to Raymond Baxter until 1978. Since then, he's lapped all other contenders.

CHARACTERISTICS: A triumph of horse-power (or should it be hoarse?) over brain-power, he often gets dangerously over-heated during the one-lap warm-up, but attempts to keep going at an average speed of 140mph throughout a race. He also makes, how can we put it, the odd mistake during a race. Once memorably characterised by Clive James as sounding like a man whose trousers were on fire.

PRETENDERS: The others are *absolutely* nowhere – there's no one to touch him – he's going into the pits.

TRIVIAL FACT: He worked in advertising until 1982, and invented the slogan, 'A Mars a day helps you work, rest and play.'

TYPICAL SENTENCE: 'And Nigel Mansell – or is it Gerhard Berger? – I can't tell – the idiotic Portuguese producer is literally not showing it – we've missed what happened – I've never seen anything like it – James Hunt…'

WHAT HE DID SAY: 'Do my eyes deceive me or does Senna's car sound a bit rough?'

PETER O'SULLEVAN

SPORT: Horse Racing
AGE: 71

CAREER RECORD: Born in Ireland, educated at Charterhouse, he started in 1946 and managed to be daily columnist for the *Daily Express and* a racehorse owner while remaining an objective TV commentator; he got excited no matter who won. Even if it was himself, no one could tell the difference, except when his Attivo won the Triumph Hurdle in 1974 and he gave it away by asking viewers to excuse him while he went to get the trophy.

CHARACTERISTICS: He manages more words per minute than most of us do in a day, and even sounds orgasmic at the end of the Allied Steel and Wire Hurdle Race at Thirsk. His powers of identification, description and analysis, while building up excitement, make him perhaps the greatest commentator in sport.

PRETENDERS: Julian Wilson, Jimmy Lindley. Enough said.

TRIVIAL FACT: When 11, he told *Express* magnate Lord Beaverbrook that he would be racing correspondent of the *Sunday Express*. He was wrong.

TYPICAL SENTENCE: Captain Frisk moves ahead of Don't Tell Ruth (80mph) but here comes Commandante (95mph) with a late run and at the line (105mph) Commandante is the winner (98mph) with Captain Frisk second (84mph) and Don't Tell Ruth coming in third (72.46mph and falling)…'

WHAT HE DID SAY: 'And Sula Bula is the winner – I heard it out of the corner of my ear.'

BILL McLAREN

SPORT: Rugby Union
AGE: 66

CAREER RECORD: Became a radio commentator in 1952, despite throwing away the BBC's invitation, thinking it was a joke. He moved to TV in 1966 but refused to give up the day job teaching under-12s P.E. in his home town of Hawick. For years, his Saturday ritual involved rising at 7 am to mark out rugby pitches, refereeing one boys' match, watching another, before driving to Murrayfield for an International. He now only likes to commentate on Scotland matches, thus cruelly condemning the viewers to Nigel Starmer-Smith.

CHARACTERISTICS: A man who can sing with his speaking voice – a rich baritone. While short on analysis (a fist-fight is 'a little argy-bargy') he is second only to 55,000 Welshmen singing 'Land Of Our Fathers' for creating atmosphere. If only his commentating was as important to him as it is to the armchair fans of rugby.

PRETENDERS: Apart from Nigel Starmer-Smith, the Edinburgh intellectuals Chris Rea (not the singer) and Ian Robertson (extra marks if you can tell their voices apart).

TRIVIAL FACT: He is addicted to boiled sweets, notably the locally-made Hawick Balls.

TYPICAL SENTENCE: 'As the referee blows the whistle for the end of the match, they'll be dancing in the streets of Ballachulish, I can tell ya!'

WHAT HE DID SAY: 'Rafter again doing the unseen which the crowd relish so much.'

DAVID COLEMAN

SPORT: Athletics
AGE: 63

CAREER RECORD: Started his marathon run on the same day Bannister broke the 4-minute mile, on 6 May 1954. From the mid-Sixties, he presented *Sportsnight With Coleman*, until it became, errrr… in fact, *Sportsnight Without Coleman*. He gave up football commentary after five FA Cup Finals and after his catch-phrase of 'one-nil!' when a goal was scored proved fatally flawed during games with more than one goal. He has never lost his job as an athletics commentator. Remarkable.

CHARACTERISTICS: His foibles are as famous as his enthusiasm. He rarely names runners from Africa or Eastern Europe (the Romanian is just ahead of the two Russians). He can encompass whole nations, even continents with one generalisation ('All Kenyans, indeed most Africans, love to front-run'). Yet he remains our best-loved sporting institution.

PRETENDERS: Ron Pickering, Stuart Storey. Surely no one can catch Coleman. Surely.

TRIVIAL FACT: He once played football for Stockport County Junior Reserves.

TYPICAL SENTENCE: 'And this time the bell – and Cram senses the Kenyans are behind him – he senses they want to win – and Ovett is literally going backwards at this stage – AND THERE GOES CRAM – HAS HE GONE TOO SOON?!'

WHAT HE DID SAY: 'When Juantorena opens his legs you can really see his class.'

HONEYSETT
Christmas with Genghis Khan

'It can be a little tedious, at times, living with an ex shot-putter.'

'How many times must I tell you, Gerald, not to hold a knife like that.'

'You think you've got problems? I've had three mountain bikes stolen this year.'

'So much for tightening up on security.'

LOVE in a BOX

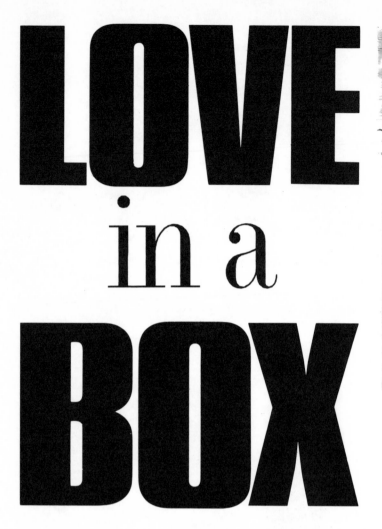

If union leader Arthur Scargill placed a lonely heart ad, how many replies would he get? Then again, how many would Page 3 girl Maria Whittaker get? JOHN HIND and STEVEN MOSCO wrote lonely heart ads for them to find out what their box-numbers would yield

'*Love is a game of secret, cunning stratagems, in which only the fools who are fated to lose reveal their true aims or motives – even to themselves.*' Eugene O'Neill.

IN THE SPIRIT of St Valentine's Day we decided to explore the romantic strategies, aims, motives and quality-control techniques of the Great British lover. The plan was simple enough. Take the personal attributes of some of the rich and famous and place them in a selection of the nation's oversubscribed lonely hearts columns. The execution was not so simple. Our first advertisement was sculpted around the details of iconic Australian soapster Jason Donovan and read:

Successful male-model type, nice bottom, bleached hair; likes a singsong, having a laugh and making money. I hail from down under (Melbourne). I'm in London for several months. Contact me please, girls. Love, Jay.

This was curtly blackballed by the sub-editors of *Loot* magazine. They wrote back to say that it wasn't good form to flaunt the demeanour of a gigolo in a lonely hearts message. The offending text, 'nice bottom' and 'likes … making money', was underlined and returned with our postal order.

More success was had with the small ads alluding to the personae of other big name stars, though *Private Eye* has still not printed our 'Magaret Thatcher' submission. We sent off details of the unmarried Christian songster Cliff Richard, the glamour model and 1988 Page 3 Girl of the Year Maria Whittaker, the 20-stone Northern comedian Bernard Manning, the radical actress Vanessa Redgrave, the miners' trade union leader Arthur Scargill, and the Australian pop singer Kylie Minogue. All were accepted, but nevertheless altered. Most censoriously *The Sport* removed our Bernard Manning-alike's reference to being a swearing widower (also that he was currently living with his mother). *Loot* magazine changed our Kylie Minogue clone's 'If your pen is out, what are you waiting for?' to the more innocuous 'If you've a pen and paper …' London's trenchantly left-wing listings magazine *City Limits* reduced our Redgrave entry's namedrop of Marx to 'marx'. Less surprisingly, all of the replies to our Maria Whittaker-double's advert in *The Sport* were opened and vetted.

Within 24 hours of publication the correspondence began arriving. Five letters per postal delivery on average, sometimes as many as 20. The replies were certainly engaging: several showed a primitive enthusiasm for psychological self-analysis, and all were erratically spelt and constructed.

Many letters were accompanied by the respondents' portraits. These ranged from nervous passport shots and over-exposed Polaroids to glossy professional 'model cards'. The letter-writers covered a wide age-range from many (s)walks of life. The majority exhibited fluctuating waves of self-glorification ('I'm known as very handsome'), optimism ('This is my 200th letter, but one to a person who I have an inkling is very special'), and intimations of lewdness ('I hope you fancy me, cos I'm very broad-minded'). All except one of our real-life lonely hearts would have no problem getting something going in the form of an active relationship. Our Arthur Scargill advertisement didn't receive one vote of confidence. There is an explanation for this. *The Sunday Times* editor Andrew Neil and his triple-Shredded Wheat hairstyle was linked with glamorous romance in the High Court recently. Mr Scargill's lack of a romantic response (glamorous or otherwise) could be because we didn't mention his own distinctive 'Mr Three-Wheats' coiffure. But there was no dearth of admirers for the likes of Miss Whittaker and Miss Minogue. Even for girth-friendly TV funny-man Mr Manning. If the way to a man's heart is really through his stomach, then some people obviously don't mind working hard to win it.

Along with lonely hearts, amorous hopefuls also use dating agencies. *Blind Date* with its match-making host Cilla Black is testimony to Britain's voracious desire for 'packaged love', as well as the increasing enjoyment of seeing people 'achieve a lover' through ludicrous, gregarious means. Take the use of third-party technology for romantic ends. Computer dating agencies now cover an eclectic range of interests and 'matching combinations', from vegetarians to fatties to professional over-50s to buppies (black urban professionals). Many agencies advertise in the national press and offer free simplified computer-matching print-outs. These act as a preliminary to a more physical (and considerably more expensive) date. Under the pseudonym Belinda Hampton we filled a free Dateline questionnaire with the essential details of the Duchess of York. We ticked, for instance, her characteristics as being: romantic, practical, conventional, adventurous. And her interests being: travelling, reading, children, homemaking, the countryside, and eating.

Sarah Ferguson's perfect mechanical match turns out – according to Dateline – to be 'Anthony' – 34 years on earth and 6' 1" tall. Anthony's musical interests are jazz, country & western, and folk. At home he enjoys listening to the radio, watching televised sport, being with children, cooking/entertaining, do-it-yourselfing, and pets. His choice of entertainments for an enjoyable evening with Sarah are theatre, concerts, opera/ballet, parties, wine bars, eateries and dinner parties. Anthony enjoys devoting time to: keeping fit, walking/hiking, the countryside, sightseeing, motoring, foreign travel and the arts. Anthony has no dislikes. For just £85, made payable to Dateline Ltd, the admittedly pregnant Duchess of York could now meet Anthony. Perhaps this would solve any concerns she may still have that there's a gentleman more suited to her hand outside her existing circles.

As for the Labour leader Neil Kinnock, we sent off all his details ('Welsh, working in politics, 5' 9", fun-loving, ambitious, generous, nervous …') to Datalink Ltd ('Britain's foremost and least expensive' coupling company), which is currently digitising 500 would-be lovers a day. Datalink, in 'computer test number D14078533', selected for Mr Kinnock a 45-year-old primary-school teacher called Louise – a woman sounding remarkably similar to Mr Kinnock's wife Glenys, and one who heartily enjoys

a sexually explicit Valentine arrives in response to one of the box numbers

pop music, museum visits, and plenty of committee work.

Encouraged by Datalink's grasp of the sensual sciences we posted a questionnaire under the guise of Cecilia Hampton. This was marked up with the attributes and tastes of octagenarian society pensmith Barbara Cartland ('age range of person you wish to meet? – 50-90 please'). Datalink's computer swiftly responded with a letter informing our Cartlandesque creation that, 'due to a preponderance of ladies over 50 seeking our unattached men', it was unable to process her form. It still recommended our unquenchably romantic authoress to contact Datelink's subsiduary company, The Sue Kent Agency, who offer a reduced oldster price of £28 (youngsters pay £83). Ms Cartland isn't guaranteed a 'preponderance' of eligible gentlemen callers if she takes this offer. But if she applied her bravura style to the self-description form she'd probably do very well. The French philospher Blaise Pascal showed a keen understanding of match-making phenomena when he noted as early as 1660, 'We never, then, love a person, but only qualities.'

Over an intense three weeks we learnt that 'out there' there is a vast, secret (and not so secret) world of loneliness. Polaroid-popping souls compose and send highly personal missives in their thousands, daily, around a mailing network that both distances them from their prey or dreams, and yet buys hearts for the price of a box-number or even a 20p stamp. It's still a romantic world and the broken-hearted can take solace: there just might be someone out there for everyone. Unless, of course, your name happens to be Arthur Scargill.

TURN OVER FOR THE RESULTS ▶

AND NOW, THOSE ADVERTISEMENT REPONSES IN FULL

	ADVERT	PUBLICATION	REPLIES	TYPE OF RESPONDENTS
MARIA WHITTAKER	**EXTREMELY** busty, slightly plump, Maria Whittaker look-alike, early 20s, loves fast cars, photography, fun, fine food, seeks attractive, go-getting man, any age, for exciting conversation, poss more. Photo pse. Anywhere.	**THE SPORT** (Tabloid newspaper) Friday 19 Jan £2 (Cost of ad)	59	Slim-built oil-industry worker, 5' 10"; Security guard from Weymouth, 26; '26, 5' 8", light brown hair, baby blue eyes'; 'I'm 37 yrs old, *very* good-looking but lacking confidence to go out and meet someone since my divorce, three years ago. I've had two.' 'Dear M W lookalike, I am a go-getting man who loves good time and food. Sorry I do not have a photo at the moment. Yours faithfully . . .'; British Coal wage consultant; Owner of three Norwich pubs; 'Sports Editor for eight newspapers'; 'Shy company director . . . In the photo I'm the blond one!!'
CLIFF RICHARD	**PRESERVED** forties male into Elvis, Christianity, seeks woman before too late!	**TIME OUT** (London listing mag) 18-25 Jan £20	3	Born Again Christian caterer, 25, from Ilford; Dental receptionist, 38, from Finchley; Head Teacher, 44, from Chingford.
VANESSA REDGRAVE	**SUCCESSFUL AGELESS** Marxist feminist actress seeks committed 'revolutionary' for close encounters of the politically sound kind, plus Albanian holidays? On your marx, get set, go!	**CITY LIMITS** (London listing mag) 18-25 Jan £17.50	5	'East London lower-middle class Jewish, lifted away, by university and the upheavals of the 60s, into 70s revolutionary politics'; TU steward, activist and course tutor; 'Zen Marxist Comedian'; 'Freelance media hack, fairly non-descript-looking'; 'Mature but ideologically confused of Letchworth'.
BERNARD MANNING	**SUCCESSFUL**, hard-working club performer, 60ish, single, slightly overweight, wishes to meet kind, sexy woman, any age, to really lavish with jokes, money, romance. Pse write. Love, big kisses. Anywhere.	**THE SPORT** Friday 19 Jan £6	6	'Anglo-French brunette, Aquarius, Roman Catholic, into suspenders and being kind, 35, from Newcastle'; 'Slim, honest and reliable Miss'; 'Lonely and very sexy' from Leytonstone; Welsh 42-yr-old 'with full figure and very nice bust'.
KYLIE MINOGUE	**TWENTY-ONE YEAR OLD** petite Australian girl, slim, blonde hair, into pop, jeans, telly, dancing, soaps and make-up, working in London 1990, would love to meet English boys/men. If you've got pen and paper, what are you waiting for? Photo if possible, love Yvonne!	**LOOT** (London/ Manchester small ads mag) 15 & 17 Jan £8 (for two insertions)	45	24-yr-old engineer in cellular radio communications; 'I'm a sort of Crocodile Dundee'; Credit controller for international publishing company; Central-heating fitter; computer programmer; 'Solicitor's Clerk, Aries'; Accountant specialising in entertainment clients; 45-yr-old teacher; Financial company clerk 'and part-time model'; Swiss finishing-school educated senior import clerk from Heathrow; London Underground worker from Islington, 23; 'Very slim and agile dancer, musician, engineer and trainee radiographer'.
ARTHUR SCARGILL	**MILITANT NORTHERN TRADE UNIONIST**, seeks politically-aware lass for stimulating conversations, meetings, conferences, pubs etc. Let's smash the new spirit of realism together!	**CITY LIMITS** 25 Jan-1 Feb £17.50	0	None.

TYPICAL REMARKS	MOST ROMANTIC/SEXUAL	MOST PRETENTIOUS/UNUSUAL
'I'm attractive, fun loving, outgoing, and I go out and get most things I want'; 'My big 'turn-on' is to see a lady wearing sexy lingerie, esp. stockings/suspenders'; 'I like to see a girl who fills out her blouse – can I come round to yours with a tape measure?'; 'Maria Whittaker makes me rock hard'; 'Eating nice food is what I like, particularly steak, roast and seafood – prawn cocktails that is'; 'So you like fast cars. Fancy a spin with me then – I have an Escort'; 'I live in the Lake District and I'm single – if you saw the Cumbrian females, you'd know why'.	'I would love to make you my very own Page Three Girl my sweetheart... most of all my newest hobbies is spending all my time with you my love... I would love this to be the year when I meet my true love and have the time of my life with you darling'; 'Please tell me what you want. Be frank. I am broadminded'; 'I have shot photos of women in various states of undress – bra and pants, topless, nude'; 'I do have my likes and dislikes. My dislikes are jumping out an airplane without a chute and my likes are stockings and sussers'; 'I enjoy giving massage, especially adore giving massage and taking photos of big busty lady'.	'I've given myself 18 months to buy my £17,000 dream car'; 'I've always been of the opinion that the difference between being at the top and sitting in the middle is *attitude*'; 'I'm looking for someone with the wit of Victoria Wood, the body of Maria Whittaker and the sophistication of Princess Di'; 'I'm a quality assurance manager of a plastics company, even though I'm only 23 years old – shows what a go-getter I am.'
'Perhaps we could meet for lunch after Church one Sunday'; 'So many people nowadays seem to have no interest in the spiritual side of life and Love'; 'I too am a Christian. And I also like Elvis! (I see no reason why one cannot combine enjoyment of "The Pelvis" with a love and respect for the creator)'.	'May I ask whether, like me, you are a virgin?'	'I believe in the family, the Police, good manners, God, and less graffiti. I do not know much about Elvis Presley but I have heard 'Jailhouse Rock'.'
'Only a failed dialectical syndicalist with a degree in workers control could appreciate your qualities'; 'Could you infiltrate my poor mind with your own brand of Marxist ideology? That would be the most thrilling'; 'I am looking for a committed Marxist for ideologically disciplined and correct but also passionate and loving encounters. I think *you* are the woman I seek'; 'My great desire is to escape Life and indulge in a little petite-bourgeois hedonism'.	'Only an SAMF actress of singular talent could get her tonsils round *that*'; 'Do you suppose they have Heartlands box numbers in Albania?'; 'We lovers of elegant socialism really ought to meet up'; 'Do write, I would love to spend an evening exploring issues with you!'; 'Please write back quickly – I can't stand the suspense.'	'Dear Ms E889 (sounds like an additive)'; 'I am a compulsive reader of anything from Gramsci to Hobsbawm'; 'I have the traditional warm red centre with a seriously green exterior. How about "proportionately unrepresentative relative to conventional political parties"'; 'I organise and run men's groups which focus on crucial issues such as the development of alternatives to male sexuality'; 'The trouble is the Marx are being moved all the time'.
'Hello successful'; 'What do you class as sexy? You have me stumped'; 'I do hope that you will like to have me as your lady'; 'I work locally and I drive a Skoda Rapide'; 'I can guess you're a comedian... I hope you are not coarse'; 'I will be honest with you. I am looking for a friend for my mother. She will kill me for writing to you but I will take the chance'; 'I am *not* fat'; 'I hope you tell *good* jokes, because I need belly laughs'.	'As for being slightly overweight – what does that matter?'; 'And I do love sexy magazines, and sexy video, and I am very easy to please'; 'I always dream of older man 'cos young men cheat and very unfaithful'; 'Give me a chance to spoil you. It will be the time of your life and then you would ask yourself where I was all the time'; 'I've often been told by friends that I'm one of the last of *the* Romantics. Trouble is I never get it'.	'I presume you are between 59 and 63'; 'You sound like the male counterpart of myself'; 'I *LOVE* you'; 'I like travelling dinners'; 'Hi, My Future!'; 'And I wear suspender-belt and stockings and I do love the colour red and black'; 'I am going to get a divorce. I hope this doesn't put you off. I won't send you a photo this time as you may be put off by my divorce.'
'I have never married and I am clean'; 'My mother keeps saying when are you going to bring a nice girl home to show off and share some of the love and affection you have'; 'I work nights in a supermarket and I'm completely bored'; 'Even though you were only seven years old when I was working and swearing with the Sex Pistols (my peak of fame and cash!) I'd be delighted to treat you to a Babycham'; 'My last relationship was complicated, as she was married... The husband got a few of the heavy boys around to deal with me. I decided to leave the company and the area...';	'*I love you and your country and your television!*'; 'I'd love to soap your suds'; 'You can tie my kangaroo down any time sheila (bad joke!)'; 'I very much look forward to meeting you. I have only just stepped out of a beautiful hot bath with my rubber ducky and we're sitting here drying in front of my blazing fireside, gazing into the flames and dreaming that you might enjoy this atmosphere with us'; 'Come for flying lessons with me'; 'God, listen to me. I must sound very conceited and big-headed. The truth is I'm on my knees.'	'Letter? Did I say letter? this is more like a *long* note'; 'What else can I tell you? Oh, I've got my own house'; 'You will have realised now that I am writing to you'; 'Dear Mademoiselle. Your note caught my eye, wondering how many awarenesses we have to share'; 'Have you ever been to Cambridge?'
Sod all.	Not a whisper.	Absolutely zilch.

MOVIES: WILLIAM GREEN
Meryl vs Miss March

Plenty of actresses have bared their all (or at least most of it) for *Playboy* magazine. Just close your eyes and think of: Jayne Mansfield, Ursula Andress, Linda Evans, Bo Derek (marry John Derek and a *Playboy* spread is as inevitable as the wedding ring), Catherine Deneuve, Joan Collins, Barbara Bach, Mariel Hemingway, Brigitte Nielsen, Sophia Loren, Brigitte Bardot and Diana Dors.

The magazine, however, likes to believe that not only do actresses take their clothes off in *Playboy*, but that people who take their clothes off in *Playboy* go on to become actresses. Mr Hefner's glossy girlie bible is extremely proud of its Playmates' film careers, routinely touting each new movie appearance with an announcement, an appropriate photograph of the performer and a reminder that Marilyn Monroe posed in *Playboy* and went on to become a movie star. In honour of that tradition, and as proof of the assertion that posing for the organ that claims to be the most tasteful of skin magazines does indeed offer a terrific boost to a young woman's career, we offer this exclusive comparison between a recent *Playboy* bunny and Oscar-winning thespian Meryl Streep.

NAME:	*Meryl Streep*
DATE OF BIRTH:	*1951*
HEIGHT:	
WEIGHT:	*Miss Streep is an extremely serious actress who does not reveal this kind of banal information*
VITAL STATISTICS:	
MARRIED?	*Yes, to Don Gummer, a sculptor*
HOME TOWN:	*The suburbs of central New Jersey*
EDUCATION:	*High School, then Vassar (a prestigious Ivy League women's college), Honours programme in costume design and dramatic writing at Dartmouth (another prestigious Ivy League College), and post-graduate studies at Yale School of Drama (yes, you guessed it, incredibly-prestigious-and-utterly-Ivy-League).*
FORMATIVE INCIDENT:	*Whilst at Yale Meryl gave a brilliant performance as Constant Garnett, a ninety-year-old translatrix in* The Idiots Karamazov, *a dazzling literary spoof by Albert Innaurato and Christopher Durang (who himself went on to be the great friend of and collaborator with Sigourney Weaver). Despite being confined to a wheelchair for the entire show, Streep gave a virtuoso display that marked her out as a star of the future.*
PERSONAL APPEARANCE:	*Meryl Streep was recently photographed for* Interview Magazine *wearing a simple black top by Donna Karan and a plain white cashmere jumper. Naturally, her hair is long and blonde, but our picture shows her in her role as Lindy Chamberlain, the mother in the famous Australian "Dingo baby" case, whom she plays in her latest film,* A Cry In The Dark. *She put on weight and wore a wig in order to make her portrayal more accurate.*
CURRENT CONCERNS:	*Like many mothers, Meryl is worried about environmental pollution and the concentration of chemicals and additives in everyday foodstuffs. On Robert Redford's recommendation, she works with the Natural Resources Defense Council, as well as having her own women's group. She is currently "trying to screw up the courage" to speak to her local Parent-Teachers Association in a bid to improve local children's diets.*
TYPICAL COMMENT BY MERYL:	*"So many people who write about the movies don't understand either the process or the creation of an actor... Most of them – even the most sophisticated – are swept away by whether it's a character they like or dislike. They confuse the dancer with the dance. It's very ingenious, really. They're like children who want to believe in Santa Claus."*
TYPICAL COMMENT ABOUT MERYL:	*"Meryl deals not just with the surface, but with the most profound levels of the characters she portrays. She invests them all with a moral sensibility, with a soul."* – Robert Benton, *film director*

NAME:	*Laurie Wood (Playboy Miss March '89)*
DATE OF BIRTH:	*1967*
HEIGHT:	*5'10"*
WEIGHT:	*125lbs (8 stone 13 lbs)*
VIAL STATISTICS:	*37-24-36*
MARRIED?	*Yes, to Jeff Wood, a former Coast Guard yeoman*
HOME TOWN:	*Sparks, Nevada*
EDUCATION:	*High School*
FORMATIVE INCIDENT:	*When she was a teenager Laurie refused to sleep with anyone, believing that she should remain a virgin until she married. This caused her to be unpopular with boys and led to teasing from her girlfriends. Nevertheless, she stuck to her guns – "I didn't want sex to be an entertainment" – leaving school with her maidenhood intact. Soon afterwards she married Jeff. She was scared; "I didn't know what sex would be." Luckily, Playboy reports, "Laurie's libido, built to critical mass by long years of discipline, surprised her. She became the kind of wife men fantasise about."*
PERSONAL APPEARANCE:	*Laurie likes to dress for her husband in black lace or gold satin lingerie. Her favourite is a garter belt, undies and a pink lace-up corset. For Playboy she wore an assortment of coats, shirts, petticoats, garters, stockings and nighties. Amazingly enough, knickers were conspicuous in their absence from the magazine wardrobe. She did not have to alter her appearance for this, her first near-nude performance. But she did have to put her fingers into some pretty interesting places.*
CURRENT CONCERNS:	*Needless to say, a girl with Laurie's conventional outlook on life was bound to be somewhat nervous at the prospect of stripping off for the benefit of millions of lecherous magazine readers. But as soon as the camera started clicking, she just thought of her husband and relaxed. "Nudity is natural," she remarked of the experience, "and I'm a natural woman."*
TYPICAL COMMENT BY LAURIE:	*"Some of my friends are not going to believe it when they see these pictures. But this is my moment – not every girl has a chance to give her husband a present like this."*
TYPICAL COMMENT ABOUT LAURIE:	*"This month Playboy presents a woman with the sex-drive, and the sex-appeal to make a birthday present of her birthday suit."* – Playboy *men's magazine*

58

chapter

3

PUNCH AND POLITICIANS

GORBY THE GREAT

Soviet satirist
VITALI VITALIEV
examines the dangerous
myths surrounding
President Mikhail Gorbachev

Liberator of Squirrels

'INTIMIDATION ABOUT impending chaos, and speculation about the threat of a coup, even civil war, can be heard. It's a fact that someone wants to create in society an atmosphere of anxiety, hopelessness and insecurity.'

That's a quotation from Mikhail Gorbachev's speech, televised nationwide last September.

So, who is the ominous Someone Rushdie who wants to subvert Soviet security? Whoever they may be, they have proved quite successful: anxiety, hopelessness and intimidation are exactly the feelings which pervade the Soviet Union at present. Or could this Someone Rushdie be none other than Mr Gorbachev himself? To test such an iconoclastic assertion, we'll have to consider Mr Gorbachev's track record in recent years.

Party people

HIS RISE to power five years ago is still an enigma. It looks as if his predecessors – Brezhnev, Andropov and Chernenko – were hastily dying just to clear the way for him. Mr Gorbachev found himself among the top ten party people under Brezhnev, who is now openly dismissed by him as the creator of stagnation. How did he manage it? How could Mr Brezhnev have harboured such a viper in his breastful of medals? Perhaps, after Mr Brezhnev's demise, Mr Gorbachev simply transformed himself out of all recognition. I don't believe in such a quick change. Especially among the ruling elite whose climb to power is still such a secretive process.

Why, then, did Mr Gorbachev introduce glasnost? Because he wanted his own personal survival and that of the rotten system of administrative command socialism. 'We'll never step down from socialism,' he keeps repeating, robot-like. I wonder why? What's so good about the system which cost the country at least 40 million innocent lives for the sake of one really big achievement – driving the world's potentially richest country to total economic collapse?

He also had another, hidden aim. Socialism was always very good for a tiny part of Russia's population, namely 'the servants of the people', meaning the people whom everyone else must serve:

Would you buy a second-hand economy from this man? Still an enigma five years on

> Perhaps, after Brezhnev's demise, Gorbachev simply transformed himself out of all recognition. I don't believe in such a quick change

60

the rulers themselves. Such a system was in no way a devilish creation of Stalin alone. Gross inequalities in the 'land of equality' began with the formation of the first 'socialist' state. These are the childhood impressions of V Kondratiyev, a prominent Soviet writer, published by *Literaturnaya Gazeta* in January 1990:

'I remember how our family was coming back to Moscow from Poltava in 1921. My father's aunt, an old Bolshevik, got us seats in the first-class carriage where the representatives of the new elite – party functionaries, Red Army commanders and Commissars – were travelling. The carriage smelt of leather, good eau de cologne and expensive cigarettes. After two years of hunger, we were dressed almost in rags. The high-ranking passengers gave us puzzled looks, they drank wine, ate delicacies (whereas there was hunger all over the country), but not a single one of them offered me, a two-year-old skeleton covered with skin, even a small piece of bread, to say nothing of chocolate which these 'masters of life' were consuming greedily in large quantities.'

Is this the kind of socialism from which Gorbachev doesn't want to step down?

Squirrel tales

RECENTLY, IN three consecutive issues of *The Sunday Correspondent* magazine, there appeared a romantic story of Gorbachev's life, written by an American journalist, Gail Sheehy. Among the photographs illustrating her article, there is one which is supposed to be especially moving. Its caption reads: 'While the Berlin Wall crumbled and as he prepared meetings with the Pope and George Bush, Gorbachev found time to feed a squirrel at his *dacha* outside Moscow last November.' How touching! But I would really prefer it if, between his meetings with the Pope, President Bush and the Dalai Lama, Mr Gorbachev would find time to feed his own country, not just one squirrel.

But can he, you may ask? I am sure he could, if only he wished to. When leaders want to introduce drastic economic reforms, they do introduce them. Suffice it to remember the NEP in the early 1920s when the huge country was fed and dressed within a year. We may also recall the 1983-1989 reforms in China which brought quick success and relative economic prosperity. The reason was simple: there was real will there – and as you know, where there's a will, there's a way. But when there is just a squirrel, there is usually no way.

No matter how hard I try, I can't see the real will for reforms in Gorbachev's case. For five years he has been feeding squirrels with nuts and his people with promises. At first he promised to eradicate drunkenness, but wound up being nicknamed Mineral Secretary, and that was that. He promised to give a separate flat to each family by the year 2000, but quickly forgot about it. He promised to combat the privileges of the elite which keep growing with every week up to the present time. And then, of course, he promised not to use force in Lithuania.

Why doesn't he keep all these promises? Simply because he is secretly happy with the current state of things. Moreover, any change in this current state of things is an immediate danger to his and his cronies' happiness. No kind of free elections or market economy has a chance in our long-suffering country while those in charge of the reforms go on living on unearned privileges. Similarly, the leaders are reluctant to introduce real reforms while privileges are there. A vicious circle.

But back to the squirrels. Take these words from the caption: 'at his *dacha* outside Moscow.' It was essential to specify which *dacha* it was, since Mr Gorbachev owns two more on the Black Sea coast, plus a plush house in Moscow. This would probably be okay for a president of a country basking in an abundance of foodstuffs and commodities. But in a state where there are only 56 officially-produced items on sale, and these items can only be acquired after many hours of queueing; in the land where millions of people still live in cellars and in the infamous communal

flats, having to share kitchens and bathrooms (if any) sometimes with a couple of dozen other families, it acquires a different meaning. As it was aptly put by Boris Yeltsin in his book *Against the Grain*, 'Gorbachev doesn't sense people's reaction. But then, how can he sense them when he has no direct reciprocal contact with the people? [Unlike with the squirrels – VV]. His meetings with workers are nothing but a masquerade, a few people stand talking to Gorbachev while all around them is a solid ring of bodyguards. These people, chosen to play the part of the 'people', have been carefully vetted and selected and are brought to the spot in special buses. And it is always a monologue. If somebody says something to him which does not fit into his picture, he is too busy putting across what he wants to say.'

As to Gorbachev's manner of speech, it has become the target of many jokes. It should be said that no Soviet leader after Lenin (who by the way had a big speech defect) could speak Russian very well. Gorbachev is not an exception here. Yeltsin writes in his book that he speaks like a market porter.

Literate or not – it isn't so important. What *is* so important is the unseeing and unhearing attitude which Mr Gorbachev strikes with most of his interlocutors. He never listens to people. And how can he when for years and years he has enjoyed a very exclusive existence: special cars and houses, canteens and shops, toilets and holiday homes. To quote Gail Sheehy again: 'Gorbachev never wanted to be a lawyer, he wanted to be a leader' and he did become a leader, though without the slightest election experience. If we had free elections in our country tomorrow, Mr Gorbachev wouldn't stand a chance. That's why he was in such a hurry to have himself 'nominated' as president by the relatively ▶

The West has fallen over itself to embrace lovable Gorby. But is Saint Mikhail's halo slipping?

I would prefer it if

President Gorbachev would

find time to feed his own country,

not just one squirrel

tame parliament with its 'silent majority' of party functionaries who had received their parliamentary seats in a similar way – as rewards for being obedient to the ruling ideology which, by gigantic efforts, has triumphantly brought the country into chaos. The smile of fiendish pleasure which momentarily flashed on Mr Gorbachev's face after being nominated as president couldn't escape anyone's eyes. Congratulations! But was there really a reason to smile? Civil war in the Caucasus, anti-semitic pogroms in Moscow and Leningrad, huge unrest everywhere else – are these good grounds for smiling? For some, probably yes, since it is only in this atmosphere of instability that the elite can hold their unearned power.

Poll axed

THERE WERE two occasions in our recent history which finally shattered my belief in Mr Gorbachev as a leader, though I had been his supporter for almost four years.

The first one occurred last October when it suddenly became known that Vladislav Starkhov, the distinguished editor of *Argumenti i Fakti* weekly, which has just received the Granada Television *What The Papers Say* award as the best paper of the year, was in danger. The reason was that this very newspaper published an opinion poll on the popularity of people's deputies. The poll was topped by Yeltsin, Sakharov, Sobchak, etc. Gorbachev was well down the list. This made him furious. He ordered his ideological chief, Medvedev, to call Mr Starkhov on the carpet (as Russian bureaucrats say) and sack him. But the editor proved a hard nut to crack. 'You have no authority over me,' he

Nice one squirrel. Gorby boosted his lovable image with the famous 'glasnuts' photo

Perestroika, meaning reconstruction, is likely to be followed by *perestrelka*, meaning shooting

told the party bosses, 'we are not a party publication.' People came out onto the streets to voice their support for Mr Starkhov, which made Mr Gorbachev think better of sacking him. Instead, the rebel editor was made to publish another opinion poll which appeared a couple of weeks later, and there of course, Mr Gorbachev came out on top. The paper had to apologise to the readers for its allegedly incorrect first poll. An interesting detail: before Mr Gorbachev's attack, the circulation of *Argumenti i Fakti* was just over 20 million copies – immediately afterwards it shot up to 33 million, thus becoming the largest circulated publication in the world. I think they should thank Gorby for such wonderful PR.

Swinging apparatchiks

THE ATTACK on Mr Starkhov triggered lots of similar setbacks for many progressive editors in the provinces. 'When they trim nails in the capital, they cut fingers in the provinces,' Nazim Khikmet, the Turkish poet, once said. For provincial bureaucrats, Mr Gorbachev's attitude was a signal to launch a major offensive against the press.

The other instance was connected with the sudden two-fold increase in the salaries of party apparatchiks and KGB agents. This was done covertly, overnight, at the time when there were heated debates at the Supreme Soviet on where to find an extra one or two million roubles to feed the poor and the homeless. As *Ogonyok* magazine (an official publication from the *Pravda* stable) put it, 'the biggest and unprecedented rise of wages for different kinds of functionaries occurred last October. The salaries of some regional party, Komsomol and trade union officials grew more than two-fold.' So now an average typist at a regional party committee is getting two or three times more than an average (even a tame) journalist. Can you imagine a bigger example of cynicism?

Silly cult

YOU PROBABLY cannot, but I can. And strangely, this cynicism comes from the West, which is falling over itself to appease Mr Gorbachev. When the Soviet troops were swarming all over Vilnius and many crucial buildings were already occupied, western politicians kept repeating like a prayer that Mr Gorbachev had promised not to use force in Lithuania. What does 'using force' consist of, then? Does it necessarily imply killing a couple of thousand students, as happened in Tiananmen Square? In fact, by letting China get away with the massacre last year, by starting to flirt with Peking only weeks after the bloodbath, the West has set a very dangerous precedent (and president as well). Driven by an instinct for self-preservation, the West involuntarily (I hope) gave the green light to the leaders of the few remaining communist countries for further repression.

Ironically, when for the first time in Soviet history our leader does not enjoy a personality cult, the West has created one for us: Gorby is great, he is the Man of the Year, the Man of the Century, the Man of Anno Domini, quite probably the reincarnation of Christ himself. On 31 March 1990, *The Times* published an article about yet another title awarded to Gorbachev in the West: now he is also 'the liberator of men's fashion in the East.' I would prefer him to remain the liberator of his own country.

Cults are ruinous. They tend to distort their subject out of all recognition. It's only natural for people to be critical of their leaders. Criticism causes improvement. But as soon as mobs in any country start shouting that their leader is great, it's the beginning of tyranny. 'Power corrupts', Lord Acton remarked. 'Blood and power make people drunk,' Dostoyevsky echoed. (Strictly speaking, it was Lord Acton who echoed Mr Dostoyevsky, but never mind.) There is not a single person on earth who can withstand the pleasant pressure of his (or her) own deification without turning into a dictator. We have had enough bloody tyrants in Russian history. We don't need to create another one.

So what's going to happen? Will Mr Gorbachev survive his country? And will his country survive Mr Gorbachev? I wish I knew. But the fact is that the status quo cannot be preserved for very much longer in a country where the economy has died a death after a painful five-year agony. Under Brezhnev, the Soviet economy could be compared to a vehicle with square wheels which sometimes, by a sort of miracle, moved squeakingly back and forth. It now looks like the same vehicle with triangular wheels (as a result of reforms). You can't go very far in such a car, can you?

The country with only 56 individual commodities on sale now bears a striking resemblance to Upper Volta, with only two major differences: the skin colour of its inhabitants, which is predominantly white, and the number of rockets with nuclear warheads, which is preposterously high. Yes, there are plenty of rockets. As well as a dozen potential Chernobyls. And if you take into account the unparalleled social apathy and the huge reserve of mutual hatred among the people, who are sick and tired of queuing for these very 56 items ... well, you can draw your own conclusions. As we joke now in Russia, *perestroika*, meaning reconstruction, is likely to be followed by *perestrelka*, meaning shooting. If all hell really breaks loose, is there any guarantee that the occasional bullet won't strike the red button? You know what I mean.

Car trouble

YES, APPARATCHIKS (Mr Gorbachev among them) are happy. The problem is that the country is now unhappy about their happiness. And if they can't find sufficient guts and pure common sense to renounce their special lifestyles (deathstyles as well, since the leaders still have their own special cemeteries) in the very near future, then any guarantees would become shaky, not only for Russia, but for the whole world.

Patience has its limits. Russian people are probably the most patient in the world, but their traditional sang-froid is running out.

> If we had free elections tomorrow,
> Gorbachev wouldn't stand a chance.
> That's why he was in such a hurry to
> have himself 'nominated' as president

As to the great liberator of squirrels and tireless feeder of men's fashion (or vice versa), I think I know how he must start. He must start by visiting an ordinary hospital for common people with its cockroaches, peeling stucco and bloodstained walls. At the same time, his wife should join a queue for the remaining 56 items – one at a time – in ordinary shops. Then Mr Gorbachev would immediately feel like introducing some real reforms, even at the peril of leaving one or two squirrels unfed.

Do we think such a prospect is a realistic one? What? I can't hear the answer ... Oh, sorry: I forgot that squirrels can't speak. They can only squeak when squeezed tightly. ■

DONEGAN
Sign Language

'See anything you don't want?'

'French but not fluently' With 1992 on the horizon, just how well can Britain's politicians converse with their foreign counterparts?

With all the buzz about a United States of Europe, you would think that being a polyglot would be all the rage in Parliament. *The Sunday Correspondent* recently chided John Major about his deficiencies in this area, but had they checked further they would have found that Mr Major is not very lonely in the monoglot club. Not that checking – when we did it – was easy. Some ministers' offices were downright abusive about the matter. Several times it seemed as if loyal staffers were going to invoke the Official Secrets Act rather than divulge information about their minister's linguistic aptitude. Chris Patten's secretary retorted, 'What's the point (of speaking another language)? We have been dealing effectively with the Continent for 100 years,' and Nicholas Ridley flatly refused to answer the question. What follows is a summary of our efforts to determine how ready Parliament is for Pan-Europeanism:

● Elle ne parle pas l'Europe

Margaret Thatcher: speaks a bit of French … but not fluently
Douglas Hurd: speaks French and Italian fluently
Tom King: speaks French fluently
Peter Brooks: speaks a bit of French … but not fluently (his secretary insists he is being modest).

● 'I'm pretty fluent in sheep, too'

Geoffrey Howe: speaks French fluently
Nicholas Ridley: considered the question a 'personal matter' and refused to answer
Nigel Lawson: a bit of French … but no fluently
Cecil Parkinson: no answer, despite repeated phone calls. 'None' assumed
Chris Patten: speaks French and Spanish … fluency uncertain. (His secretary assumed because Mr Patten vacationed both in France and Spain that he was fluent, but she would not confirm this with Mr Patten.)

Neil Kinnock: speaks a bit of French, German and Spanish, … but isn't fluent in any, nor in Welsh, incidentally
Robin Cook: Not hot on modern languages but speaks Latin and Ancient Greek fluently

● 'They never taught us foreign in Sheffield'

Roy Hattersley: none
Bryan Gould: French. (He may have become rusty, according to his wife, but once spoke the language fluently.)
Ken Livingstone: 'none' we assume as call was not not returned
Tony Benn: none
John Prescott: speaks a bit of French … but not fluently
Paddy Ashdown: speaks French and Mandarin Chinese fluently.

● Too busy with the medicine to bother with languages

David Owen: none

It's not exactly impressive, is it? But never mind: if there's one thing that senior European politicians have in common, it's that whenever they are interviewed for British news programmes they speak … beautiful English

'All right, have it your way, it's something to do with the greenhouse effect.'

POLLS APART

PUNCH LOOKS BACK AT THE NEXT ELECTION

Two safe predictions can be made for Britain in the not too distant future: 1) There will be a General Election. 2) Someone will win it. Beyond this, who can say whether it will be Labour or the Tories?

Punch found two MPs who were brave enough to envisage the terrible possibility of being on the losing side.

Overleaf, each declares his vision of a 'probable scenario' to the world.

Outspoken journalist and Labour MP AUSTIN MITCHELL predicts Margaret Thatcher's likely opening moves in the first 100 days of her Fourth Reich.

Tory rebel and rising media star JULIAN CRITCHLEY imagines the dawn of a new era under Prime Minister Neil Kinnock. No one could be found to describe a victory by the Liberal Democrats

IT'S NEIL AT No. 10

Days 1-10. In which Neil wins, but Maggie refuses to budge

'Oh darling, it's finally come true. Our dream home.' Neil and Glenys collect first prize in the national raffle

ON THE LUNCHTIME television news on Friday 6 June 1991, viewers were shown Mr Neil Kinnock being driven to the Palace in order to kiss hands with his sovereign. Although there were still some rural constituencies to declare, Labour had already won a comfortable majority of seats in the new Parliament. Mr Peter Snow, whose trousers remained resolutely at half-mast throughout a very long night, had announced at 4 am, '1991 is another 1945'. Mr Brian Redhead from *Today* had claimed that 'the 12 "wasted years" years of Tory government have come to an end', and Mr Kenneth Baker had conceded defeat standing in the Great Hall of Conservative Central Office in the midst of a crowd of weeping girls, all of whom were called Fiona. Mr Michael Heseltine said he was ready for any eventuality.

The cameras followed Mr Neil Kinnock back from the Palace as far as Downing Street, only to find the Iron Gates shut fast against him. It was understood that Mrs Thatcher, who was declining to recognise what she called 'the nation's ingratitude', had secured the gate herself, and was refusing to quit No. 10. She had told Lynda Lee Potter of the *Daily Mail*, 'We shall not be moved.' Two large Pickfords vans could be seen parked in Whitehall. As Mr Bernard Ingham had disappeared, having, on the early evidence of a swing to Labour, burnt his uniform, Sir Robert Armstrong, the Cabinet Secretary, had called for Lord Whitelaw. Willie, who had been lunching at Pratt's, was let into No. 10 by the garden entrance: in the meantime the new Prime Minister retired to the Walworth Road whence he issued the first list of his new Cabinet.

There were few surprises. The television bulletins showed pictures of Gerald Kaufman on the steps of the Foreign and Commonwealth Office. 'I am standing in Ernie Bevin's shoes,' he boasted. Mr Roy Hattersley went to the Home Office with the courtesy title of Deputy Prime Minister. Mr John Smith brought a touch of Scottish rectitude to the Treasury. Mr Kenneth Livingstone was a surprise choice as Minister without Portfolio. Miss Glenda Jackson and Mr Austin Mitchell were appointed joint chairmen of the Labour party.

On the evening of 9 June Mr Neil Kinnock made his first Prime Ministerial broadcast. 'We are at the dawn of a new era: the dark age of Thatcherism is past.' The pound lost five cents against the dollar and fell as much against the Deutschmark. Lord Whitelaw was glimpsed scrambling over the garden wall of No. 10. 'It has all been too much for Mrs Thatcher,' was his only comment.

A week later Helmut Kohl, the first Chancellor of the Fourth Reich, flew into London with an offer to shore up the pound. After a siege lasting almost a week (the gas, electricity and finally the telephone were cut off) Mrs Thatcher emerged from No. 10. After difficult negotiations conducted by Sir Alfred Sherman, on behalf of Mrs Thatcher, and Mr Peter Mandleson, it was finally agreed that she could keep the carpets and curtains. The Iron Gates were thrown open and the Thatcher caravan made for Fort Dulwich. 'I shall return,' said Mrs Thatcher to Mr Jimmy Young. Mr Michael Heseltine said he stood ready for any eventuality. 'I would be happy to serve the Tory party in any capacity,' he said, speaking from his humble home near Banbury.

Days 10-50
Mr Heseltine stands by

Pleading an excessive work load ('we have to clean out the Aegean (sic) stables'), the Prime Minister said that he would ▶

MAGGIE'S BACK!

Days 1-10. In which Baroness Beaconsfield is relaunched

Is it Prime Minister Maggie back again, or just 3-2-1 host Ted Rodgers after the operation?

T'WAS NOT A FAMOUS victory. More a defeat which could afford a good ad agency. But enough of Saatchi's 'Thank you Britain for saving Britain' ads, and *The Sun*'s 'Britain Kicks Kinnochio' headline. Mrs Thatcher had turned her usual stance of running against her own government into a personal vendetta. Now, as a past mistress at putting what she didn't understand in language everyone could follow, she announced that she had been vindicated. 'The people have voted for change. We are their dynamic for change. We must now lead the change back.'

Graciously, she declined to be deterred by the fact that the electorate had proved itself less worthy of her than it had once been. 'The people have rejected socialism and renewed their mandate to me by making mine the largest single party. I accept their request to lead Britain into the 21st Century'. Dismissing the loss of her Finchley seat as 'a temporary inconvenience which frees me from trivia', the Prime Minister ennobled herself as Baroness Beaconsfield, sent for the Queen and informed Her Other Majesty of her intention of carrying on as Prime Minister to build 'one nation' from the House of Lords.

'Noble work'. The clarion was answered by Lord Ingham of Hebden Bridge, recalled from the *Yorkshire Post*, Lord Watkins of Blaby, currently privatising Gosplan, and Lord Bell of Bouffant, PR to Mr Boris Yeltsin. Their advice was unanimous: relaunch.

The Great Relaunch – or *relancement* as its compere, Lord St John, called it – generated two spectacular media events: Home and Away. The Away Day was staged at the Imperial War Museum. To the backing of massed choirs of Young Conservatives, Baroness Beaconsfield drove at the head of a three-hour parade of mothballed tanks and delivered a rewritten version of Henry V's speech before Agincourt, producing immediate protest from the French embassy, Mr Michael Heseltine, and Miss Glenda Jackson, shadow theatre critic.

The Home launch required a reopened mental hospital, rescued before being sold, repainted and filled by a thousand grateful lunatics collected from London doorways. 'Give me your poor, your hungry, your huddled masses yearning to be free and I will intern them,' intoned the Prime Minister, unveiling the new 'light touch' welfare policy, 'from each according to his inclination, to each according to his (government-assessed) need.'

Days 10-50
Sir Geoffrey moves house

With the tone skilfully set, Baroness Beaconsfield applied herself to putting the Cabinet together, helped by a unanimous call from the 1922 committee for all good Conservatives to come to the aid of the party. Mr Edward Heath, Father of the House, made a moving offer of support. Meanwhile Mr Michael Heseltine (Deputy Foreign Minister and plenipotentiary to Brussels), Mr Norman Tebbit (Military Governor of Scotland), Mr John Major (Foreign, Home, Employment and Environment Secretary) and Sir Geoffrey Howe (with official residences at Cardiff Castle, Caernarvon Castle, Pembroke Castle, and Barbara Castle) were accepted after pledges of fealty.

Mr Nigel Lawson became Chancellor of the Exchequer on a two-day-a-week basis on a full salary to supplement his earnings from Barclays. The bank's logo was displayed on the despatch box whenever their Chancellor spoke. The panel installed for this purpose was also rented out to other organisations eager to advertise their support for the new government and by the Department of ▶

IT'S NEIL AT No. 10

◄ answer PM's Questions on Tuesdays only; his wife would perform on Thursday afternoons. Chancellor Kohl, still in London in his brave attempt to shore up the pound (which had lost a further 50 cents against the dollar), said that he was prepared to accept the entire contents of the V&A 'on permanent loan' in Baden-Baden. Mrs Thatcher, who had remained incommunicado inside Fort Dulwich, made a brief public appearance. She told a small crowd of Monday Clubbers which had gathered on the glacis of her home, 'Je vous ai compris', or something that sounded very much like it. She was wearing her blue and was supported on either side by Mr Peter Lilley and Mr George Gardiner. Mr Michael Heseltine, who was photographed on horseback wearing pink, said that he awaited the nation's call. 'I am at its service,' he proclaimed from the saddle. Mr Roy Hattersley published a collection of light essays entitled *Second Fiddle*, and Mr Edward Heath's long-awaited memoirs *If You Wait By The River Bank Long Enough* (*The Body of Your Enemy Will Float By*) was serialised in *The Independent*. Mr Kenneth Livingstone made a speech complaining of the betrayal of socialism.

Days 50-100
Neil sheds a tear

The Prime Minister published his first honours list. Sir Harry Secombe and Mr Jack Petersen were sent to the Lords. Miss Ruth Madoc was made a Dame Commander of the British Empire. There were knighthoods for Mr Aled Jones, Mr Alan Watkins and Mr Max Boyce. Accused of racism by Lord Tebbit of Chingford, the Prime Minister defended himself at length on nationwide television. 'Did I not weep when Nelson was freed?' he

asked. Mrs Thatcher, in a statement issued on her behalf from Fort Dulwich by Sir Marcus Fox, spoke of her second decade of service to her country. Mr Michael Heseltine, when asked whether he contemplated standing against Mrs Thatcher for the leadership of the Conservative party, said, 'No one should be in any doubt as to my intentions. I am ready to serve my party in any capacity.'

As a gesture of support for the pound, Mr Dan Quayle took a suite of rooms at the Savoy Hotel. Chancellor Kohl, whose battle to shore up the pound against the Deutschmark had been greatly appreciated by Mr John Smith, was given Blenheim Palace for his exclusive use while in the United Kingdom. Mr Kenneth Livingstone returned to the back benches claiming that the Labour government had lost faith with the people. He was replaced as Lord Privy Seal by Mr Anthony Banks. Mr Cranley Onslow, the chairman of the '22, announced that there would be a leadership election. Lady Howe threw her husband's hat into the ring. Mr Kenneth Baker published yet another anthology of verse. Mrs Thatcher, who was borne into committee room 14 on a throne on the four corners of which were Lord Whitelaw, Mr Colin Moynnihan, Mr Peter Morrison and Mr Michael Portillo, said that Britain would join the EMS 'when the time was ripe'. The value of the pound continued to fall. The BBC was given over to the playing of martial music. Mr Austin Mitchell resigned as part-chairman of the Labour party in order to become a disc jockey on Sky Television. 'In that way I can keep in touch,' he said. 'It was no joke being chairman of the people's party.'

A motor car sticker was spotted in the vicinity of Dulwich with the legend 'Come back Maggie, all is forgiven'. ∎
Mr Julian Critchley is the Conservative MP for Aldershot.

MAGGIE'S BACK!

◄ Trade and Industry, taken over by Saatchi in 1991.

All other posts were put up for sealed tender bid without quality threshold, just as before, so the real surprises were those appointments from outside the Tory party. Mr David Owen joined the Cabinet as Secretary of State for Defence and chairman of Cabinet committees ('David will replace my Willy' the PM said). He brought with him the vote at his command, plus the good wishes of Miss Rosie Barnes. The Rev Ian Paisley became leader of the House. After prayer and consultation with the Orange order, Mr William Molyneux became Secretary of State for Northern Ireland provided all mention of Green policies was eliminated.

Parliament opened to a Queen's speech delivered by Prince Andrew, whose company (HRH Photo Services) had undercut the bid of British Monarchy PLC. The state opening was tastefully choreographed by Prince Edward, with music by Mr Andrew Lloyd Webber specially adapted from *Evita*. Highlights of the speech included the abolition of the Community Charge for all but Labour voters, residents of Finchley, and Rottweilers, and an announcement that Britain would withdraw 'when the time is ripe' from the European Monetary System which the Conservatives had joined to dish Labour. 'Maggie Charts The Way Ahead' said the *Daily Mail*. 'A Brave Programme for the New Britain' commented the *Express*. *The Guardian* was unable to make up its mind.

Mr Neil Kinnock announced that Labour would reserve its position until Phase 18 of the Policy Review had been completed. Mr Roy Hattersley stepped down as deputy leader to devote time to submitting a suggestion to *Punch* for a new column and completing his 836-page novel, *Scenes from a Yorkshire Foetus: Weeks 7-28*. The party, withdrew from Parliament for the process of

choosing a new leader between Mr Dennis Skinner (voted TV MP of the year) Mr John Smith, Mr Gordon Brown, Mr Jack Cunningham, Mr Bryan Gould (already elected leader of the New Zealand Labour Party in absentia) and 38 members of the Tribune Group, but before the election could be completed the Scottish members withdrew to set up an independent assembly.

Days 50-100
More confusion for Maggie

In the ensuing confusion, the Government won an underwhelming majority in the Commons. In the Lords no one dared speak against it in the face of the basilisk glare of Baroness Beaconsfield. David Owen had her hired out for the filming of another Jeffrey Archer novel. In the geriatric ward of the Constitution, business carried on as usual with the Baroness disturbing the sleep of the diminishing and increasingly senile membership, but addressing herself mainly to Lord Jimmy Young. And the TV cameras. Mr Nigel Lawson took time off from Barclays to put interest rates back to 25% after their pre-election fall.

Outside, few noticed. Television news and current affairs programmes had been replaced by quiz shows in the contract bids of 1992. Newspapers clamoured for the reduction of parliamentary salaries since members had so little work to do. *The Guardian* finally made up its mind. British democracy was not dead. It just smelled funny. In the Lords, Baroness Beaconsfield smiled frequently for the cameras, now all locked on her, lowered her voice another octave and looked better every day. By a reverse Mr Dorian Grey syndrome, the picture looked worse for the country. But the City discounted that. As it had everything else. ∎
Mr Austin Mitchell is the Labour MP for Great Grimsby.

Blimey, Cedric, couldn't you have found somewhere better for us to doss down for the night!....

Damp streaming down walls.... Ceilings collapsing....

Wet rot, dry rot, fungus, bloody cockroaches.......

Hardly a pane of glass anywhere — Bloody freezing...

Bloody rats! Christ! — Of all the places you had to choose....

....a bloody junior school!

Political performers (clockwise): Labour pollster Glenda Jackson; bewhiskered broadcaster Sir Clement Freud; silver surfer Ludovic Kennedy; acting president Ronald Reagan; and piano-playing lensman Denis Healey

BRINGING THE HOUSE DOWN

With Glenda Jackson MP now a distinct possibility, ANTHONY LEE reports on the stars who've followed the well-worn path from performing arts to politics.

DENIS WINSTON HEALEY is throwing in the towel at the next election, and the House of Commons will lose the best honky-tonk piano player it never had. As the Paderewski of the Parliamentary knees-up, Mr Healey knows, as do many private citizens with more than one string to their bow, that politics has demeaned if not demolished his true calling. If only he had perfected his piano playing first.

Never mind, Mr Healey may disappear but, the electorate permitting, the equally creative Glenda Jackson will enter the Commons as the Labour MP for Hampstead and Highgate. One can only hope that she makes a more convincing representative for the People's Party in real life than Penelope Keith does in her latest TV 'comedy', *No Job for a Lady*, even if the televising of the Commons' proceedings has made the gap between reality and fantasy even less perceptible than ever before.

Meanwhile, it is only a fortnight since the dashing Vaclav Havel, a fine writer and an inspiring politician, came to Britain as President of Czechoslovakia. As the world's best living example of the artist-turned-statesman, he was fawned upon by our own Lady Harold and Antonia Pinter, two would-be intellectual leaders who lack either the talent or the moral fibre of their Mittel-European mentor. But to be fair to the Pinters, they have never attempted to inflict themselves upon the voters of this, or any other country, limiting themselves to cocktail parties and journalism as vehicles for their philosophies. Others, however, have been less modest.

A slew of celebrities around the world has felt zealous enough to inflict their ill-gotten fame on the democratic process itself. Shortly before the Horowitz of the Hustings announced his impending retirement, Sebastian Coe – who so thrilled us all by running very fast, in public – was adopted as Conservative candidate for Falmouth and Camborne. The ability to shift one's position with the greatest possible speed may well be a useful qualification for 20th-century legislators. If Mr Coe is elected he will find himself in athletic company in the House: Menzies Campbell, Liberal-Democratic spokesman on defence, ran in the sprint relay at the 1964 Olympics long before he ran for Parliament. He runs neither fast nor in public any more.

High office need not necessarily be closed to sportsmen. Christopher Chataway ran a little less speedily than Mr Coe in the early 1950s, and still managed to become Minister of Post and Telecommunications in 1971. But Mr Chataway had one advantage over Mr Coe: he was a TV personality in the days when few people owned televisions and few people on television had any personality. As an early ITN starlet, Mr Chataway demonstrated the allure of becoming a politician for those who cross-examine them; the gamekeepers have an almost orgasmic regard for the poachers if not for the game. Mr Chataway entered Parliament in 1959 (along with You Know Who) and since then the Tory benches have been graced by a bevy of broadcasters: Winston Churchill *grand-fils*, Tim Brinton, Dick Tracey, Sir Geoffrey Johnson Smith, and the incumbent MP for Falmouth and Camborne, David Mudd. Labour can meanwhile boast Bryan Gould, Roderick McFarqhuar, Bryan Magee, Austin Mitchell and Ednyfed Davies (yes *that* Ednyfed Davies).

Shrewd statisticians will spot that the Liberal Democrats are somewhat disadvantaged. True, the hirsute gourmand Sir Clement Freud did represent the Isle of Ely and Cambridge NE for 14 years, while still speaking, without hesitation, repetition or deviation, on radio's *Just a Minute*, a skill he wisely foreswore in the Palace of Westminster. Two of Mr Chataway's colleagues at ITN tried their luck with the Liberals; if the voters of Rochdale (1958) and Hereford (1959) had been a little more, er, liberal, we might have been spared the inexhaustible effusions of Ludovic Kennedy and Sir Robin Day.

Sir Robin's recent protestations of his own comparative poverty indicate a rather rosy view of parliamentary remuneration. What did he imagine he would have amassed from duties as a humble legislator? Brian Walden, Robert Kilroy-Silk and Matthew Parris have all forsworn the ballot-box for the goggle-box. Did they know something Sir Robin does not?

Television is a recent launching pad for politics. But as Mr Havel's reception in the capitals of the world might suggest, literature has a far longer pedigree. The next president of Peru may well be her most famous novelist, Mario Vargas Llosa, who would thus become the first Latin American head of state to govern his country from a flat behind Harrods. Throughout history, writers from Demosthenes to Jeffrey Archer have opined on public affairs, but few have had the sense of humour to engage in them; Mr Archer remained *hors de combat*, having emerged from the chrysalis of economic decline as a literary butterfly of unparalleled fragrance.

Such becoming modesty has not afflicted those bastions of American literature, Gore Vidal and Norman Mailer. The former first ran for Congress in 1960 under the banner 'More With Gore',

BRINGING THE HOUSE DOWN

Go ahead, make me mayor. His Honour Clint Eastwood, the former Mayor of Carmel

though more of what we, and possibly he, have yet to discover. The latter's involvement, like his literature, was more inflammatory. As a candidate for the New York mayoralty in 1969, Mr Mailer offered a unique qualification: he was the first person to run for public office who had attempted to murder his wife by stabbing. Mr Mailer's platform included proposing New York City as the 51st State of the Union; his running mate, the Irish-American columnist Jimmy Breslin, subsequently demonstrated his own grasp of diplomacy by greeting the (then) National Security Commissioner, Zbigniew Brezsinski, as a 'Polish **********'. Mr Mailer lost the race to Kennedy-clone John V Lindsay, but the latter's victory had its own grisly denouement. Long after his own political fortunes had declined

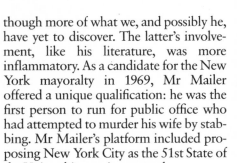

A slew of celebrities around the world has felt zealous enough to inflict their ill-gotten fame on the democratic process itself

into benign bankruptcy, Mr Lindsay cropped up in a cruel Otto Preminger film called *Rosebud*, playing an American politician (none too convincingly). I once chided Mr Preminger with this opportunistic casting. 'What a suggestion!' came the bright-eyed response. 'I chose him for his acting ability'. The film bombed.

Ronald Reagan is the apotheosis of the politics/showbiz symbiosis, but he is not the first thespian to reach high office. When Congressman Richard Nixon ran for the Senate in 1950, he was opposed by Helen Gahagan Douglas, a former Broadway leading lady who had starred (somewhat prophetically) in a 1935 film as Rider Haggard's 'She Who Must Be Obeyed'. Mrs Douglas, a Democrat, enjoyed the public support of the Screen Actors' Guild president Ronald Reagan. Mr Reagan acted well, privately working for Nixon, who won the Senate seat and a lasting epithet from his opponent: 'Tricky Dick'. Actor and tap-dancer George Murphy, Reagan's deputy as SAG vice-president, took his multifarious talents to the US Senate in 1964, having first done an obligatory stint as an FBI bagman – if only fictitiously – as the star of the 1952 spy thriller *Walk East on Beacon Street*. Successful US mayors have included Clint Eastwood (Carmel, California, 1986-88) and Salvatore Philip Bono (Palm Springs, California, 1988-). The latter's political career could hardly have been predicted from his warbling as the Sonny half of pop duo Sonny and Cher.

If international fame seems wasted on such humdrum domestic diversions, purely local talent can lead to grander things. Namdamuri Taraka Rama Rao, chief minister of Andhra Pradesh and a key Indian opposition figure, was also the country's foremost matinée idol for 30 years, starring in some 300 films. Lately he has taken to wearing some of his screen costumes on the campaign trail. Having specialised in playing Hindu deities, his saffron

robes and specially built chariot might well whet Charlton Heston's appetite for a political career post *Ben Hur/Moses*.

Europe's modern goddess at the temple of Thespis is Mrs Jules Dassin, aka the moussaka-munching songstress Melina Mercouri, the recently removed Greek Minister of Culture. Mercouri scored her greatest international hit in *Never on a Sunday*, winning an Oscar nomination for her portrayal of a golden-hearted whore catering to the populace of Piraeus. She capitalised on the movie's politics, if not her role, when she became Parliamentary deputy for Piraeus in 1977. Over lunch in Athens some years ago, Mercouri mentioned that both her father and grandfather had been prominent politicians. 'The poison was in the blood,' she purred, eyeing her cocktail. Discussing a planned interview in London, I said I would send details via the Greek embassy. The Delphic features dropped. I was told to deal instead with a well-known showbusiness PR agency. But surely she was the Greek Minister of Culture? 'Yes. But I'm also Melina Mercouri.' A clear case of having your *baklava* and eating it.

Iceland's first female president, the tongue-twisting Vigdis Finnbogadòttir, had an excellent apprenticeship. She taught French on TV and was the director of the Reykjavik Theatre Company. All the world's a political platform, it would seem.

In Brazil, Señor Silvio Santo is a Leslie Crowther-lookalike who fronts an all-day (yes, *all-day*) game and talk show on the country's second most popular television network. Señor Santos is not only the network's chief asset but also its proprietor; his programme is everything a budding politician could wish for as a springboard. Within days of entering the presidential elections, he commanded 46% in the polls. The electoral commission then stepped in, since directors of public utilities cannot run for public office, and TV networks are public utilities. Señor Santos protested that he could not be disqualified as a director because he wasn't one; he simply owned 98% of the stock. The electoral commission stood firm and his political career was over.

In Italy the most famous face in Parliament belongs to La Cicciolina ('Sweetie Pie', born Ilona Staller). Other parts of her anatomy are equally famous since, prior to politics, her métier was pornographic videos – a medium in which she achieved some considerable success. Her ability to bare her bosoms at election rallies is thought to have played a greater part in her victory than her analysis of the Common Agricultural Policy. Our own Leaderene may well have cause to consider emulating La Cicciolina's strategy if she is determined to fight another two elections. ∎

PYNE
Pynes's people

'For heaven's sake, Geraldine – if I was interested in that
sort of thing I'd watch the new Dennis Potter serial!'

'Great news! We've got you a job
playing left-back for Wimbledon!'

'Spurs are dominating the centre of the park…'

MR PRESIDENT, WE PRESUME

In which RANDI HACKER and JACKIE KAUFMAN meet Mr and Mrs Bush, chase squirrels with Millie the Killer Pooch, and take the President's personal White House tour…*

*Regular readers please note: this is *not* an imaginary interview. This is completely genuine – the real McBush

'Here's where I live … up there,' said George Bush, President of the United States, pointing with the First Finger towards the third floor of the White House private wing.

'See that window on the top? See that first low floor, then that next floor? Then the one above it that has the window that goes like a circle, only it's only a half-circle? See? That's our living-room and on this side, that's our bedroom. No, no, no! That's not our bedroom. That's … see the one where the window is all blacked out? That's the bathroom.'

There it was, the authentic voice of a decisive US President, describing his home to three black schoolkids from an elementary school in Washington DC. We were there to do a story for a Time Warner children's magazine about the nation's ultimate work-out facility – the White House.

Our research showed that almost every president since Teddy Roosevelt has added some kind of sports or exercise equipment to the First House. Teddy Roosevelt put in a tennis court. Ike installed his own putting green on the South Lawn. JFK splashed in an indoor pool built by FDR, used by DDE and LBJ and turned into a press room by Richard M. Nixon. Ford put in an outdoor pool. Sir Ronald Reagan had a weight room installed in the private quarters. America's 41st president has added a state-of-the-art horseshoe pit.

To give it the childhood twist, we wanted to bring a group of kids over to work out with the President. How could George Bush turn down a public relations opportunity involving children and physical fitness? He couldn't. That's why, four months after we wrote a letter to Presidential spin doctor Marlin Fitzwater, we were on our way to Washington.

The appointment was for 3:30, Tuesday, 3 October. We arrived 15 minutes early and found the White House hopping. And no wonder – it was coup day down in Panama.

always see in news photos of the Oval Office. A Presidential film crew, a Presidential photographer and the Time Warner photographer covered the meeting from every conceivable angle. Lights! Camera! Action! It's live from the White House!

The kids froze. But our President knew what to do. He turned every question Jackie asked him into a kind, gentle, slightly confused lesson for the kids.

'You know what they call football in South America and Europe?' he said. 'They call it soccer. They call it football. They call it soccer football.'

In no time at all, the kids felt right at home. One asked if he'd been in every room in the White House. The President motioned them over to a wall of windows, stood with an arm around one kid's shoulder and gave his inimitable room-by-room description.

Jackie's hopes for one of George Bush's famous tours of the private quarters soared. Since he was inaugurated our President has taken congressmen, campaign contributors, a television news crew and even a few ordinary citizens into his bedroom and bathroom. But no. By now, the coup in Panama had completely collapsed (see Day At A Glance overleaf) and ▶

**The man who married his mother?
George and Barbara relax at home**

Now you might think that when Commander-in-Chief Bush heard some military officers were shooting it out with Noriega's bodyguards he'd cancel all appointments, order some coffee, take the restricted access elevator to the Situation Room and huddle with his advisers. After all, our President said he'd love to see Noriega toppled by Panamanians. But instead of personally monitoring a situation he wished for out loud, on camera, on the record, the whole uprising only put him 45 minutes behind schedule.

That meant our 3:30 interview was pushed back to 4:15. We didn't mind. While the kids waited, they sipped Cokes wrapped in Presidential cocktail napkins and asked assorted Secret Service personnel and public relations officers questions like 'Does Mrs Bush have to clean this house herself?' and 'Where does the maid sleep?'

Meanwhile, the fabled White House Press Room was a flurry of activity. Reporters signed up for Presidential PR trips. Cameramen checked their focuses. One fourth estater

snorted in the fourth row. Through it all, the Associated Press telephone hot line remained strangely silent.

Every once in a while the Public Address system provided America's newshound élite with the information that helps keep them at the top of their profession:

'The President of Mexico will be leaving. This photo opportunity will take place at the Northeast Entrance.'

'The President's revised schedule is currently being circulated.'

'Anyone who wants to view the table settings for tonight's state dinner, please meet your escort at the double glass doors.'

Since only four of us were invited into the Oval Office, Randi scampered off to see the Ladybird Johnson china in the State Dining Room and at 4:15, Jackie and the kids headed for a rendezvous with history.

The First Host himself greeted them at the door. George Bush is taller and more genial than expected. He greeted the kids and guided them over to those chairs and couches you

Overheard on the South Lawn

Barbara Bush is devoted to Millie. They appear on magazine covers and television shows together all the time. When Millie had her pups in the First Bedroom, Barbara made George move out. Throughout America she has rapidly gained a reputation as a pet-loving woman. Here, in a myth-shattering exclusive, is a verbatim conversation between Barbara Bush and her squirrel-killing dog as she tried to persuade Millie to join her photo opportunity.

'Here, Millie! Come here, Millie! Here, Millie! Come on here, Mil! Millie! Here, Millie *Millie! Here, Millie!* (thin whistle) Now, Millie, get out of here, out of my shadow! No! Millie! Sit! Stay! Oh, Millie, just stay! Mil! Turning your back on horseshoes! *No! Stay!* Uh uh! Just stay! Stay! Stay! One shot! We're not asking much! *Stay Millie!* C'mon, Millie! You're out! Good girl, Millie!'

Marlin Fitzwater wanted to get these kids out and get on with some damage control.

So after chatting about sports for a while longer, the President said to the kids, 'Here's how a President works'. He picked up the handset of his power phone and confidently punched one of the 50 buttons.

'Bar?' he drawled. 'We got three kids here visiting us. Why don't you meet 'em down by the pool?' He hung up and told the kids Mrs Bush would come out with Millie, the First Pooch. He also told them a little bit about his dog.

'You know Millie is trained,' he said. 'She's a hunter so she's a *kind* of dog. So she has killed five squirrels here – that's five *confirmed* kills – that means someone's seen 'em.' The kids looked scared. 'Oh, she's a very friendly dog,' the President reassured them. 'She wouldn't hurt you.'

Then he sent them out to meet Millie and wished them luck.

Minutes after reaching the Gerald R. Ford heated outdoor pool, a brown and white spaniel came streaking through the First Firs. It was Millie, in hot pursuit of some more confirmed kills. Barbara Bush was heard before she was spotted.

'Millie! Millie!' the First Lady's voice wafted over the shrubbery. 'Which way did she go?' she said as she stepped on to the pool deck. Her photographer joined the Time Warner photographer so that coverage remained continuous. No opportunity wasted.

Mrs Bush leaked the exciting news that she is ghostwriting a book for Millie. It seems that Millie has quite a lot to say about a dog's life in the White House. So while Millie was doing more paws-on research for her chapter on confirmed kills, Mrs Bush decided that a picture of Millie with the three black kids was essential. This resulted in a classic tug-of-war between celebrity and ghostwriter.

Millie just wanted to chase squirrels. Mrs Bush wanted Millie to pose and the kids were

terrified that Millie would take a bite out of them. Confirmed kill number six? Gulp.

'She won't bite,' Mrs Bush reassured the kids. 'She's the one dog in America who hasn't found anyone she wants to bite yet'.

This failed to put the kids totally at ease. Mrs Bush nonetheless persisted and commanded, cajoled and otherwise bullied Millie into taking advantage of this photo opportunity. (See Overheard on the South Lawn.) Soon it was time for us to go.

We hooked up back in the Press Room where Randi was all aglow from her tour of the State Dining Room. 'Everyone has four wine glasses!' she said. 'And there are white satin matchbooks that say "The President's House" at each place!'

As we turned in our security clearance badges and passed out through the tall iron high-security fence, we knew this had been a day to remember. Even though Randi couldn't get one of those Presidential matchbooks, we had learned something valuable about democracy, fitness and formal table settings.

Day At A Glance

8:15 a.m. *Noriega's Mercedes Benz arrives at his headquarters in Panama.*

George Bush meets with Brent Scowcroft, his hawkish National Security Adviser and Dan Quayle, his pretty boy Vice President in the Oval Office.

Jackie and Randi jog past the Reflecting Pool near the Lincoln Memorial on the Mall in preparation for their big meeting.

9:00 a.m. *Rebel forces take Noriega prisoner and control military headquarters. American war helicopters hover overhead and observe the coup.*

George Bush meets with his rotund Chief of Staff John Sununu and Dan Quayle, his goofy Vice President in the Oval Office.

Jackie and Randi munch on their toast and drink coffee while honing their Presidential question list. Showers follow.

10:00 a.m. *First reports reach the US that rebels have control of Noriega's headquarters.*

President Bush and his impeachment insurance Vice President Dan Quayle greet Mexican President Carlos Salinas de Gortari on the South Lawn of the White House.

Jackie and Randi want to travel light. They leave their bags at Union Station so they don't have to take them to the Oval Office.

Noon *Rebels announce that Noriega will retire. The broadcast is abruptly cut off.*

White House spokesman Marlin Fitzwater interrupts President Bush's meeting with Mexican President Salinas de Gortari. Fitzwater discreetly

hands Bush a note about the coup. Bush politely shows it to Salinas.

Malapropist Vice President Dan Quayle's whereabouts are unknown.

Jackie and Randi are about half-way through the four-mile walk from Union Station to Capitol Hill.

1:00 p.m. *Noriega loyalists begin to shoot their way toward their leader even as desperate rebels call the US military base in Panama saying they will give the Americans Noriega back in return for some military support.*

President Bush and Salinas are still meeting.

Joke-bait Vice President Dan Quayle is currently eating lunch with some big-wig senators in the Capitol Building.

Randi and Jackie ask a uniformed Secret Service guard where a citizen can get a decent sandwich and a Coca-Cola with ice around the White House.

2:00 p.m. *Noriega's forces are victorious and the rebels are quashed. Noriega himself shoots the rebel leader in the head.*

Bush says so long to Salinas and finally huddles with the hawkish Scowcroft, James Baker, his ambitious Secretary of State and tough guy Dick Cheney, Secretary of Defense. Meanwhile the Soviet Defence Minister Dmitri Yazov is cooling his heels in a waiting area.

Faux-graduate Vice President Dan Quayle is still busy with his lunch date.

Jackie and Randi clear security in time to see President Salinas speak to American reporters in Spanish, get in his limo and leave.

3:30 p.m. *Noriega is back in charge. The leader of the coup is dead. Other rebel soldiers flee to American military bases.*

Bush bids the Soviet Yazov dasvedanya *for now.*

Sated Vice President Dan Quayle finally heads back to his office for a 'top level' meeting with Mexican President Salinas.

Jackie and Randi are told that the President is 45 minutes behind schedule.

4:15 p.m. *Arrests and executions of rebels are successfully under way in Panama.*

Bush greets Jackie and the three kids at the door to the Oval Office.

Rich-boy Vice President Dan Quayle meets with President Salinas.

Randi views the four wine glasses at each table setting in the State Dining Room and considers swiping some matches. ■

'It doesn't work.'

'I think it's a heat-seeking missile.'

DESPERATE DAN

First it was President Reagan the actor. Now it's

Vice-President Quayle the comedian.

RANDI HACKER and JACKIE KAUFMAN

look at the comic effect of Dan Quayle

The vice-president of the United States walked into a grubby breakfast bar during an informal walkabout in Washington. He looked about him for a moment, smiled broadly, then turned and offered his hand to the first woman he saw. 'Hi, I'm Dan Quayle,' he said. 'Who are you?' The woman looked at him icily. 'I'm your bodyguard,' she replied.

The story, one of many doing the rounds of America at the moment, may or may not be true. What matters is that J. Danforth Quayle III has at last forged himself a role in the difficult job of vice-president. In America's declining years, he has become jester to the nation. There is a book of his best-known sayings, *The Dan Quayle Quiz Book*, and he has even started telling jokes against himself. After one foreign trip he told reporters: 'Before I left, the president called me into his office and said, very slowly, "Dan, good relations with these Asian countries are very important to us – but I'm sending you anyway."'

Despite an aide's admission that Quayle starts from 'a low base of knowledge', foreign trips are the vice-president's speciality. After a tour of Latin America, he spoke of his regret that, 'I didn't study Latin harder at school so I could converse with these people.' In the Pacific, he called Pago Pago 'Pogo Pogo' all day long. On Samoa he told islanders: 'You all look like happy campers to me. Happy campers you are, happy campers you have been, and as far as I am concerned, happy campers you will always be.' He held a flamethrower backwards in Central America, and talked of the need for peace. Back home in Alaska, he told how he had taken up the case of a worker hurt in the Alaska oil spillage. 'I talked to one woman who had experienced a concern about the irritation she was having on her face and eyes,' said the syntax-impaired VP. 'And I expressed concern to the Exxon official here and they're going to do something about it. That is something in a very constructive basis that I was able to do,' he said decisively.

Quayle, as far as anybody can make out, has firm views on defence. This is one of them: 'Right now, we have a theory of mutually assured destruction that supposedly provides for peace and stability and it's worked,' he told the City Club of Chicago. Fine, but then he went on: 'That doesn't mean we can't build upon a concept of mutual assured destruction where both sides are vulnerable to another attack. Why wouldn't an enhanced deterrent, a more stable peace, a better prospect to denying the ones who enter conflict in the first place to

have to reduction of offensive systems and an introduction of defensive capability? I believe that is the route this country will eventually go.' According to the normally cautious *New York Times*, 'He left his audience shaking their heads in apparent confusion.' Only apparent confusion? To anyone else it seemed that there was no doubt about it at all.

What is worrying is that defence is supposed to be one of Quayle's best subjects. He assures reporters that his eight years as a member of the Senate Armed Services Committee made him a knowledgeable statesman in matters of weapons and things. 'I got through a number of things in the areas of defence,' said garble-ready Dan. 'Like the importance of cruise missiles and getting them more accurate so that we can have precise precision.'

It is precisely because of a lack of precise precision in the speeches of Dan Quayle that President Bush was asked if he would be choosing a new running mate in 1992. Bush made it perfectly clear that the Quayle thing was not a problem. If Bush decides to run for re-election, Quayle will be his man.

This may sound like mutually assured destruction at its finest, but consider this: a vice-president like Quayle is the best impeachment insurance a president could have. One of the most popular Quayle jokes is this:

'What are the most frightening six words in the English language?'

'Dan, I don't feel too good.'

We would not be surprised if George Herbert Walker Bush just leaned back in his black presidential Oval Office swivel chair and chuckled when grammar-resistant J. Danforth Quayle III went to Hawaii and said: 'Hawaii has always been a very pivotal role in the Pacific. It is in the Pacific. It is part of the United States that is an island that is right here.' We bet Bush felt even more secure when his thought-light vice-president told the press: 'If I had to summarise my position vis-à-vis the Soviet Union, you'd have to put me down as an agnostic.'

Bush can feel yet more certain that his own position is safe with every occasion that the depth-free Quayle goes on the offensive. 'I stand by all the misstatements,' the defiantly-dumb Dan once remarked. He recently attacked his critics thus: 'They have to deal with me, and the way I look at it, I'm the vice-president. They know it, and they know that I know it.' We know it too. We also know that most US vice-presidents who have run for president have won. Frightening thought, isn't it? ■

Randi Hacker and Jackie Kaufman live in Vermont and are regular contributors to Spy, Rolling Stone and National Lampoon. Dan Quayle lives in Washington.

THE QUOTES OF QUAYLE

On himself:

'The way I look at it, I'm vice-president'.

On Hawaii:

'Hawaii has always been a very pivotal role in the Pacific. It is in the Pacific.'

On Samoa:

'You look like happy campers to me . . . and as far as I am concerned, you always will be.'

On the San Francisco earthquake:

'The loss of life will be irreplaceable.'

On thinking:

'Some people spend a lot of time thinking: should I do this or should I do that? I don't.'

On the House of Representatives:

'You can get a bunch of guys and go down to the gym and play basketball. You can't do that in the Senate.'

On human rights:

'The US will work towards the elimination of human rights.'

On the family:

'Republicans understand the importance of bondage between parent and child.'

Now turn the page for the ultimate Quayle Quiz . . .

TEST YOUR SKILL WITH THE QUAYLE QUIZ

The American vice-president has crossed the world 'speaking' about many things. See if you can pick out the authentic Quayle Quotes from the ones we made up in this quiz.

1) What did Dan Quayle have to say about the 20th Century?

a) 'We all lived in this century. I didn't live in this century.'

b) 'This is a great century. It is a century that we are in. It is the 20th Century.'

c) 'A century is 100 years. And that is how long this century has been and will be.'

A dense, bulbous, virulently orange vegetable. But what is he holding?

Has he wasted his mind?

2) During the 1988 Presidential Campaign, what did candidate Quayle have to say when asked if he still believed America should slow the pace of the strategic arms talks?

a) 'I don't know if it means we should slow them down but maybe we should consider not moving it as fast.'

b) 'Strategic arms, in fact, are the talks that reduce arms in a conventional and strategic sense.'

c) 'In the Bush Administration, obviously, there will be strategy development. Whether the strategy gets into this or not, I don't know.'

3) When asked if women who have become pregnant as a result of rape are entitled to choose an abortion, what was Dan Quayle's response?

a) 'Doctors in the medical community would, in fact, agree that rape leaves the women in a state of mind that it is difficult to decide.'

b) 'Rape is a terrible crime. It is a crime that is terrible because it is against the law and against the woman.'

c) 'I understand that immediately after a rape that is recorded, that a woman normally, in fact, can go to the hospital and have a D&C. At that time, that is before the forming of a life. That is not anything to do with abortion.'

4) Which of the following shows Dan Quayle's understanding of the environmental crisis on Earth?

a) 'We are, obviously, working to grasp the environment by the horns and, in fact, do something about the environment here on Earth.'

b) 'Now we have an international treaty, a treaty that is commonly referred to as the Montreal Treaty. For the first time we are talking about the impact of CO_2 on the ozone layer. That's progress for the environment.'

c) 'Earth is a planet. It's a planet in the solar system. It's a part of the solar system that is a planet that is right here.'

5) Addressing the United Negro College Fund, white boy Dan Quayle bungled their slogan 'A mind is terrible thing to waste.' What did he say?

a) 'What a waste it is to lose one's mind – or not to have a mind. How true that is.'

b) 'And when you have a mind, and you, in fact, waste it, isn't that a terrible thing?'

c) 'Wasting your mind is indeed a terrible waste.'

Answers: 1) a; 2) c; 3) c; 4) b; 5) a.

Did he live in this century?

MEMOIRS
ARE MADE OF THIS

Politicians never die, they simply write their life stories. With newly retired Nigel Lawson and Norman Fowler in mind, FRANCIS WHEEN advises on the essential ingredients of the successful political memoir

WHEN NIGEL LAWSON resigned as Chancellor of the Exchequer last autumn, it was reported that he was likely to write a book about it all. When Norman Fowler joined him on the backbenches in January, many newspapers announced that we could now expect Norman, too, to start writing his memoirs. Why this confident speculation? Not because either man had said anything at all about his literary intentions, but simply because *that is what politicians do*. They fight their way up the greasy pole, make a hash of things in government and then retire to the backbenches or a Sussex farm and compose an autobiography which explains what a splendid job they did. Francis Pym, Lord Carrington, Jim Prior, Willie Whitelaw and Norman Tebbit all did it; up in Lapland, no doubt, little Lapps do it; and it therefore seems reasonable to assume that Nigel 'Niglet' Lawson and Norman 'Crikey' Fowler will, in due course, do it too.

If you are a politician who is past the sell-by date, there are several good arguments in favour of writing your memoirs. First, it provides a 'contemporary source' for future historians, thus ensuring your immortality. In the shorter term, it gives you another burst of publicity at a time when you might otherwise have been slipping out of public consciousness into the black hole inhabited by Chuter Ede and Ray Gunter. Just when we'd all but forgotten Denis Healey, for instance, last autumn he was on the

television more or less continuously for about a month, simply because he'd written his memoirs. (What little TV time Healey did not fill was occupied by Edwina Currie, Robin Day and Ludovic Kennedy – all plugging *their* memoirs.) Finally, there is the dosh: Lawson might reasonbly expect a £100,000 advance for his autobiography, and even a ferrety little non-entity like Fowler could probably get £50,000.

So let's assume that Nigel and Norman will shortly be setting finger to Amstrad. What advice can one offer to them and any others who might be taking the plunge? First, get the front cover right: there must be a big, boring mug-shot of the author, and a dull, clichéd title. It is bad form to call your book anything memorable or original, so study the masters of the *genre*: Lord Hailsham (*The Door Wherein I Went*), Jim Callaghan (*Time and Chance*), Douglas Jay (*Change and Fortune*), Oswald Mosley (*My Life*), Leo Amery (*My Political Life*) and, most admirable of all, Anthony Eden (*Memoirs of the Rt Hon Sir Anthony Eden KG, PC, MC*). Aim for something like *A Varied Life*, or *In My Time*. Do not imitate Duff Cooper, who in a fit of absent-mindedness called his memoirs *Old Men Forget*.

Next the dedication. To your wife, of course; but in the case of men like Lawson and Fowler, who have both been married more than once, it's important to get the right wife. The first spouse – the one you traded in for a younger model – should not appear in the book at all.

And so to the text. First sentences are the most important: they

have to grab the attention. Our helpful chart on the following pages shows how four of the past year's memoirists handled this tricky task. After page one you can be as tedious and mundane as you like, since the reader is hooked.

How you fill the rest of the book is up to you, of course, but some conventions must be observed. You should complain that the BBC was always grotesquely unfair to you – describe it as a hornet's nest of vipers – but, at the same time, show your states-manlike magnanimity. 'In spite of everything,' you will write, 'I bear no grudge.' Mention, too, how well you got on with MPs on the opposite side of the House; 'We may have had our disagree-ments, but they respected me.' With colleagues on your own ben-ches, however, you can be as rude as you like. 'Fanatics', 'Infantile posturing' and 'Out of their tiny Chinese minds' are just some of the phrases you may find useful.

You must emphasise that you too have what Denis Healey calls a 'hinterland': in other words, that you aren't a narrow-minded philistine with no interests beyond acquiring ministerial cars and an official residence. Perhaps you once went to an opera; if so, be sure to mention it. Quoting poetry always impresses people, so dig out the *Golden Treasury* that you won as a hand-writing prize in the fourth form and find some verses which seem to encapsu-late your own struggle to forge a better, braver, nobler world. And

if you have ever met any distinguished figures from the Arts, tell us about it. Even Sue Pollard is better than nothing.

Finally, what about love-life? Though you may think that accounts of bedroom romps will help to sell the book, experience suggests otherwise. The two raciest memoirs by politicians in recent years – Woodrow Wyatt's *Confessions of an Optimist* (plenty of womanising) and Tom Driberg's *Ruling Passions* (plenty more of the other thing) – were not conspicuous on the best-seller list, whereas Willie Whitelaw's yawn-a-minute *The Whitelaw Memoirs* sold by the megaton. Sex is permissible only in the chapter about those 'difficult' adolecent years, where you can describe how you were seduced by George Melly on an art-room sofa at school. Assuming you were, that is. You may also reveal that on your 22nd birthday you drank 15 pints of Babycham and were sick all over your then girlfriend's carpet. It was a long time ago, you explain, and you have grown out of that sort of thing.

Assuming you have, that is. ∎

Francis Wheen is the former editor of The Observer's Pendennis *column and regular contributor to* Private Eye. *He has just com-pleted his long-awaited biography of Labour MP Tom Driberg, published by Chatto & Windus.*

Now turn to page 84 for our aide-mémoire guide ☞

David Steel havana good time with bleeched clubster Peter Stringfellow

Denis Healey gets his manuscript accepted by Kinnock Publishing

AGAINST GOLIATH
David Steel's Story by David Steel (Weidenfeld & Nicolson)

Opening words:
'David Steel was shot dead outside his house in front of his wife and child. The date was 20 December 1686. Doubtless there have been times when some wished that his descendant might suffer the same fate.' Three pages later admits that there's no proof he is descended from that D Steel after all.

Early influences:
'I collected all of Arthur Ransome's *Swallows and Amazons* books. There was no television but I was a devotee of radio's *Children's Hour* and the *Just William* series.'

School record:
Unsatisfactory. 'I frequently got into trouble . . . and was beaten by senior sadists clad in their brief authority as prefects . . . my school work suffered through lack of interest. I preferred the company of my devoted pet monkey, Gibber, and Alsatian dog Duke.'

Early love-life:
Spurned romantic advances while in Moscow with party of Scottish students in 1960: 'I was invited to a dance by a Russian girl who on the third time round this pool opened her mouth to reveal a smiling set of stainless steel teeth and said "I will give you my body for your sweater".'

Gay interlude:
In Moscow for Andropov's funeral: 'David Owen and I were billeted with two of the attachés but meantime were given a room to change out of our winter woollies before lunch. We were in the middle of struggling out of our long johns when Denis Healey blundered in by mistake. His vulgar humour got the better of him. "Ho, ho, ho, so this is what the Alliance is all about".'

Party animal:
At a banquet in Shanghai, he asks what a particular dish is. 'It's bean soup,' his host explains. Quick as a flash, Steel revives the old gag: 'I don't wish to know what it's been – I want to know what it is now!' Host fails to get joke. British diplomats not amused either. Steel's explanation of his indiscretion: 'I must have consumed too many of the powerful cups of warm rice wine.'

Uncomradely remarks about colleagues:
Many hints at the difficulty of working with the other David. 'David Owen and I filmed pieces in the hall for a party political broadcast, David being in slightly tetchy mood as he always seemed to be with television crews. Afterwards Judy and I sat with Bill and Sylvia Rodgers, who seemed not to be on speaking terms with David and Debbie Owen.'

Cultural name-dropping:
Boasts that he was at school with Roger Whittaker (of 'Durham Town' and other unforgettable hits of yesteryear – 'though when the singer and I met a year or two ago in a TV studio we had to admit we didn't remember each other at all.' Also mentions that he is 'a life member of Ronnie Scott's jazz club.'

Most surprising revelations:
When his black labrador had puppies, he gave one of the litter to President Ceausescu of Romania 'as a thank-you after an official visit'. Steel adds: 'By all reports it still lives in the presidential palace and is a favourite of the elderly autocrat. The Romanian embassy in London has to dispatch tins of its favourite food and biscuits in the diplomatic bag.' Where is this poor pooch now?

Least surprising revelation:
Groping for the *mot juste* to describe China, Steel serendipitously finds it: 'Inscrutable was the word.'

THE TIME OF MY LIFE
by Denis Healey (Michael Joseph)

Opening words:
'No comet blazed when I was born. But there was a storm all over England. Virginia Woolf records in her diary that it was "not actually raining, though dark. Trees turned brown, shrivelled on their opposed sides, as if dried up by a hot sun. No autumn tints".'

Early influences:
Cinematic. 'I used to sit in the penny seats on the front row of the Cosy Corner picture house; giant images of Tom Mix and Buck Jones reared above me in distorted perspective with the piano thundering away . . .' Also much influenced by detective Falcon Swift and his assistant Chick Conway in *The Boy's Magazine*.

School record:
Attended Drake and Tonsons' Kindergarten in Keighley, 'which the actress Mollie Sugden also attended'. It was there that he endured 'the greatest humiliation of my childhood': one afternoon he returned to school from home after lunch still wearing a pinafore. 'I had to hide weeping in the cloakroom, until the teacher found me and took it off.'

Early love-life:
At Oxford he was friendly with 'many girls' in the Labour Club and had the hots for Edna Edmunds, 'the Zuleika Dobson of St Hugh's', his future wife. In 1987 Edna was a Booker Prize judge: 'While I was walking on the downs she was reading or riffling through some 120 modern novels. She learned more about sex in those two months than in over 40 years of married bliss with me.' Say no more.

Gay interlude:
The boy Healey went on holidays in Cornwall with his classics teacher. 'In the end I realised that his interest in me was not purely intellectual, so I ceased these visits.'

Party animal:
After crashing into the back of a parked car one night, went to police station in Tottenham Court Road to report the accident. 'I was trembling with fury when I spoke to the Sergeant on duty. He wrote down my report and as I turned to go, a taxi-driver who was also at the desk said: "'Ere, this fellow's drunk." The breath test showed a positive result.' Less well publicised was the urine test, which showed a negative result.

Uncomradely remarks about colleagues:
Not as many as you would expect from an old bruiser. One fellow-minister in the Callaghan government, David Owen, is said to suffer from 'insecurity', 'arrogance', 'spikiness' and a 'rebarbative personality'. Another, Tony Benn, is merely 'a political ninny of the most superior quality'.

Cultural name-dropping:
At the age of 18 Healey became one of the first people to read Samuel Beckett's *Murphy*: 'Indeed by introducing *Murphy* to Iris Murdoch at Oxford I may have dislodged the pebble which started her avalanche.' Modest, eh?

Most surprising revelation:
Terror of the dark. 'For years I used to sleep with the sheet over my head, breathing through a tiny opening over my mouth.'

Least surprising revelation:
At Oxford, Denis Healey once mentioned to fellow-undergraduate Ted Heath that someone had gone away with a girlfriend for the weekend. Heath was horrified: 'You don't mean to say they are sleeping together?' Healey said he thought they might be. 'Good heavens,' Heath gasped. 'I can't imagine anyone in the Conservative Association doing that.'

AGAINST THE TIDE:
Diaries 1973-76 by Tony Benn (Hutchinson)

Opening sentences:
'*Wednesday 17 January 1973*. Nothing on television but Edward Heath's press conference at Lancaster House, with the world's news media gathered, to announce Phase 2 of the pay and prices freeze. Parliament has been totally pushed to one side and now MPs simply sit at home watching television...I feel I am living in a dream world at the moment.'

Early influences:
None mentioned, but in a previous volume of diaries Benn revealed that his youthful reading included *Our Island Story*, *Our Empire Story in Pictures*, the 1945 Labour election manifesto and the 1947 India Independence Bill.

School record:
Benn went to Westminster public school. All he says about this is: 'Of course the whole of Westminster is my village. That's where I was born, went to school, where Father and Mother were married, where Father died and where his memorial service was held, and where I work. It is a strange place, Westminster...'

Early love-life
Married young, and is still touchingly devoted to his wife. Typical is the entry for 12 October 1976: 'We have had such a marvellous life together and her radicalism and support and determination have really kept me going. I couldn't have managed without her.' All together now: Aaaaaaahhh.

Gay interlude:
Takes close interest in Thorpe affair, siding with Jeremy Thorpe against 'this decrepit, sad, blackmailing, former male model, Norman Scott' (13 March 1976). After Thorpe's resignation in May 1976, Benn has another go at 'Norman Scott, that awful male model', adding: 'It is terribly sad for Jeremy.'

Party animal:
The teetotal Benn drinks 25 pints of tea a day, plus an occasional cola or 7-up; his idea of a perfect meal is 'Coke and a plate of sandwiches'. Here is a Saturday night knees-up *chez* Benn in June 1973, for 60 guests: 'It went on until about two in the morning, and it was jolly and friendly. We agreed to form the 'Twenty-Five Club', committed to the nationalisation of the twenty-five companies.'

Uncomradely remarks on colleagues:
'What a bloody awful man [Harold] Wilson is, cheap and nasty.' (11 March 1977, while Benn was a member of Wilson's Cabinet.) Benn then served under Jim Callaghan, – 'very crabby'.

Cultural name-dropping:
None at all, except for a brief appearance by the woman who later became famous as Sybil Fawlty, at the first National Community Action Conference, in Bristol, Saturday 9 June 1973: 'Before I went on there was a good little play produced by Prunella Scales, a TV actress associated with the Socialist Labour League. I was due to speak at eight o'clock and my slides didn't work for some time, so there was a lot of ribald laughter.'

Most surprising revelation:
'*Wednesday 17 November 1976*. Tonight I began reading *Mein Kampf*, which was written by Hitler in the 1920s, long before he came to power.'

Least surprising revelation:
'*Sunday 26 December 1976*. Caroline gave each of us a copy of the *Communist Manifesto* in our stockings, published in English in Russia, and she gave Josh a book called *Marx for Beginners* and gave Hilary Isaac Deutscher's biography of Trotsky.'

UPWARDLY MOBILE
by Norman Tebbit (Futura)

Opening words:
'Whatever control we may have over the time, place or manner of our departure from this world, we have no influence at all over our arrival. The 29th of March 1931 was not the best time to be born.'

Early influences:
'I had read all Leslie Charteris's 'Saint' books by the time I was 12.'

School record:
Teachers at Edmonton Grammar 'will live forever in my mind', especially 'Miss Emery, Miss Henderson and George 'Gussy' Locke who recognised in me a wordsmith.' Clever old Gussy.

Early love-life:
Almost non-existent. The 20-year-old Tebbit did go out for a while with Wendy Craig, later the star of many immortal TV series (*Butterflies, And Mother Makes Three* etc). However...

Gay interlude:
'...I remained far more fond of the company of other males than of girls. Life was so full that I hardly had time for girls, anyway...it was all too much effort.' Long accounts of male-bonding with fellow-pilots – 'mostly bachelors' – during his days in the Royal Auxiliary Air Force (early 1950s). 'The squadron was the first love.' Get the picture?

Party animal:
You bet. In his 20s, Tebbit's 'liking for a good drink and pranks' tended to 'land me in trouble'. Lots of 'hard drinking and wild parties' in the mess and in pubs. 'Rough cider (tanglefoot) was cheap and good though it certainly lived up to its name.' Tebbit and his chums, 'like most people at that time, had a relaxed attitude to drinking and driving...Amongst members of both the flying club and the squadron, driving accidents and car write-offs were almost a part of life!'

Uncomradely remarks about colleagues:
During the Falklands War, weedy Francis Pym 'in true Foreign Office style pursued every avenue which might lead to an accommodation with Argentina.' Most venom is saved for Ted Heath, who from the early 1970s onwards was 'a political and electoral liability'. Heath's government was nothing more than 'a mish-mash of ill-considered centralist and socialist hand-to-mouth devices with no intellectual nor political cohesion.'

Cultural name-dropping
Apart from Wendy Craig (*qv*) only two artistic heavyweights cross his path: Jimmy Savile ('I came to realise there was a lot more to him than the showbiz personality') and Jeffrey Archer ('It is only fair to say that the appointment of Jeffrey Archer as my deputy raised quite a few eyebrows').

Most surprising revelation:
'Geoffrey Howe proved an excellent chairman, his splendid sense of mischievous irreverent humour, which is seldom seen in public, cheering us on.'

Least surprising revelation:
While working as a BOAC pilot, Tebbit reveals, 'my refusal to fudge won me few friends'.

AS TYRANTS GO BY

Following the downfalls of Ceausescu and Noriega,

ANTHONY LEE examines the ignoble tradition of

bloodthirsty dictators and their fates

I t is to the credit of the United States government, not to mention the cackhandedness of its military operations, that General Manuel Noriega is currently a guest of the Miami judicial system, rather than luxuriating in some other sedate sunspot, enjoying the $300m odd he is alleged to have siphoned from Panama.

At least he is out of the Vatican's hair (or should that be *biretta*?). The Yuletide devotions of Joe Sebastian Laboa, the papal Nuncio, could scarcely have been improved by the constant counterpoint of Jimi Hendrix, Roger Daltrey and Led Zeppelin; Messrs Daltrey and Co. might well have a valid claim for defamation in being defined as a military means of offence, but that is their business. Ours is yet another deposed dictator to dispose of, made redundant at a time when the market is overstocked.

Defining a dictator is never easy. Today's despot is yesterday's darling, but a regular turnover in US presidents can work wonders on long-term memory and foreign policy. Noriega can count himself lucky that he is in Miami. Personally, I recommend the Bayside Development, should he need a few designer artefacts to accompany his military togs, or the odd souvenir for the wife and mistresses on his release – at current estimates, likely to be just in time for the third millennium. But just in case he gets off (we must all be prepared) where will he go? Various countries operate retirement schemes for former despots. Which should he choose?

Certainly not Romania. Dictators are a difficult species to contemplate, and the Romanians chose not to contemplate the Ceausescus at all. 'The population had everything it needed,' opined the Grand Leader of the Peoples of Romania at his final appearance. Not as much, though, as the *Conducator*, whose palace afforded an entertaining post-Christmas away-day tour for the populace, not least those 200,000 whose homes were demolished at 48 hours' notice to accommodate it.

In accordance with dictatorial tradition, the Ceausescu clan had salted away a little nest-egg for their retirement, rumoured to be $400m in Zurich gold. Elena Ceausescu also adhered to the principle of despotess as foot-fetishist, maintaining a shoe collection quite as extensive as that of the Widow Marcos. Imelda's life is still scandalously blighted by the fraud charges brought upon her immaculately coiffeured head by her late husband's alleged ▶

Opposite: **9 ruthless rulesters (clockwise from top) – Fidel Castro, Idi Amin, Fulgencio Batista, Baby Doc Duvalier, Augusto Pinochet, Jean Bédel Bokassa, Ferdinand Marcos, Nicolae Ceausescu, and (centre) Alfredo Stroessner**

THE GREATER THE POWER, THE MORE DANGEROUS THE ABUSE ...

HEAVY MEDAL FANS FIELD MARSHALL AMIN DADA AND GENERAL BOKASSA

◄ billion-dollar retirement fund. Imelda lives, in her own words, 'in penury' – actually a $2.5m (rented) abode in Hawaii.

Honolulu is much-favoured as a watering-hole for this class of political retiree, once the US helicopters (so what's wrong with Dan Air?) have ferried them out of trouble. It was the last resort, and resting place, of Dr Syngman Rhee, who was the first President of the South Korean Republic until an ungrateful populace gave him the heave-ho in 1960. Obituaries of this lifelong anti-Communist paid tribute in equal proportions to his fight for a unified Korea and his rather indelicate (that is, ruthlessly bloody) methods of achieving it. True to his calling, Dr Rhee was accused of improperly appropriating £3.5m. 'That's the first I've heard of it,' replied the doctor, when asked to account for the sum. Perhaps deafness was a problem, for Dr Rhee was reported to have gone to Hawaii for health reasons. Presumably a desire to avoid having one's private parts hacked off by the mob is the healthiest reason of all.

History has not been kind to Koreans. The immediate past president of South Korea, Chun Doo Hwan, is (par for the course) facing charges of corruption, but has been forced to endure a far more horrendous exile: South Korea itself. Having been exiled there for a time, I have some sympathy for his plight; Chun retreated to a remote Buddhist monstery, there presumably to polish,

in holy isolation, such elegant turns of phrase as 'an unfortunate accident' – his term for the deaths of 200 civilians at the hands of troops during a 1980 student uprising. President Chun has always been a shy man. One American correspondent had his television camera removed when he dared to film Chun's back during the president's inspection of the new Olympic stadium. Chun apparently harboured the impression that his almost hairless dome was not visible from the front.

In North Korea Kim Il Sung, Syngman Rhee's old adversary from Korean War days, still gibbers nervously over statues of himself, the profusion of which almost outnumbers his subjects. Other despots have to hack it in foreign climes. The ailing Shah of Iran was reduced to incommodious shufflings as he sought a place to settle: few friends then for the man who, just weeks before, had the world as his pen-pal. By February 1986, when Jean-Claude 'Baby Doc' Duvalier fled Haiti, having decided (according to his taped message) 'to pass the destiny of the nation into the hands of the military,' an estimated $750m had, reportedly, already passed into the hands of the Duvalier dynasty. US MercyAir performed another rescue mission, depositing the Duvaliers in that most inhospitable of hell holes, the French Riviera, with a promise to pick them up when (wink, wink) a permanent place of exile had been located. The Duvaliers remain in France to this day, prime symbols of the *liberté* and *egalité* enjoyed under Mitterrand socialism. As politicians the Duvaliers may have been lethal; as (*soi-disant*) penniless refugees, they are miracle-workers. According to some reports, they have been living, appropriately enough, *chez* that international socialite Adnan Khashoggi, who currently sports an electronic tag to ensure his continued presence in the US, though for matters other than acting as the Duvaliers' landlord.

The French government has finally taken an interest in the Duvaliers' schizophrenic expenditure, but Baby Doc's lawyers have rightly argued that the French courts have no jurisdiction over the Duvaliers' dealings in Haiti. Indeed, any other interpretation of the Penal Code might imply that the French had suddenly developed a mood of impartiality. For was not France home not only to the Ayatollah Khomeini, during his exile from Iran, but also to that entertaining figure of post-colonial African politics, Jean Bédel Bokassa?

In 1965 the former French Army officer seized power as President of the Central African Republic and rode the waves of French funding, Israeli trade and South African aid. But despots frolic on the surf of power without suffering the undertow of sanity. Bokassa declared himself President for Life, in fitting reward for his enthusiastic commitment to judicial excellence. When the organised mutilation of thieves failed to curtail crime, he simply led a ritual beating, in which three men died and 43 others were maimed. No advocate of secret justice, Bokassa had all the bodies put on public display for several days.

In due recognition of such sterling work, the President in 1977 appointed himself Emperor Jean Bédel Bokassa I, in a coronation ceremony costing $25m (one quarter of his empire's annual budget). Utilitarian in the extreme, he even found a use for the imperial sceptre: it came in handy for poking out the eyes of a rebellious schoolchild. The nature of his rebellion? Refusal to buy overpriced school uniforms from one of the Emperor's wives shops. The Emperor's reign came to an end in 1979, during a trip to Libya; he retired to an 18-room chateau near Paris until 1987, when he pitched up in his old empire, was tried, sentenced to death, and reprieved to a life of forced labour.

That Bokassa's favourite wife was Romanian proves that there is irony in history; that his best friend was Idi Amin confirms that history is full of farce. Amin was so impressed by Bokassa's medals, spilling down his jacket like so much gilded puke, that the Ugandan *eminence grise* had himself a set minted overnight. Amin's own reign of terror included the usual prodigious blood baths, but he also shared with Bokassa a taste (*sic*) for cannibalism. This dietary refinement he inflicted on other people, rather than partaking himself, or partaking *of* himself: victims were obliged to indulge in an innovative version of nutritional recycling, being forced to consume their own flesh. In 1979 Amin fled Uganda and found refuge in Libya, but moved on for ten years to Saudi Arabia (a reward for his support of Uganda's Muslim minority) until January 1989, when the Saudis decided he was a luxury they could no longer afford. Fundless, he headed for Zaire, after which his progress became about as predictable as his mental state.

If Amin could find his way there, he – and indeed Noriega – might consider Brazil. Noriega's movements are currently as restricted as were those of the distinguished research scientist Josef Mengele at the end of World War Two; Mengele supposedly ended his days in throbbing São Paulo. Noriega reportedly employed Brazilian witches to rid himself of his enemies – a stratagem which his present predicament proves to have been less than efficacious.

The Brazilian authorities are at least experienced in dealing with statesmen of Noriega's calibre. One of Brazil's Amazon neighbours, Paraguay, was ruled for 34 years by General Alfredo Stroessner, who – in time-honoured fashion – ran the place as a family fiefdom. For 32 of those years, Paraguay was in a state of emergency, though since Stroessner had declared this condition, we must assume he did not consider himself its cause. While foreign journalists were not overly welcome, Paraguay under Stroessner was not inhospitable to members of the governing classes: whole echelons of the Third Reich are believed to have received safe refuge. The General was also a generous man. Brazil, not content with ravaging its own rainforests, was allowed to colonise and plunder within Paraguay. In February 1989, a coup terminated the General's beneficence. But what was to be done with him? Could he perhaps go to Chile, where his old friend Augusto Pinochet was completing a mere 16 years in the family business?

Astute analysts will know that Brazil maintained its reputation for egalitarian protectionism, and extended to Stroessner the same security of tenure long granted to that vibrant media personality, Ronald Biggs.

Stroessner's successor is one General Andres Rodriguez, who happens to be the father of Stroessner's daughter-in-law. Furthermore, since Rodriguez has already amassed a fortune considered incommensurate with a general's salary, we might conclude that any family reunion might be done over cocktails in São Paulo, rather than at a criminal court in Asuncion. They might yet be joined by another General, Pinochet, who next month will finally relinquish all duties as President of Chile, and at the tender age of 73, begins an eight-year term as commander of the army – a post he thoughtfully bestowed upon himself prior to his political retirement.

So what about Colombia, whose economy of nasal stimulation might appeal to a person of Noriega's interests? If so, he should be careful to remain unlisted in the Bogotá telephone directory, a precaution which Ronald Biggs failed to have taken in Rio, the last time I looked. Miami might not be so bad after all. Cuba's last elected prime minister is there, but then, much of Cuba is in Miami. Batista left there to start his Cuban coup in 1952, and it was to Miami that Fidel Castro fled. In 1959, when it became Castro's turn to collect Cuba, Batista returned to Miami.

Just outside Orlando, there is an alligator farm called 'Gatorland'. Given the sunshine state's propensity for theme parks, perhaps it could accommodate one more, devoted to dictators – 'Tatorland' let's say. For a mere $20 or so, interested followers of international affairs could watch (in carefully reconstructed surroundings) Bokassa prancing around in his medals and crown; Imelda trying on shoes for shopping sprees; Stroessner reviewing endless troop parades, and Noriega attending to his mistresses. Vatican advisers would doubtless be able to provide wise counsel, being quite savvy about tourist moneymakers.

A sense of humour is, after all, a quality sorely lacking among most despots. Ceausescu at least made his views on humour quite clear. Anyone cracking jokes about the President of the Socialist Republic of Romania got two years in the nick. Yet one grand jest went unpunished, possibly because nobody considered it funny. In 1978 Nicolae Ceaucescu was awarded an honorary British knighthood. True, it was withdrawn upon his fall, but if we assume it was meant with no humour at all, then Noriega's course is clear. Welcome, Manuel. England awaits… ■

Amin's reign of terror included the usual bloodbaths but he also shared with Bokassa a taste (sic) for cannibalism

SKODA
TEST AREA
→

'I liked it so much I bought the company.'

'I think somebody's trying to kill me.'

chapter

THE CARTOONISTS ART

CARTOONS
By de la Nougerede

'Sorry I can't help you – I'm a stranger here myself.'

'Nothing personal, Pooh, but we figured you'd fetch a fortune on the open market.'

'I'm afraid it's terminal – Her Majesty the Snow Queen, is suffering from global warming.'

'Understaffed?!! – I've carried out five operations this morning and I'm only the janitor!'

$\mathcal{A}$ CARTOON BONANZA

Introduced by Miles Kington

Cartoonists are different from other people, like writers for example. They think that prose is funny grey stuff that separates the drawings. They know that writers always become editors of Punch *but they don't care because they also know that people always turn to the cartoons first and don't always go on to the articles. You could have an issue of* Punch *devoted only to drawings but not one entirely full of prose. That's why cartoonists look so pleased with themselves.*

No, that's not the reason, actually. The reason cartoonists tend to look happy is that they have just come to London away from the strange place they live in and for the first time in a long time they have a chance to get together and make merry. I always noticed at Punch *that after a* Punch *party the writers went home, usually by themselves, whereas the cartoonists, as if unable to admit that festivities had finished, went across the road to the nearest pub and carried on the party there at their own expense. Sometimes I used to follow them. I was the only writer there.*

Many rounds were bought me. This must be, I thought, because they were all naturally grega-rious people but now, looking back, I realise that they had nowhere else to go. Their homes were all in Leicester or the Wirral or Sussex.

Most of the time they spend hunched over a drawing board feeling lonely and unwanted, so quite naturally they take the chance of a get together when they can, and they associate London with the good life rather as Welsh rugby supporters do. They feel as little inclined to come and live in London as Welsh rugby fans do. Quite often cartoonists do make the big break from their own home town but then they go and live somewhere as unLondonlike as possible. Larry moved

'Morning.'

from Birmingham to Stratford on Avon. Bill Tidy moved from the steppes of Lancashire to the wastes of Northamptonshire. Or was it Leicester-shire? And how can they tell?

Cartoonists do not in my experience talk about cartooning. For 10 years I worked next to the art room here, and the art editor and deputy had constant arguments about whether Dutch painters or Italian painters were better (a stupid argument, as temperamentally one was northern and the other Mediterra-nean). Cartoonists would come in and talk about drink, or art, or money, or how much Mike Heath really earned, but they never talked about cartooning, except perhaps to wonder what kind of car David Langdon thought he was drawing. That's why they all look happy. No, it's not, actually. The reason they all look so happy is that they have noms de plume like Mac or Chic or Pont or Sprod. This means they can never be recognised. A writer may go somewhere and give his name, expecting to be recognised, and nobody there has heard of him. A cartoonist gives his name, but doesn't care if it doesn't ring any bells, because that's not the name he's famous by. So while the writer is going through a depressive fit at his failure, the cartoonist is

'It says he's an egotistical, shallow, insincere little bore and if he's not careful he could end up with his own chat show!'

already ordering his first drink.

I remember now. That's why they're all so happy. They all have the best drinking story. I can remember listening to McMurtry telling of the night he fell asleep in Piccadilly underground, missed the last train and stayed all night. I can remember Ross Thomson waking up at the seaside in a train (he didn't live at the seaside) going into a phone box to explain he was at the seaside to a disbelieving wife and furiously holding the receiver out to the sound of breakers to convince her. I can remember someone saying 'Have you heard what Frank Dickens did the other night when he was pissed?' and everyone gathering round afraid to miss the latest Frank Dickens story. I can remember the first time I was ever invited to a Toby dinner – the *Punch* cartoonists' banquet. Someone at the dinner said to me: 'We don't have a loyal toast, we just wait till Sprod falls over.' And it was true too.

One thing I ought to tell you about cartoonists. They don't like sending off just six good drawings to editors because they know editors like to reject something, and it's a bit hard to have three good drawings come back. So they put in four or five others to be rejected. And very often they are the ones that get taken, by the Editor, who is a writer and therefore knows nothing about the art of cartooning.

Maybe that's the real reason cartoonists have a small smile about their features. Consciousness of being a superior race. ∎

HALDANE
Designer victims

"It's not the kind of bird table
I had in mind, Roger."

"One gets a better class of zombie in here these days."

TIE RACK

"I think we should have done more market research."

"Miss Dawson, phone the architect and find out which of us is the right way up."

"He insisted on having his superhero suit designed by Giorgio Armani."

LARRY
Open that door!

RODIN'S MAFIA VICTIM

RODIN'S DULL COUPLE

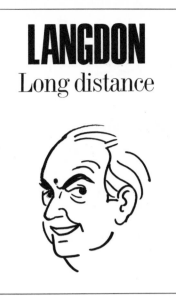

LANGDON
Long distance

'And anyway, how can the market inspector tell they're NOT souvenir bits of the Berlin Wall?'

'I'm against. So there's hardly any point in putting it to the vote.'

'The word is, skip this audience. HM's busy on her Christmas message to the nation AND the Commonwealth.'

'A wee bit premature, darling – refurbishing No. 10.'

'Have a heart, dearie – it's too cold for kerb-crawling.'

MYERS
In memoriam

'It happens to be the only part of my body that's not ticklish.'

'It's said he just LOVED company.'

'He invented dental floss.'

'Sometimes I wish you would just sing in the bath.'

'He always had this great passion for letting truth be known.'

LOWRY

M O RNING

(Neville Brody sings the blues…)

'Hey brother! Are we bad, or are we baaaad?!!'

'How do you like it? We redesigned the logo.'

'Stands the church clock at ten to three and have they still got Led Zeppelin's 'Stairway to Heaven' on the Student's Union jukebox?'

Museum

PALAEOLITHIC
NEOLITHIC
YONKS AGO

'Wow! Culture shock.'

'Hi! We're the media.'

'No, Daddy. This is Mr Shithead.'

'Dalmations always confuse me. I can never figure out which dots are their eyes.'

MILLER & CO.

'There's a gentleman here to see you in high-tops.'

'Spare us the sermon, Harry. Just say no.'

'You don't have to take any. I can cope with rejection.'

GET IN LANE NOW

↑ WE'LL BE HERE AGES   ↑ SHOULD HAVE STAYED WHERE I WAS   ↑ OTHER LANE IS MOVING FASTER   ↑ PUSHING YOUR LUCK   ↑ SOME-ONE WILL LET ME IN

THE MAN ON THE CLAPHAM OMNIBUS

PYNE
Pynes's people

'Spare an old yuppie the price of a Perrier water, guv?'

'We can't be far from London now'.

HUSBAND
Thuggy bears

'I'm desperate for a cause.'

'That was funny when he said he'd get his big brother.'

'Son, it's about time you knew — we adopted you.'

'You spoil that dog, Roy.'

'Miss Dovely, you'd better
cancel my appointments
for the rest of the day.'

'Jesus Christ, Nobby, slowdown.'

JACKSON
All cut up

'Original oak beams, delightfully situated in the centre of the village – it all sounded so good in the estate agent's brochure.'

'If you ask me – Mrs Tiggy-Winkle should never've got the job in the first place.'

'Arnold wants to be a revisionist historian when he grows up.'

'He's done it! He's done it! He's finally created a butter that spreads straight from the fridge!'

'The condensation's pretty bad tonight…'

SCHWADRON
Myth-takers

TRUTH, HONOR, INTEGRITY

'And so the prince and princess lived happily ever after until the tabloids started speculating on their marital problems.'

'Anger, covetousness, gluttony and sloth haven't been all that bad to us, Renselow.'

FLIGHT INSURANCE

100 YODELS FOR EVERY OCCASION

'It's from a vitamin company. It's addressed to you, Your Royal Sluggishness.'

'I don't care if one of the boys did order it. Go away.'

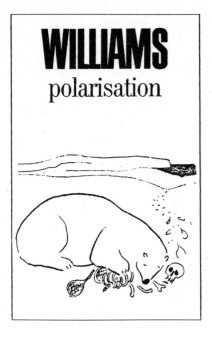

WILLIAMS
polarisation

'The batteries! The batteries!'

'Damn! Forgot to turn the blanket off.'

'Hey!'

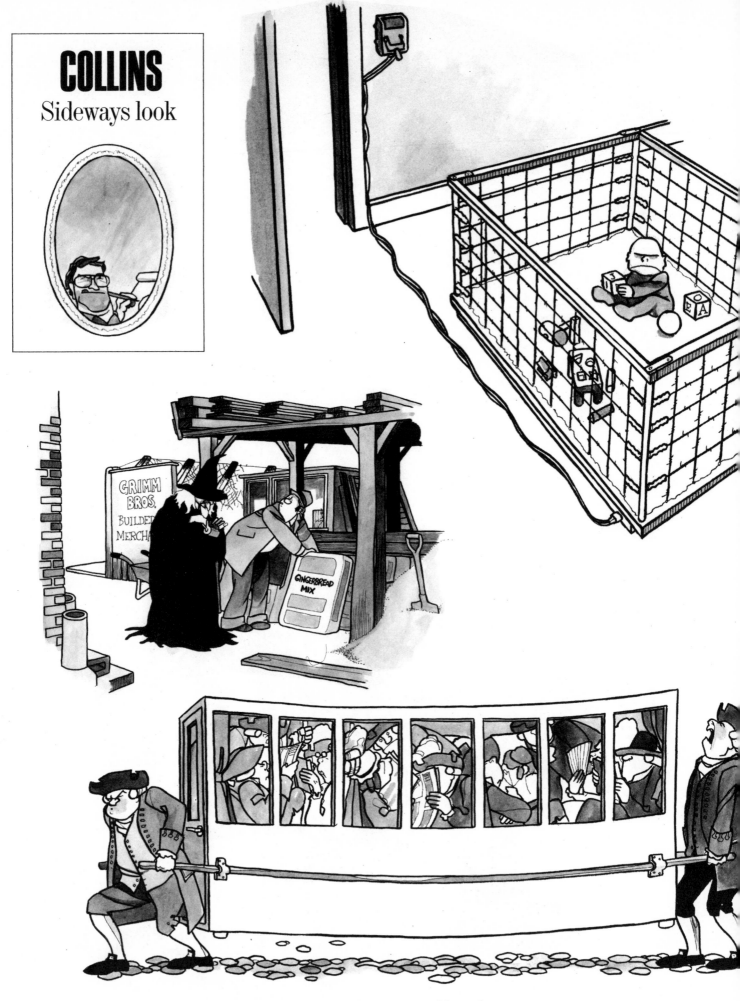

COLLINS
Sideways look

'I'ATES the bloody rush hour...'

'Good to see that you haven't lost
your sense of humour, Mr Bembridge'.

SHOW
BOX

chapter

5

TRAVEL, TRIALS   AND TRIBULATIONS

> Living in the country isn't about *Country Living*. It's about the dangers of mad cows, low-flying jets and village fêtes. STEPHEN PILE explains why he's giving up chasing the rural dream

OUT OF FARM'S WAY

WELCOME, OH FOG and smut. Hello crowds and sweet pollution. Come, pretty traffic, let me kiss thee. I have left rural England for ever (and I mean *for ever*. In future I don't even want to see it through a train window. I shall wrestle with other passengers to pull the blinds down.)

On the day we left Miles Kington rang. 'You sound euphoric,' he said. 'Your wife sounds very euphoric.' She was singing and howling and practically hysterical with the joy of it. Miles has just moved from London to Limpley Stoke, a move that would stagger Italian farmers (they won't even live on their farms because it is so boring. They prefer to commute out from Florence). He said that it was horses for courses. 'Some people like knitting. Others like …' No, no, hold it there. I am a friend and fan of Mr Kington, but I have to put my foot down here: the countryside is nothing whatever like knitting.

People do not spend their whole lives dreaming about throwing in their jobs and leaving London to knit. There are not idyllic and seductive pictures of knitting on every advert, label and wrapper. We are not sold the idea day after day that knitting is somehow more pure, good, real and wholesome than our normal town life.

An idealized version of the countryside is sold to us up hill and down dale at every possible moment. And what is the result? Throughout world history migration has always been from the country to the town and for very good reasons. (The Samaritans have 2½ times more calls from the rural than the urban population.) But now for the first time ever millions are going in the opposite direction. Are they mad?

And now you will look at me and say, 'Well, you're a rational man. You knew the countryside was a bunch of pesticide-sodden fields joined together by motorways and subject to an everlasting planning ruction, a tree-filled suburbia and backdrop for estate agency where nothing of interest has happened since the Creation. So why did you go?'

Ah, well, now we come to the main thrust and point. Blow the trumpets. Turn the spotlight: *J'accuse Country Living*. Like the Moonies, this glossy magazine leads perfectly sane middle-class people to behave in staggering ways. For years I read this publication with its roses over the door, its beautiful young couples seen in their expensively renovated homes and its never ending columns by Brian Redhead. Mr Redhead looks like every Morris dancer you have ever seen, wittering on about preserving hedgehogs and saving absolutely everything in sight.

'The Aga is a way of life' the magazine said and I believed it. 'Happiness is not possible without exposed beams.' Oh, I remember all the articles. 'Should one buy a paddock?' by Caroline McGhee (yes, one should). 'Give your child a perfect country childhood' by Libby Purves. How to buy a pony. Entertaining the village. Carefree cooking. Making the most of your porch. Ragging and rolling till you're sick of it. Oh how we laughed.

Then one day we had a baby and years of brainwashing took effect. The paddock factor seized us by the throat. In our mind's eye apple-cheeked infants ran in past the roses along the Aga underneath the dried flowers and up to the stripped pine table to eat home-baked carefree cakes. So off we set to Upper Podley (I have changed the name – just slightly – to protect the guilty. The innocent need no protection). And what did we find?

For a start, in rural England there are more media folk than ▶

OUT OF FARM'S WAY

◄ milk churns. One of the most distressing features of *Country Living* magazine is the regular appearance in it of Paul Heiney dressed like an escaped extra from *Far From The Madding Crowd*. He is always in there telling us about how he breeds horses or grows mangel-wurzels (no really). And every time he is dressed in period boots, a collarless shirt, chunky cord trousers and a check waistcoat with a watch chain. Do they send up a team of wardrobe assistants or does he actually walk round Suffolk dressed like this? And who is he kidding? We all know he is a television presenter and Electricity Board advertiser, not Gabriel Archer.

In the bookshops I notice a new work entitled *Bel Mooney's Somerset*. Ms Mooney was born in Liverpool and has spent her working life on London newspapers. I have spent hours gossiping with this dear woman in the office and we have even been out for lunch. Not once during this whole period did she ever so much as mention Somerset. She always seemed to be staying in her London flat to get away from it. Why hasn't she written a book called *Bel Mooney's London Flat*? It would be much more to the point.

All of these newly rural journalists contribute to *Country Living*'s 'Scenes From A Provincial Life' column, dealing with their first days and hours surrounded by rural bliss. In it they always meet the bluff farmer next door who is full of wisdom. A year later they are writing large features entitled 'My Norfolk,' saying how their beloved county is under threat from developers and road builders.

Of course, the only reason they are having this 'idyllic' life and are boring the rest of us to tears with the details is because they can roar up and down the motorway to work in London at the drop of a hat. How many trees were chopped down, farms ruined and villages blighted so that Brian Redhead can get to Broadcasting House for six o'clock on Monday morning?

In fact, rural England has been dying for as long as anyone can remember. William Cobbett was the first to spot it in *Rural Rides*. It was dying because of the Enclosures Act. Then it died when the railways opened and it died when the railways closed. It died when everybody left and it died when everybody came back. But the dying had to stop and rigor mortis finally set in between 1984 and 1990.

In the early 1980s – before *Country Living* came into existence – you could still pay 40p at the village hall to see the Podley Players, a bold amateur troupe, give a generous selection of a playwright's lines, occasionally in the order which he intended. These fine actors were not shackled by a script. They saw it as a springboard, a point of reference during a long night, a skeleton on which to hang jokes of their own or the ad libs of an evening. In the wardrobe they had a camel suit and liked to use it in every production, regardless of the play. *Hamlet* upon the battlements would not be safe from that camel.

But since 1985 the *Country Living* readers have moved in (the magazine started in 1984). The first thing they did in Podley was to hijack the drama group. Now the standard is semi-professional and you have to wear a dinner jacket for the opening night of a Harold Pinter.

The Freke Arms used to be a genuine, beat-up country pub in the village square with a glass-cased pie-warmer and no real ale at all. ('No call for it round 'ere. Locals prefer the fizzy.') But now it has been horse-brassed from top to bottom and is acclaimed annually by Egon Ronay for its caviar and borscht. Bills of £30 or £40 a head are quite common.

Every time there is a barn dance or fête the villagers (some of whom have lived here as long as six months) get out the same old hay bales. There are only six in the whole village. At Upper Podley barbecue night the hay bales are the only way of telling you're not in Sloane Square. Behold the chic rustics in their waxed Laura Ashley caped drover's coats and their Liberty scarves.

I once saw two elegant women going out for a walk. They tiptoed gingerly out of Honeypot Cottage wearing taupe cotton designer jodphurs, knee-length lace-up boots, wide-brimmed hats and floral wraparound shawls. They walked halfway across a rutted, uninteresting field, then turned round and went back in again. So bracing, darling. Nobody but nobody knows anything about rural matters. (If a foal is born in Podley half the village turns out to video the occasion. It's like a press conference for Madonna.)

In our village the only ambition of the rector is to get the congregation to call him 'Roger'. Sadly, this is the one thing they are not prepared to do. They have not spent half-a-million pounds on a house (with paddock), given their children a country childhood and spent the whole afternoon hanging dried flowers just to say 'Hello, Roger' every time they see some drip vicar. No, they want to cycle past with fresh bread in the pannier, tinkle the bell and say, 'Morning, rector, lovely day.' It is part of the rural idyll. They have paid for it.

Our experience has not been blissful at all. What is this myth that the countryside is wonderful for children? They never see an animal because they are all locked up in battery farms. They can't get into a field ('KEEP OUT') to run freely through it. My daughter just lay on the floor, sucking her thumb, bored to tears, watching Dumbo videos, because the countryside had nothing more to offer. Its facilities and rewards are nil.

And the Aga, oh yes the Aga. It's a way of life all right, particularly in the summer. It heats the food, heats the house and heats the water. The piping heat warms the dream cottage day and night. The only problem is that between May and September, with temperatures reaching 80 degrees outside, you have to walk round stark naked with all the windows open. The kitchen is like a Burmese rubber plantation. The only alternative is to stop cooking altogether and use cold water till the winter months return. Now the greenhouse effect has left us with only a couple of hours of genuinely cold weather a year, an Aga seems a bad investment.

As for exposed beams, why doesn't *Country Living* do a feature about how you can hear every word as clear as day in the room above or below. If somebody is in bed you have to whisper in the sitting-room. If you are exchanging intimate chatter in the bedroom you might as well use a tannoy. The explanation is that the Tudors did not intend these beams to be exposed. They quite sensibly covered theirs up to retain the heat and insulate the sound. But some pioneering design nitwit in the 1940s thought it would make things look altogether older if they were exposed. And, of course, we all followed. ►

◀ As if exposed beams were not enough, everything in the village is thatched, including the fitness centre which is packed full of pastel tracksuits and Nautilus equipment and peroxide blonde instructors shouting 'Do it' in time to a tape. Even the saloon bar in the Freke Arms has just been thatched. It looks like Polynesia: the hut where Gauguin died.

Christmas was a let-down. Automatic security lighting has been the death of carol singing in rural England. We set off with shepherd's lamps dangling from our crooks. (They gave no light whatsoever so we had torches in our other hand.) The moment you open a gate and start walking up the drive a light goes on in the hall. When we opened the porch door a burglar alarm went off that would raise the last six rectors.

Noise in the countryside is intolerable, not least from the shooting fraternity. On Saturday mornings business syndicates engage upon the mass slaughter of everything that moves. If you stand in the garden it sounds like the Somme. The only thing that can (and does) drown out these sportsmen are the low-flying military jets which are such a feature.

The village community has been dead for 50 years. You've got more chance of contacting Dame Nellie Melba on a ouija board than seeing your neighbour

I think there was a protest meeting about that. But then there was about everything: protest is now the main rural pastime. I went to one meeting at which the people who lived at the Old Schoolhouse, the Old Bakery, the Old Shop, the Old Saddlery, the Old Mill, the Old Forge and the Old Rectory got together to discuss the fact that the village community is in grave danger of dying out. (A developer wants to build 300 houses and a bus station on Snotte's Bottom Green, which they found unacceptable.)

The fact that the community has been dead from the eyeballs up and down for the past 50 years does not seem to have dawned on them. You've got more chance of contacting Dame Nellie Melba on a ouija board than seeing your neighbour. They move in, renovate the cottage, extend it to three times the original size, build a six-foot wall round the garden, switch on the burglar alarm then go to Australia for six months ('We've got a house out there.') Furthermore, it is my view that, authentically, a bus station could only improve Snotte's Bottom Green.

Then in September they discovered that mad cow disease had been caught by mice. Oh terrific, terrific, now we've got mad mice on top of everything else.

In February we woke up to a typical winter's morning: it was baking hot and there was a breeze gusting at 120 mph. We opened the window to find that the entire forest had blown away. At this point we decided that our rural idyll was at an end.

Basically we are moving back to London so we can go out for a walk. In the countryside it is not possible to do this. All the land belongs to somebody else and you can tramp dust-filled, weary, tarmac-ed lanes all day, avoiding pantechnicons and hurtling Range Rovers, trying to find a footpath. We had to get into the car and drive along a dual carriageway for 20 minutes to reach one.

But now the nightmare is over. My children have pink cheeks for the first time in ages. We walk around the city streets with gratitude, knowing that there are theatres and crèches and parks and pools and every civilized facility known to man. But, lo and hark, a beauteous traffic jam has formed beneath my window. I must away and hug it. ■

Stephen Pile is author of the successful Book of Heroic Failures.

TOWN AND COUNTRY

'I've just heard the first cuckoo of spring cough.'

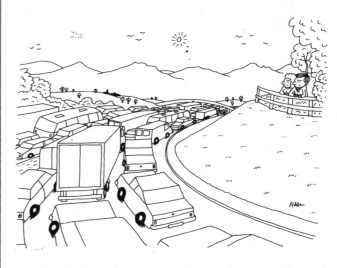

'It's been designated a motorway of outstanding natural beauty!'

'It's an unemployment blackspot, of course.'

Around the world with the Duchess of York

Punch takes a holiday-by-holiday look at Fergie the globe-trotting Royal

The world has lost a great holidaymaker. For years vacation fans the whole world over gasped in admiration as the Duchess of York reacted to her newfound royalty by going on the longest awayday spree anyone had ever seen. She was a phenomenon – a one-woman *Wish You Were Here*.

As plain Sarah Ferguson she had been happiest skiing in Switzerland (those were the days, of course, when there was snow in Switzerland). But marriage to Prince Andrew broadened her horizons; here was a *Blind Date* whose prize seemed to be a never-ending round-the-world tour. In 1987, for example, she got away on ten separate trips. She once racked up 99 days holiday in a single year, a figure that may very well be an all-time record.

But now all that has changed. Despite a Civil List increase that takes her annual remuneration from a strictly Tourist Class £68,000 to a Club World-style £155,000, the Duchess has thrown away her brochures and settled down. Her days are now spent on royal duties (up from 55 in 1988 to 200 last year), the supervision of her new home, Southyork, the care of her daughter Beatrice and preparations for her new baby. As if to confound her critics, her hard work has been combined with a slimline figure. So much so, in fact, that she is now being accused of looking pale and drawn when she should be rosy and blooming.

The proof of her sobriety is the fact that in the whole of the 1990s to date, the Duchess has only managed a quick break with the Royal Family in Norfolk, during which she swam with Princess Diana in a King's Lynn health club and restricted herself to the Sandringham Diet.

We at *Punch* belief that Fergie's achievements deserve a permanent record, a memorial to a woman who took the motto 'work hard, play hard,' and made half of it her very own. This is no sneering profile. You will find no references to the Duchess's sex-life or her supposed predeliction for dirty jokes. Let other magazines stoop to that level. We shall confine ourselves to the facts.

A DUCHESS ON HOLIDA[Y]

1986
JULY North Atlantic for her honeymoon in the Azores

1987
JANUARY Norfolk: Three weeks hunting and shooting in Sandringham.
    Switzerland: One week skiing at Klosters.
FEBRUARY Switzerland: Two more weeks skiing at Klosters.
MARCH France: Two days of shopping in Paris.
    Caribbean: Ten days at Robert Sangster's Barbados pad.
JUNE France: A quick trip to Bordeaux.
JULY Canada: Thirteen days in the Northern Territories. The Duchess comes face to face with a 'giant man-eating grizzly bear' and is reputedly not enamoured of her wilderness experience, crying on the phone to her mother in Buenos Aires.
AUGUST Scotland: Three weeks killing grouse at Balmoral. The Duchess and Princess Diana sneak off for a Jacuzzi in a nearby town, and cause a public palaver.
SEPTEMBER United States: Four days in Connecticut. The Duchess is frightened by a 12-foot snake.
    Indian Ocean: Seven days holiday following an official tour in Mauritius. Arguably the Duchess's most notorious freebie. The tab was conservatively estimated at £3,500 for accommodation alone and was allegedly picked up by a South African hotel chain.

1988
JANUARY Switzerland: The Duchess goes to Klosters for the first of three skiing holidays in as many months.
FEBRUARY France: Meribel for a change.
MARCH Switzerland: Klosters the old favourite. Then…
MARCH United States: The Duchess goes to Hollywood as patron of UK/LA '88 festival. Unfortunately Tinsel Town's top stars all snubbed the York's farewell party on the royal yacht. Not even John Travolta

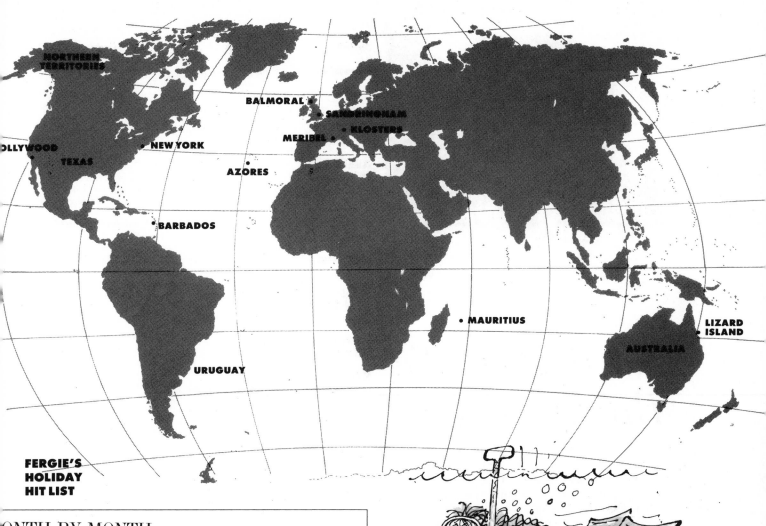

NORTHERN
TERRITORIES

BALMORAL •
• SANDRINGHAM
• KLOSTERS
MERIBEL •

OLLYWOOD
TEXAS

• NEW YORK

AZORES

• BARBADOS

• MAURITIUS

LIZARD
ISLAND

AUSTRALIA

URUGUAY

**FERGIE'S
HOLIDAY
HIT LIST**

ONTH BY MONTH

appeared to dance with Fergie as he did with Princess Diana in New York. All that is except Joan Collins, who met the Duchess for the third time in five days. The English papers fume over her dress sense, lavatorial remarks and references to Prince Andrew. But at the ambassador's party in Palm Springs, Frank Sinatra sings just for her.

OCTOBER Australia: A six-week visit begins controversially as the Duchess decides to leave the recently born Princess Beatrice behind. She is severely criticised by the television personality Esther Rantzen. Things get worse when the Australian press attack the Duchess's 'waddle'. Prince Andrew is described as having the expression of a man 'making a slow recovery from a kick in the soft extremities'. In answer to criticism that she was not seeing enough of her baby, the Duchess extends the trip by ten days 'to be alone with Andrew'. 'Bea lovers' are not amused.

1989

JANUARY France: The Duchess pops off for a quick skiing holiday, but has to be back in time for the memorial service for victims of the Clapham Rail disaster.

APRIL Scotland: A short holiday in Scotland 'to be alone with Andrew'.

JULY Canada: Thirteen days during which the Duke and Duchess adopt an endangered Beluga whale.

OCTOBER Switzerland: Weekend partying on her 30th birthday.

Uruguay: A trip to restart the Whitbread Round-the-world Yacht Race. A furore is caused by revelations that the Duchess attempted to secure free airline tickets for herself and several members of staff.

NOVEMBER United States: A short visit to Texas followed by Christmas shopping in New York. The Duchess returns with 51 bags of excess luggage (for which she should have been charged £2,146), and is reputed to have spent £32,000 in three hours on the last day.

Australia: Off for a luxury holiday on Lizard Island 'The most beautiful place in the world.'

READERS KEEN to follow Fergie around the world may care to know more about a few of her favourite resorts. Our *Punch* pocket guide says the following…

SANDRINGHAM. Norfolk is very flat, and life at Sandringham doesn't appear to be any more exciting. Bored young members of the Royal family have been known to call London friends to bemoan the sparkle-free atmosphere of Christmas chez Windsor.

BARBADOS. Jolly nice, but go out of season. For the two months either side of Christmas, prices rocket. Fellow holiday-makers range from rowdy package gangs bored with Torremolinos, to celebrities such as Michael Winner, Michael Caine, Julian Lennon and Chris 'Dire' Rea. It is hard to say which group the sensitive reader would find more objectionable.

MAURITIUS. Great fun if you happen to like South Africans, for whom it is an Indian Ocean Ibiza.

KLOSTERS. Mr Punch cannot understand why sane people would spend fortunes to career down mountains on plastic planks. If you feel you must, Klosters is as good a place as any. But beware, it is full of people who closely resemble the Duchess of York, but without the saving grace of royalty.

LIZARD ISLAND. Prince Charles called this craggy Australian island, ringed with coral reefs and white beaches one of the most beautiful places on earth. There are 32 private suites with leafy verandahs, an excellent restaurant and a well-stocked bar. Book me a ticket, Bruce. ■

The V&A: Lady of Spain we adore you...

Showdown on the Brompton Road

The Brompton Road, in the heart of London's Knightsbridge, is home to two magnificent institutions – Harrods and the Victoria and Albert Museum. One is a world-famous department store, recently taken over by the Al-Fayeds, a family of Egyptian financiers. The other is a museum – recently taken over by Mrs Elizabeth Esteve-Coll, a Spanish sea-captain's widow. Both takeovers have been met with howls of outrage and controversy. So just how similar are these two behemoths?

Harrods: Over to you Al-Fayed?

Name	The V&A	Harrods
Location	*Department store just off Brompton Road, London SW3 (Cromwell Road SW7)*	*Department store on Brompton Road, London SW3 (though phone book listing says, "Knightsbridge, SW7")*
Royal Warrant	*Founded 1851 by Prince Albert*	*By Appointment to Her Majesty the Queen*
Admission fee	*"Voluntary Donation" on the way in (50p suggested minimum)*	*No admission fee, but hard to get out without making involuntary donation at Way In (£50 suggested minimum)*
Acquisitions policy	*Bought for the Nation*	*Anything Money Can Buy*
Mark-up	*Date, artist's name, origins, materials*	*Price in £ sterling*
Stock availability	*Most items one of a kind; production runs may have ceased in 3000 BC*	*We don't have that style in your size, sir, but we can order it in by next week*
Customer salutation	*Please do not touch*	*Would you like some help? (tone of faux-incredulity)*
Kennel service	*William Wegman's Weimaraner currently boarding in the Twentieth Century Gallery; Earl of Dudley's Newfoundland, Bashaw, resides in Room 120*	*Lower ground, entrance via Door 10, Hans Road. Kennel space for 18, all species, during shopping hours only. Dog bowls and fresh water provided gratis.*
Crockery	*Islamic, Far Eastern, European, featuring Meissen, Bernard Leach, Wedgwood; Levels C and D. Not guaranteed dishwasher-proof*	*China and Glass departments on 2nd floor. Wedgwood Collectors' Pieces include Dancing Hours bowl, white on black jasper, 26cm, 10.25" diameter, £696.75.*
Bedding	*Great Bed of Ware Mahogany, maker unknown, 16th-century, Room 54. Could sleep 6 comfortably. In need of new mattress*	*Third floor. Does not currently supply four posters. Closest available: Relyon Camelot Sprung edge divan set, kingsize, 7'0" x 7'0", £3362*
Ladies fashions	*Yes, Costume Court on ground floor but no changing rooms*	*Entire 1st floor, though lamentably short on whalebone corsets and bustles*
Beauty parlour	*None*	*Fifth Floor*
Cafeteria	*The New Restaurant, attached in Henry Cole wing. Cure for Modern Art (Earl Grey, Lapsang Souchong, Rose Pouchong flavours): 55p*	*Cafe Espresso and West Side Express on ground floor Georgian restaurant and Way In cafe on 4th floor, etc. Egg salads served strictly free of repro female nudes*
Late nite	*The V&A Club, Wednesday evenings, 6.45 p.m. to 9.30 p.m.*	*Wednesday until 7 p.m.*
Custodians' uniform & services	*V&A Security Services, navy single breasted suit with three silver buttons and peaked cap with black patent "leather" peak. Will show you to the 14 and 30 bus stop if you ask nicely*	*Lime green double breasted coat over matching trousers, with ten gold buttons, and matching peaked cap with black patent brim. Will hail taxis and open your limousine doors*

● **There's nothing wrong with modern art that a good cup of tea won't cure.**

"The man from the Mafia...he say Yesss!"

'Let's face it – us March hares aren't going to compete with Mad Cow disease.'

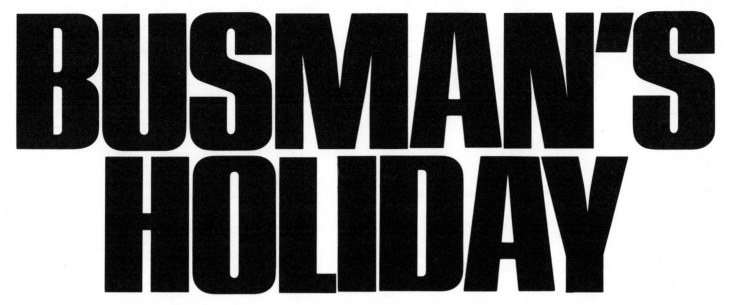

BUSMAN'S HOLIDAY

LAWRENCE SKILLING took a double-decker to Russia with some hard-drinking Aussies.
He met a spy named Boris and a Stalinist called Natasha. *Summer Holiday* it wasn't

I stepped into an Earl's Court hotel room to be greeted warmly by the people with whom I would spend the next 28 days in a converted double-decker bus. 'You're not a bleeding Pommie bastard, are you?' said one. I looked around. I was the only person not wearing a T-shirt with a koala, kiwi, kangaroo, map of Australia, or 'God Bless Oz' on it.

'No, I'm Scottish actually,' I replied.

'They're just Poms in skirts,' said my travelling companion to be, with a crooked smile to show that this was all just fun. I laughed politely.

Altogether there were about 20 of us. Thirteen males, two New Zealanders, two Pommy bastards, a driver, a courier, and 16 Australians. The men were big in that special beer and steak way, with lots of moustaches. Even the ones who were shaven looked as though they had moustaches. The women were much the same – except scrawnier in a feral, wild dingo sort of way. Most of them were younger than me but looked at least five years older due to the ravaging ultra-violet of Australia's sun. In fact, women isn't an apt description: female men would be better. There was an exception, but she turned out to be an English migrant who had been sheltered indoors under damp cloths for most of her life.

Diane, our courier, scared me. She had a monolithic quality about her, and seemed ideal for the job, as was De-Hy, the driver. Named thus for being permanently alcoholically dehydrated, De-Hy was the perfect foil to Diane. A dead ringer for particularly macho lager commercials, he could drive for 14 hours at a stretch, drink his passengers under the bus, and then terrorise them. De-Hy was an icon to us all.

The bus, in which we would cross Scandinavia and the Soviet Union, was named Ben. A London Routemaster, it had been shortened in height and had most of the upstairs seats ripped out to make room for three-tier bunk-beds. Downstairs there was a rudimentary kitchen and a few seats. All of the seats could be converted into beds by laying cushioned boards between the gaps. Each person had a small shelf as storage space. Bags (compulsorily soft) were crushed, empty, under the seats. This wasn't the trip for a Paul Smith linen jacket, or indeed the sort of person who would wear one.

Before we boarded the bus Ralph was sick, earning him lots of kudos. To celebrate setting off, everyone started drinking. It was,

after all, mid-morning. By the time we got to Dover, Shaz and Sue had consumed a bottle of Baileys Irish cream and a bottle of Bacardi between them. Much to everybody's admiration, they were sick on the ferry.

To an Australian, chundering is a reaffirmation of life; a proud, patriotic thing to do. To make friends with an Australian, vomit copiously in front of him. I was unpopular with my fellow travellers as I was not sick once. Now and then I mentioned feeling quite queasy, but that was not enough.

Our first proper stop across the Channel was at Ostend. With gasps of relief the Australians piled into a Flemish supermarket to buy 'tinnies', schnapps, vodka, brandy and other essentials. Virtually everybody, including the courier, was well oiled when we got into Hamburg to investigate brass bands and Reeperbahn prostitutes. In the latter field, as in everything else, the Germans are way ahead of us: Hamburgers have the benefit of large supermarkets where Helmut Newton-style women can be examined. If you don't pick one, one will almost certainly pick you. No vicarious sightseeing is allowed.

On bus holidays, there is an allotted time for everything – even visiting prostitutes. As we regrouped at the bus, nobody would actually admit paying for sex, though Pete, the hunky male mascot of the tour, did proudly tell us how he'd ended up having a cup of coffee with 'an amazing woman' in a strange little bar. ▶

about to board the bus, London.

Sight seeing in Hamburg.

◄ 'How much did you pay for the coffee,' somebody asked.

'Two hundred marks, why?' That is just over £70. Until that point, Peter seemed to think that the German mark and the Italian lire were linked in value.

One thing my fellow travellers could not be accused of is stinginess. In order of importance, they spent their money on:

1) Alcohol
2) Hard Rock Café sweatshirts, in any city that had them
3) Other sweatshirts
4) Dolls in native costume
5) Tasteless pottery
6) Small silver charms
7) Postcards (two-dozen each)

The local inhabitants sensed this profligacy. However, only one of our number was robbed, and that was in Copenhagen, next stop after Hamburg. What Derek apparently did was to wander into Copenhagen's equivalent of Brixton wearing a luminous track suit in Australian red, white and blue plus a slouch hat, as favoured by Paul Hogan. He sauntered up to a bench, on which five mohawked punks were sharing a syringe, adjusted his $1,000 Pentax and pulled out a full-size map of the city. The punks attacked him, probably out of sheer irritation. Derek responded by kicking off his Nike trainers and running barefoot back to the bus. The shoes were all he lost. He never explained why he left them behind.

Perhaps to make up for this unpleasantness, Derek had a romantic adventure a few days later in Stockholm. He was once again in his neon track suit and consulting his street map when a girl, in halting English, offered to show him around. She showed him around the town before showing him around selected parts of herself at the psychiatric hospital where she lived. Derek swore blind that she was a nurse.

Scandinavia was intimidating in its cleanliness, perfection and efficiency. It was also expensive. But everybody was attractive and spoke English – even the one down-and-out I encountered. My fellow travellers didn't like it much since a can of beer costs the same as a hi-fi and is nearly unobtainable. It goes without saying that Scandinavia has one of the worst drink problems in the western world.

Things got better when we crossed the Finnish border into Russia. It was grey, it was squalid, it was miserable, it was like

Touring Copenhagen.

coming home. Perhaps the reason I liked it so much was that everybody else hated. it. Once the bus had been stripped for drugs, we were introduced to Boris, our Intourist Commissar. He was to remain with us for our entire stay in the Soviet Union. One hour after boarding the bus, he was totally and uncontrollably drunk. Until that moment, the biggest thrill in Boris's 20-year life had been drinking battery acid in the army. He groped every woman on the tour, even Diane, then he was sick. The Australians would have loved him after this, but he spoiled everything by crying in a most middle-European fashion. The embarrassment. Luckily, after a few more Bacardis, he passed out and was put in an upstairs bunk. He had drunk only a fraction of what the bus's hard-core drinkers had put away in an evening. In addition to Boris, Intourist provided another spy (I mean guide) at every major town we visited. We had about four others, all called Boris.

All the stories you hear about Russia are true. The description 'Upper Volta with rockets' is oft used, but spot on. In Moscow's showcase GUM store, you can buy busts of Lenin, hats, pieces of nylon, 1965 Dansette record players, and Elton John records on the Melodia label. And that's it. A food store would have

Arriving at the Russian border.

poisonous Russian beer (the worst in the world), cherry juice, packets of fat, and jars of spaghetti bolognese in yellow slime with the lids half rusted off. Toilets on the main roads (two-lane switchbacks in pot-holed gravel) would be sheds filled with excrement.

I loved it. The people were so keen to trade or talk they would quite often run after the bus. Perhaps to compensate for the bleakness of life, Russians are enthusiastic about sex. In public places, women would stare appraisingly in a way which just doesn't happen in Britain unless you've got some interesting cold sores. One night, in a campsite disco outside Kallinin, the appalling Peter and I found ourselves dancing with a couple of girls. After the band had finished the Status Quo songs, and we couldn't buy any more vodka, we asked them back to my chalet. Along with the girls came Igor, a student of English to act as an interpreter.

What followed was a very strange evening. Drinking several bottles of blackmarket Russian champagne (the Australians had bought so much that four bunks were given over to storage) we haltingly learned about each other. Both the girls, Olga and Natasha, were hardline Stalinists who thought Gorbachev was a mincing nancy boy who was selling out the great Soviet. Their eyes did twinkle as they said this, though. Igor was a bit more liberal, espousing a modicum of restraint for state mental care policies. In between the translation of our political aberrations, he told me privately how much he loved Natasha and bemoaned the fact that she saw him only as a friend. By this time, Natasha and I were getting discreetly tactile, and I was getting Igor to tell her that I thought her eyes had the still, deep wonder of the Black Sea. I was drunk. Pete, meanwhile, was rampaging around on the ox-like body of Olga, who must have weighed at least 16 stone. Five minutes more of this and Igor said that he was going outside 'for a

Visiting the Hermitage Museum, Leningrad.

little while'. His voice shook slightly as he spoke. After spending my entire life in the Igor role the situation had pathos and piquancy. I felt guilty afterwards, but glad that I'd hired the one-rouble chalet as an escape from sleeping on the bus.

Meanwhile, my fellow travellers carried on drinking and having sex with each other. The only cultural contact we had was when Mike was sick in the Hermitage Museum in Leningrad. In vomiting terms it could be compared with the 'Ring Cycle'. Mostly, Mike managed to find a window to puke out of, when he wasn't being chased by the aghast female curators. However, on the last couple of occasions, the windows wouldn't open. So Mike was sick on the glass, splashing display cases of priceless Tsarist baubles underneath. Soon after this, he was helped to the exit. Ultimately, Mike won the tour 'Chunder Chart' competition by throwing-up about 30 times – 20 times higher than average. For this he won a bottle of alcohol.

I wasn't drinking nearly as much as the others, but I still got run-down into a permanent state of sore throats, coughs and sneezes. The latter condition wasn't helped by one couple whose night-time lovemaking on the bus, inches away from my head, would raise clouds of dust. The male half of this particular pair wouldn't acknowledge the girl during the day because he didn't want to be associated with the 'silly tart.' The physical strain was also compounded by no sleep at night. It's hard to believe now, but the partying and boozing on the bus went on till about 4am nearly every night. The bus would leave whatever campsite it was on at between 7 and 8am. Those who thought they could escape the ongoing good times would be blasted in their bunks with an air horn or simply the banks of 60-watt speakers relaying the full volume Midnight Oil, Bryan Adams, Tracey Chapman etc, from downstairs. I got to hate Tracey Chapman *soo* much. In addition, you would often be woken by some blind drunk kicking you in the head as he squeezed into your bunk, not even aware you were in it.

During the day I would either doze on the bus or in the gardens of the museums I visited. I remember having a particularly good sleep outside Oslo's Munch museum – all that unashamed madness was strangely comforting at the time.

The Munch museum, Oslo.

And so the holiday ground on. The bus began to break down regularly as the normal 40mph cruising speed became too much of a strain. Leaks in the roof opened up and some beds were best avoided if it was wet outside. For miles on end I would lounge at the back of the top deck with Mani, the other Brit (via Bangladesh), and Derek, still in his tracksuit.

Outside, the big nothingness of Russia gradually became more recognisable and European as we headed west. Poland was a good country. Appealingly miserable like Russia but with more in the shops and big sprawling street markets, black in nature. Change a few pounds into zlotys and you end up with a wad of currency inches thick. Unlike the USSR there are antique shops and traders selling stuff which is actually worth having. And so cheap! A dress in a Warsaw store works out at 40 pence. A bottle of fantastic plum vodka, 25 pence.

Now that communism has disappeared for ever, all this wonderful disparity will vanish. These drab, yet strangely exotic countries will all simply be like Austria. In the meantime take western cigarettes, brand-named plastic bags, rock band T-shirts and good digital watches. Forget jeans. You'll get much less for a £30 pair of 501s than you would for a £4.99 'Anthrax' T-shirt.

In return, you'll be offered fur hats, Red Army belts, uniforms,

Shopping in Warsaw.

sex and lots of junk money. The latter is fairly useless in Russia but in the right place you can use it to buy overpriced Soviet gold. The best Bloc item I bought was this great 1930s style 'Pakema' watch which was retro without trying.

It was hard getting used to being in the West again. When we visited a supermarket in West Berlin after two weeks in the East it was an unsettling experience. Such affluence! It seemed very wrong that one could buy over 25 different sorts of chocolate.

With only a few days left before returning to London, it occurred to me that I had never been so alienated from a group of people. Well, not since school anyway. To my busmates I was a cynical, non-partying, unclean (some days I didn't shower; Australians do it twice a day), non-drinking, superior bastard of a Pom. One drunken evening, Sheena, wife of Tim, the one witty chap on board, had a real go at me.

'You think you're so frigging special, don't you?'

Sheena must have had a lot on her mind, because 48 hours away from London she had a capsule nervous breakdown. Despite not being a terribly popular person this seemed to put the other Australians into a decline. Instead of reaching a crescendo, the partying tailed off into simple drab alcoholism. 'Moose', a real 'rager', put away his horned Viking helmet (with the condoms on the horns), and sexual activity fizzled out. When 'Ben' arrived back in Earl's Court we could almost have been mistaken for a tour from the Methodist Holidays Guild. Almost. ∎

Lawrence Skilling's last piece for Punch *was an inside look at hamsters. He is currently recovering from carsickness.*

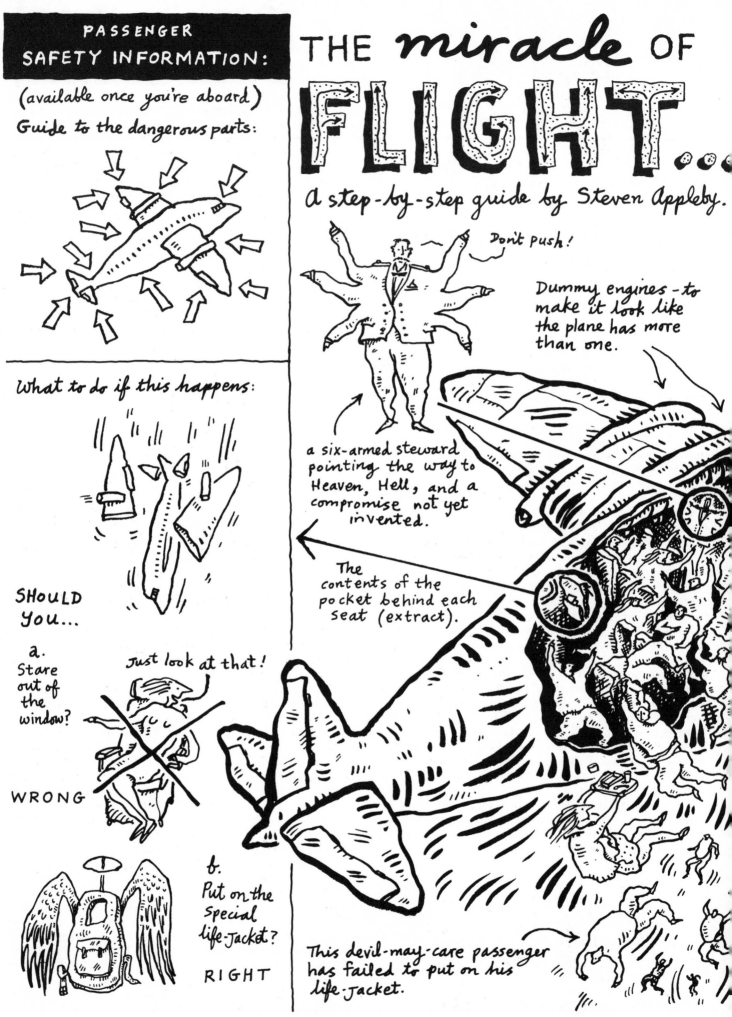

what you're missing while you're stuck in that departure lounge!!

i- An idealised version of air travel:

Let's look for faces in the clouds...

The interior panelling, in plastic, goes yellow and fragile with time like the inside of a refrigerator.

Ejector seat in operation. Unfortunately the roof door has failed to open.

ii- The realistic approach:

look Sir! acute turbulence ahead!!

Splendid! ha ha ha ha...

Scalding hot cup of 'tea', Sir or madam?

Kitchen

Bah!

Old stewardess - hired to reassure passengers that air travel prolongs life.

THE FUTURE...

Everyone on the planet will have a personal aeroplane the size of an elephant which will hover above each house until summoned by its owner's whistle.

It will run on free solar energy and travel as fast as a thought.

C.R.A.S.H

The 'porcupine' flying suit is all the rage this year!

On cloudy days or at night it will plunge down out of control and burst through the roof.

The engine. It can be seen that someone has cut away the protective casing. No wonder it isn't working properly. Experts will also notice that it is facing the wrong way.

© SAI 1989

133

NOW make your very own cut-out-and-keep: JET PLANE KIT!

Please note! Some of the pieces are depicted out of proportion to one another. These larger and smaller items have the effect, when assembled, of creating a breathtakingly realistic aerial scene *in perspective*! Air travel comes vigorously alive in your sitting room...

a.

undercarriage - discard. f.

WING no. 2 - glue to plane or hang separately.

c.

Optional tail section - can be left attached to plane, or cut off along dotted line and suspended separately.

vi munch...

v auto Pilot

P.O.P.!

Try to cut the flames out in a convincingly flickery sort of way.

a. iv

It's safer than driving.

i

ii iii vii viii woof?

Thread string through heads of plummeting passengers i - ix.

134

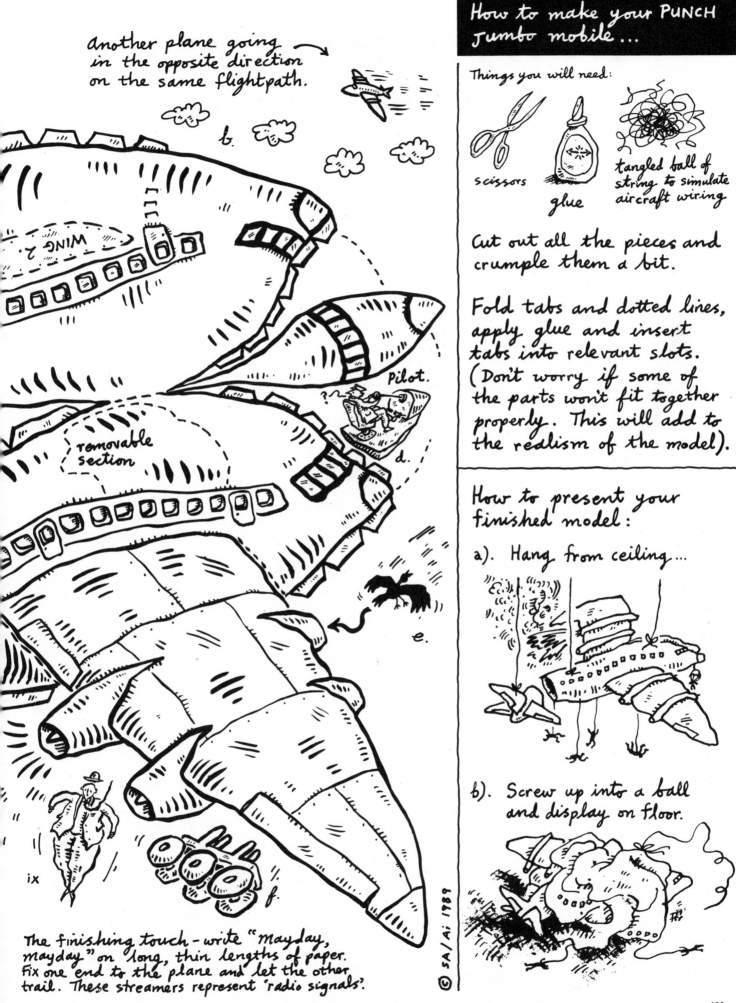

Another plane going in the opposite direction on the same flightpath.

b.

WING 2.

removable section

Pilot.

d.

e.

ix

f.

The finishing touch – write "Mayday, mayday" on long, thin lengths of paper. Fix one end to the plane and let the other trail. These streamers represent 'radio signals'.

© SA/Ai. 1989

How to make your PUNCH Jumbo mobile...

Things you will need:

scissors

glue

tangled ball of string to simulate aircraft wiring

Cut out all the pieces and crumple them a bit.

Fold tabs and dotted lines, apply glue and insert tabs into relevant slots. (Don't worry if some of the parts won't fit together properly. This will add to the realism of the model).

How to present your finished model:

a). Hang from ceiling...

b). Screw up into a ball and display on floor.

135

Prince and the revolution

TOBY YOUNG escorted Prince Paul and 1,000 condoms to Romania

The last man nearly ruined this place,
He didn't know what to do with it.
If you think this country's bad off now,
Just wait till I get through with it.

His Excellency Rufus T. Firefly, President of Freedonia

'All great events and personalities in world history reappear,' wrote Karl Marx. 'The first time as tragedy, the second as farce.' He was thinking of the events of 1851, when Napoleon's idiot nephew seized control of the French state. However, it is equally applicable to the current sequence of events in Eastern Europe. *Battleship Potemkin* may have been an appropriate monument to the Russian Revolution, but there won't be any need to make a film about the recent revolution in Romania. It's already been done. It stars the Marx Brothers and it's called *Duck Soup*.

At any rate, that was the impression I got after taking a day-trip to Romania during the midst of the current upheavals. Organised by the Relief Fund for Romania, it was ostensibly an opportunity for the western media to report on the country's urgent need for food and medical supplies. Romanian hospitals are unable to cope with the stream of casualties flooding into their wards and it is estimated that the country will run out of food within a fortnight. However, the original purpose of the trip was quickly obscured by the extraordinary collection of individuals who had managed to secure themselves a place on it.

The list included: George Tecuciama, a 39-year-old Romanian exile, bringing over a personal computer for the National Peasants' Party disguised as a food parcel; Larry Adler, the 75-year-old mouth-organist, bringing over 1,000 condoms donated by Richard Branson; and Prince Paul Hohenzollern, a Parisian estate agent, bringing himself over with a view to being installed on the Romanian throne. 'It would be good for tourism,' he explained. It came as no surprise that Peter Tweedie, leader of a British medical supplies team, had been left behind at Gatwick Airport.

Not that Her Majesty's Press was under-represented. After all, what important news story would be complete without the tabloids? 'I was up till three o'clock last night drinking Lambuzi,' claimed *The Sun* photographer. 'We only came because it's a junket.' Luckily *The Sun* reporter was better

prepared. 'Look,' he exclaimed holding up a copy of that day's *Times* which carried a story about Romania. 'Now I know how to spell Ceausescu.'

The presence of *The Sun* reporter and his colleagues was a cause of some concern to Mark Burca, the organiser of the trip. He suggested that when we arrive at Bucharest airport we pay our respects by observing a minute's silence. 'Otherwise,' he explained, 'they might think we're a razzmatazz media circus.' Unfortunately, this advice fell on deaf ears. The moment the plane touched down, the hacks spilled out on to the tarmac to photograph unsuspecting members of the public holding up copies of their newspapers. Prince Paul, on the other hand, who had never before set foot on Romanian soil, treated the occasion with the gravity it deserved. He held a press conference. Eventually, Mark Burca managed to persuade everyone to observe a minute's silence. This was a touching moment, particularly when it was interrupted by Larry Adler, who took advantage of the opportunity to give a rendition of *The Star Spangled Banner*.

After being ushered through customs we were met by three coaches, one going to an orphanage, one to a hospital, and a third to the Inter-Continental Hotel. Here was an opportunity to witness the food and medical supplies being distributed first hand. Naturally, all the hacks chose to scramble aboard the coach going to the Inter-Continental.

Once on route, we were treated to a guided tour by a hero of the revolution. 'Welcome to Romania, free Romania…' Prior to the events of 22 December our guide had worked for the Ministry of Tourism and had had to churn out the same propaganda for 20 years. Consequently, he was taking full advantage of his new-found freedom. 'On the right you see traditional peasant village, well laid out, nice church in centre. On the left you see disgusting modern building built by the fascist Ceausescu where no one want to live. This we will pull down.' Soon we were approaching the town centre. 'As you can see there are many bullet-holes here. This is where the revolutionary youth of Romania died fighting the dictator Ceausescu.' At this, one of the photographers was overcome with emotion. He leant over to Imogen Edwards-Jones, a 21-year-old reporter for *The Indy*, and said. 'D'you fancy a shag in the snow?'

When we arrived at the Inter-Continental Hotel our guide announced that those who required light refreshment should make their way to the German Bar, whereas those who wished to meet the National

Larry Adler greets Mr Brucan

136

Salvation Front, the revolutionary government, should remain on board. 'I make sure you all get an exclusive,' he said. By the time the coach resumed its journey the only people left on board were me, a large-nosed hack from the *Evening Standard*, and Larry Adler.

At the government's headquarters we were taken to the office of Silviu Brucan. Larry Adler claimed to know him from his days as the Romanian Ambassador to the United Nations in New York, and his close links with the Ceausescu regime make him one of the most controversial figures in the National Salvation Front. In addition to being their adviser on foreign policy, Brucan is the author of a theoretical defence of the new government's position entitled *No '-isms', No Party*.

He was a small, yellow man who looked a bit like Yoda, the Jedi-master from *The Empire Strikes Back*. He was clearly immensely busy and hadn't the faintest idea who we were. He turned to Larry Adler first. 'Why have you come?'

'Silviu, don't you remember me? We used to spend all those evenings together in New York. It's Larry Adler.'

'No, I don't remember you.' Larry looked crestfallen.

'I've come all the way from England to bring you 1,000 condoms.' He looked at Larry Adler as if he were mad.

'These I cannot use.' He then pointed at his Chief of Staff, Florin Badinici. 'But maybe he can use them.'

'Yes,' replied Florin. 'I make revolutionary balloons.'

Next it was my turn. 'You also bring me condom?' inquired Silviu.

'No, I'm from *Punch* magazine.'

'Never heard of it.' I decided to try another tack.

'I'm also a student.' His eyes lit up.

'What you study?'

'The theory of democracy.'

'Ah,' he said, slapping me on the back. 'With the theory we have no problem. It's with the practice we have a problem.'

The highlight of the trip came when Larry Adler decided it was time to give Mr Brucan the benefit of his experience. After all, Larry Adler has been a friend of the rich and famous for the best part of a century and knows a thing or two about how to run a country. 'This is a little something I composed myself,' he said. There followed a quick burst of *Romanian Rhapsody*.

'Ah,' cried the member of the Council of the Executive and author of *The Dissolution of Power: A Sociology of International Relations and Politics*. 'Now you are talking.'

On the flight back I sat next to George Tecuciama who had just seen his father for the first time in 13 years and assured me that the days of the National Salvation Front were numbered.

'What about Prince Paul?' I asked.

'I told my father that we had Prince Paul with us and you know what he say? "Who the f*** is that?"'

The following day *The Sun* carried a photograph of two bemused Romanian women staring at a copy of the paper. The headline read: EASTENDERS 'GODMOTHER' JULIA MOVES OVER TO ITV. ■

Cheques should be made payable to 'Relief Fund For Romania' and sent to Bank of Scotland, 16/18 Piccadilly, London W1.

The resemblance between the political situation in Romania and that of Freedonia, the fictional eastern European state featured in *Duck Soup*, is uncanny.

FREEDONIA	ROMANIA
Freedonia is run by Gloria Teasdale, a wealthy American widow, who has sexual designs on Groucho Marx.	Until recently, Romania was dominated by Elena Ceausescu, an overbearing matriarch, who, according to highly-placed government officials, required sex every 16 minutes.
As President Rufus T. Firefly, one of the laws Groucho announces is: 'No one's allowed to smoke, or tell a dirty joke.'	Securitate agents used to identify potential dissidents by telling anti-Ceausescu jokes. If anyone laughed they were placed under surveillance.
At one point, Groucho escapes an angry mob by leaping on the back of Harpo's motorbike.	In his panic to escape the demonstrators on the night of 22 December, Ceausescu ended up sitting on the knee of his helicopter pilot.
In the course of his administration, President Rufus T. Firefly announces that chewing gum is forbidden. He then proceeds to move his jaw in an exaggerated fashion.	In the course of his administration, President Ion Iliescu announces that the Communist Party is illegal. He is himself a member of the Communist Party.

And now, for everyone stuck in Terminal Two,

Punch proudly presents a whole new concept in

entertainment – the In-lounge Movie. Written and

directed by MILES KINGTON, ladies and gentlemen...

AIRPORT '89

The scene is a large terminal building in a large airport. In what country? Who knows – all airports are set in the same country. Yes, it's Duty Free country, where the men all speak English with American accents, and the girls are all dressed in uniforms from a cigarette advertisement, and they all smile the whole time except when dealing with the public. Enter Brad, a security guard. He is showing round Tom, whose first day in the job it is.

Brad: ...And this here is Katie, who handles the check-ins for Deutsche Gramofon Gesellschaft.
Tom: I thought that was a record company?
Brad: Yeah, well, so many opera stars jet around the world these days... Katie, this is Tom, it's his first day in Security.
Katie: Hi. Which newspaper do you work for?
Tom: I beg your pardon?
Brad: Just a joke we have round here. If we see someone we don't know, we assume he's a journalist disguising himself for a scoop. "I Entered Flight Control Tower Disguised As Colin Moynihan!"
Tom: Did you?

Brad: No, that's just a ...well, never mind. Anyway, after Katie has weighed the baggage it goes down the conveyor belt behind her out of sight. Now, there's a persistent belief among the public that as soon as it vanishes, skilled luggage handlers open every suitcase, spot an object of value and abstract it before closing the suitcase as skilfully as before, so that the holidaymaker does not notice it until two days later and blames it on the hotel staff. There is not a word of truth in this.
Tom: Not at all?
Brad: No. What actually happens is that the luggage handlers open the cases, spot the valuables and make a note of the details *so that they can open the cases on the return journey.* Makes sense.
Tom: Why?
Brad: Because the owners will have bought more stuff abroad meanwhile. Hey, you're pretty stupid, aren't you, Tom?
Katie: I think he's pretty cute.
At that moment an Arab in flowing robes comes up to Brad and asks him a question. Brad takes him on one side.
Katie: You mustn't mind Brad, Tom. He's not

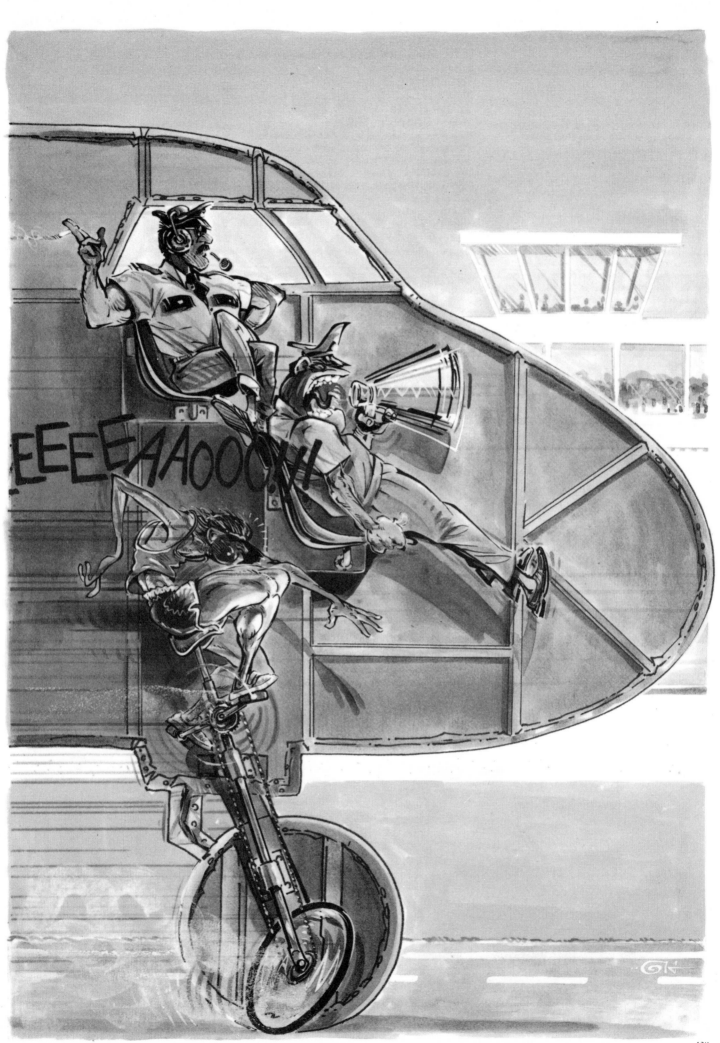

been the same since…

Tom: Since what?

Katie: Well, he was once an air steward, until they found…

Tom: That he was smuggling?

Katie: No. Worse than that. They found…

Brad returns before we hear what can possibly be worse than smuggling.

Tom: That was very impressive, Brad. I didn't know you spoke Arabic.

Brad: I don't. And nor does he. Don't let those flowing robes fool you – he's another of our security guys called Delbert. He had a small problem for me to sort out, that's all.

Tom: What problem?

Brad: His robes were caught in his trouser belt and he couldn't take a pee.

A man walks past holding up one of those sticks on which there is one of those notices bearing the name of the man you would like to give a lift to. This one says 'Mr Salman Rushdie'.

Brad: Hey, you! Come over here.

Mr Salman Rushdie's Putative Chauffeur: Are you calling me?

Brad: Yes, I am. What did I tell you yesterday?

Chauffeur: You said I was to stop taking the piss and to get the hell out of the airport and if you saw me again you'd break both my legs.

Brad: Right.

He gives chase as the man flees.

Katie: It's all right – he's not really a chauffeur. A lot of people with nothing to do like wandering around with those notices; it's like a club, really. Yesterday his notice read 'Mr Terry Waite'. Well, that's going a bit far.

Tom: Tell me about when Brad was an air steward. Did they catch him putting a short measure of vodka in the Bloody Marys and keeping the profit himself?

Katie: No, it was worse than that. Apparently…

Brad returns, panting.

Brad: Well, I broke his stick. That's a start, any-

way. Now then, Tom…

He is interrupted by alarm bells and bleeps and sirens.

Tom: What in God's name is that?

Brad: It's a Level Three Alert. He'll be coming this way.

There enters a fabulously rich billionaire, attended by upward of 40 but downward of 50 aides and equerries, attending to his every whim, spraying his cordless phone, laughing at his funny stories, etc. This vision of wealth passes on, leaving a flurry of dollar bills behind.

Tom: But who was he?

Brad: Oh, he's the guy who comes by every week to inspect the prices in the Duty Free Area, and put them up. I believe they are now on average double what they charge in the High Street, but the punters still buy. It's crazy.

Tom: How many levels of alert are there?

Brad: Good question, Tom. I'm sorry I called you stupid just now. It's just that I've been under a lot of stress recently, ever since I stopped being an air steward, and…and…I'm sorry, what was the question?

There is the familiar 'bing bong' presaging a public announcement. The public address clears its throat and speaks.

P/A: Will Mr Colin Moynihan please go to the 'Friends of Pamella Bordes Celebrity Lounge'? Will Mr Colin Moynihan please go to the – oh, I'm sorry. He's here already. We hadn't noticed him. Please ignore that message. **('Bing bong.')**

Tom: What was that all about?

Brad: It's a sort of semi-reserved lounge area, half-way between the VIP lounge and the ordinary punters' waiting area. It's for people who are almost famous.

Tom: Like Mrs Gro Harlem Bruntland?

Brad: Who? Yes, probably. **(Another 'Bing Bong' from the public address.)** God, I

love that noise. No matter how banal the information, I always have to listen.

P/A: Have you *quite* finished?

Brad: Yes. Sorry.

P/A: *Thank* you … Calling all passengers on Flight MAN 109 Manganesian Airways to Harare. Here is an announcement. Manganesian Airways have finally gone bust. All passengers on Flight MAN 109 are therefore requested to go to Door 29, where a coach will commence the overland safari to Harare via Yugoslavia and the Sahara Desert. Thank you, and good luck.

'Bing Bong'

Brad: A Level One Alert is the finding of unattended luggage, or more than three suitcases going round on the carousel over an hour after the flight has unloaded. Level Two Alert is a passenger refusing a body search, or insisting on more than five. Level Three you have seen. Level Seven…

Tom: What about Four, Five and Six?

Brad: We don't talk about them. They were lost in a rather nasty terrorist attack last year at Gatwick. Level Seven is a man in Arab robes talking with an Irish accent. Level Eight is no kosher breakfasts on El Al. Level Nine is a sighting of a football supporters' club pennant. And Level Ten is the most dangerous. Any idea?

Tom: Full-scale terrorist attack?

Brad: Fact-finding visit by Paul Channon.

A sudden hubbub, as 40 or 50 typical British holiday-makers gallop past in a vague conga formation. They all have sun-tans, sombreros, little straw donkeys, frayed jean shorts, bright yellow duty free bags, and girlfriends called Karen. Several of them are waving flags inscribed 'Malaga is English!'

Katie: God, I pity the airline they're flying on.

Brad: Ah, but they're not flying. You'd be amazed how many cheap package tourists just come here for the day or the weekend these

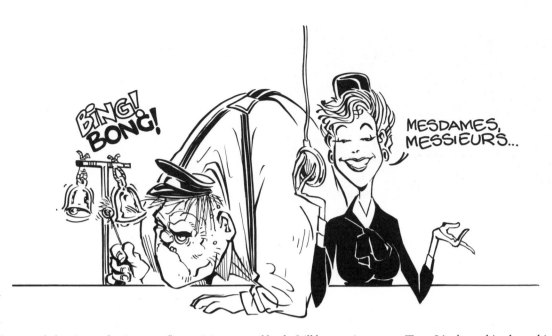

BING! BONG!

MESDAMES, MESSIEURS...

days, and parade around the airport having a great time without actually going anywhere. We have a small pool 'n' barbeque area for them if they stay over three days, and of course the complete souvenir service, so they can pretend to come back from wherever they choose.

Tom: But has Paul Channon ever actually found a fact?

Brad: Pardon?

Tom: These fact-finding missions by Paul Channon. Does he ever actually find one?

Brad: Tom, I'm sorry I called you intelligent just now. I rather think you may be stupid after all. Ministers never, ever find facts – all that happens is they are handed facts by their entourage, rather in the same way as little boiled sweets are handed to airline passengers just prior to a landing or…or…

Tom: Or posterior to take-off?

Brad: Tom, I'm sorry I called you stupid just now. Your Latin grammar is impressive.

flew to Moscow and back. Still he wasn't uncovered. But by that time he was getting the hang of flying and rather enjoyed it, so he stayed as a co-pilot and never went back to the *Express*. **(More alarm bells and sirens.)** My God, that's a Level Eleven Alert! I've never known one of them before!

Tom: What does it mean?

Brad: It means, "Crazed, fully armed terrorist heading this way in a camouflage jacket, holding people hostage and demanding the release of all his friends in prison, also a million pounds, and a hot breakfast. You will recognise him by the camouflage jacket."

Enter a crazed terrorist. The terrorist in camouflage jacket, etc. Everyone shrieks, faints or runs.

Tom: What do we do?

Brad: Are you crazy? We don't do anything. We leave this sort of thing to the security people.

Tom: But we are the security people!

Tom: It's about this place, this airport. There's something very odd about it. Everyone we have seen is either security in disguise, or a chauffeur, or a pilot, or check-in girls, or day trippers, or the man fixing Duty Free prices…

Brad: So.

Tom: There are no passengers. *No one is actually flying in or out of here.*

There is a sudden silence round Tom. Everyone turns and looks at him. He backs off a little.

Brad: You're right. And I'll tell you why. Because this isn't a real airport. This is a fake airport built by the government to trap terrorists in. They come here thinking they're going to travel, but what they don't realise is that everyone, and I mean *everyone*, is a security person in disguise. Only the one person who isn't in on the secret is the guilty person. And that person is…

Tom: Yes, who is he?

Brad: *You*, Tom. You alone had no idea what was going on. You are the odd man out. Sorry Tom. Goodbye, Tom.

They all advance threateningly on him.

Tom: Well, for God's sake, at least tell me first why you had to stop being an air steward!

Brad: It's quite simple. They discovered I wasn't gay. Do you want to tell me who Mrs Gro Harlem Bruntland is?

Tom: She's the Prime Minister of Norway.

Brad: Is she now? Well, well. Maybe you were intelligent after all. Goodbye, Tom.

They close in on him and grab him and start shaking him. He screams. The noise wakes him up, in the waiting area at Gatwick Airport. His friend Gary, sitting next to him, puts a hand over his mouth.

Gary: Blimey. You having a nightmare or something?

Tom: No. Yes. I dreamt that nobody was flying in or out of the airport and we were all zombies, and I was about to die.

Gary: Well, it's true. They've just announced another six-hour delay, due to Spanish air controllers, and we could all die for all anyone cares. I quite feel like it, actually. But I think I'll have a drink first. You coming?

Tom: Yeah, all right.

Airport '89 is coming to an airport near you soon. Don't miss it. You won't. ∎

"We have a special pool 'n' barbeque area and a complete souvenir service, so they can pretend to come back from wherever they choose"

At that moment a pilot flanked by two assistant pilots walks into view, and greets Brad cheerily. The three of them walk on, rather like a surgeon and his two minions going off to do a vital operation, except that top surgeons wouldn't care to be seen in dark glasses.

Katie: God, he's so dishy.

Brad: Mmm, but only when he's on duty.

Tom: Who is he? One of the pilots?

Brad: Yes, but he has a very strange background. He used to be a *Daily Express* journalist and was sent here in 1986 to prove how easy it was to masquerade as a co-pilot. He got on a flight to Madrid, and back again.

Tom: What happened then?

Brad: Nothing. Nobody spotted him. So he

Brad: Are we? Damn, you're right.

Heroically, almost vaingloriously, he hurls himself on the terrorist who turns to meet him. He holds out – is it a gun? A grenade? A sword? No – it's a hand. He holds it out and shakes hands with Brad. They go off into a corner and talk together.

Tom: I – don't understand.

Katie: Oh, he's another security guy in disguise, just testing the arrangements. By the way, the reason Brad stopped being an air steward …

… too late. Brad returns.

Tom: Brad, there is something I have to ask you.

Brad: It's about why I stopped being an air steward, isn't it?

Tom: No.

Brad: Go on. You intrigue me.

141

LAAGER AND LIMEY

MATTHEW CAMPLING
on South Africans in the UK

AS NELSON MANDELA came ambling out of prison last week, the same thought struck thousands of his compatriots — maybe the time had come: maybe they could go home again. These were not the aged warriors of the ANC, these were the white South Africans who had spent the Eighties dusting off their British passports and heading back to the old country.

For the past decade, and especially since the declaration of the State of Emergency in 1985, Anglo-Saxon South Africans have been making the Great Trek to London. They've said goodbye to their servants and swimming-pools and said hello to a life that is altogether less luxurious.

On arrival here, many South Africans go to great efforts to make contact with distant members of their families. This cushions the depression that overtakes them once they realise that life will never be the same again, that the weather is lousy, they they will never find anywhere reasonable to live. They come armed with a long list of names, telephone numbers, and huge

over-optimism. South Africans seem to believe that anybody living in London must be a success. Touching, isn't it?

For example, Deanne, newly arrived, telephones Michael. In South Africa he was the Features Editor of a major magazine. In London he started out cleaning toilets at £2.50 an hour. Now he's earning £8 an hour doing some word processing work for a temp agency. Deanne opens with some flattering Power Conversation. 'Basically,' she says, 'I want you to tell me how I can be useful to you.' Michael would like some help with cleaning and ironing, but is too polite to say so. Having only recently graduated from his own Power Conversations, he guesses she is talking about journalistic help.

'I'm not working in magazines any more,' he says. This is the first step on Deanne's road to reality. 'But can you type? I could speak to my agency about getting you a temp job?' There is a gasp at the other end of the line.

'You own an agency? I didn't realise.' The road to reality will obviously be a long haul.

Later in the conversation, the subject of why they left inevitably crops up. Michael sighs. How do you express the years of spiritual depressions, the memories of police harassment, the bleak despair, and the viciousness of his white compatriots. 'Yes,' agrees Deanne, 'and you had to wait six months to get paid for freelance work.'

Britain is not the easiest destination for a South African. Australia is warmer, Canada is bigger. But many of the anticipated wave of emigrants, the de Klerkies, still believe that London is their spiritual home, and the Queen their spiritual leader. They believe they will be able to find an unfurnished one-bedroom flat in central London for £50 a week, they believe that South Africans do well in London, and above all they believe that they never supported apartheid.

Most of the non-Afrikaans de Klerkies will arrive clutching British or EEC passports. You only have to have an Irish grandfather and you are in the pink. However, some arrive without Right of Abode. This is a big mistake. From lives of privilege and security they will be plunged into a situation that will seem to them like that of the Vietnamese boat people, unwanted in a strange land. They become, rather ironically, part of the black economy, and desperately scheme their way around the immigration rules, either by seeking political asylum or finding somebody to marry them. Sometimes they live in poverty that approaches squalor. Two Trekkie families were so poor that they could only afford one bath a week between them. The children would use the water first, followed by their mums, the laundry and finally the men.

Life, of course, is not so grim for all South Africans. Sir Mark Weinberg, chairman of Allied Dunbar, has actress and businesswoman Anouska Hempel to comfort him in moments of homesickness. Nigel Hawthorne has become the epitome of all things gloriously British. Richard E Grant, star of *Withnail & I*, is carving out a successful acting career. Alastair Morton, perhaps with more to worry about than most, is carving his way to France as co-chairman of the Channel Tunnel.

Whether or not politics was a major motivation in coming to England, some South Africans do blossom into political flowers. A playwright whose output back home was restricted to domestic comedies can now be contacted 'only through the ANC'. Janet Suzman, Yvonne Bryceland, and Anthony Sher have also embraced their South African roots and prospered.

What comes as a bit of a shock to South Africans — apart from the weather, the standard of living, house prices, and the traffic — is that racial integration is not quite as complete in Britain as they anticipated. Kept in isolation by censorship back home, they genuinely believe that things are different elsewhere. It only takes one conversation with a cabbie who works cheerfully and announces, 'Yeah, we got trouble with blacks too,' to let them know that racism is sadly inescapable.

Still, things are not all bad. There's a butcher in Richmond who supplies boerewors, biltong and imported newspapers. And there is a pub in Chiswick where a boereseun-in-exile gathers a few friends around for a drink. Quite a few friends, actually. One South African said that half his university graduation class had found their way here. And there is always a scratch existence or better. One modern-day Trekkie, Sir Michael Edwardes, was chairman of British Leyland. But he has managed to put his past behind him and now runs Tryhorn Investments.

South Africans are good mixers on the whole. They integrate, even if that integration destroys the illusion that England is a free country, awash with memories of the Goons and Winston Churchill. It is only when two or three get round a table does the home-sickness come out – after all, before the National Party created apartheid in 1948, it was arguably the most beautiful and abundant country in the world.

The exiles gradually lose touch with the situation back home – until, of course, a total stranger with their telephone number arrives to sleep on their floor. 'Basically I want to know what I can do for you.' Take my advice – for the next year get a new number. ∎
Matthew Campling's family took him to South Africa in 1963. He returned to Britain, with a few telephone numbers, in 1986.

BOERN TO BE WILD

So, how can you spot the South African in your neighbourhood? Well, anyone who introduces themselves by the following Afrikaaner names is bound to be a Trekkie…
Men: Fricke, Boetie, Klass, Gerrit
Women: Sanie, Koekie, Anneline, Sussie

Other tell-tale signs come from the way they dress. Many South African women did not catch up with mini-skirts until the early Seventies. Having done so, however, they became so enamoured of these little nothings that they've never worn anything else. The South African mini, however, is not your modern lycra number – floral crimplene is still *le dernier cri*. The skirt is often teamed with the South African woman's favourite accessories – bronze handbags and gold shoes. Another top item is the **doek** or headscarf – very popular with farm girls everywhere.

The giveaway garment for men is the safari suit, worn – and this is the key – with shorts. These are teamed with knee-length socks, into the top of one of which a comb is tucked. This is a perfectly normal outfit in Johannesburg. It is, however, more obtrusive in Peckham.

South African slang is somewhat limited. One reason for this is that the government does not encourage the free-thinking exuberance from which slang usually emerges. Euphemism and distance are the order of the day. South Africans do not talk about apartheid: they talk about **the black problem**. They do not refer to civil war: they refer to **the unrest situation**. Other terms include…

come right=pull yourself together
pause a bit=hang on
main ou what counts=man of influence
the main ou=very popular
a right doos=a complete dickhead
a gif chick=a pretty girl
scat=darling
magna hilda reeva=revolting
yo kny=to bonk, screw or shag
kuck=crap
a moffie=a gay man
a lettie bag=a gay woman
a b.m. (abbr. baby-maker)=a heterosexual

South Africans like to pick up British or American trends and adapt them for life on the Cape. London's Sloane Rangers became Johannesburg's **Rosebank Rangers**. Similarly, New York's Jewish American Princesses have their equivalents in SA's **kugels**. Their menfolk are known as **bagels**.

Some idea of the contrasts faced by South Africans who abandon the sundappled swimming-pools of home for the mean streets of London can be gleaned by this fact: you know you've done well in South Africa when David Hicks redecorates your… servant's quarters. Sorry, Sussie, but it isn't quite like that here.

THE WILDEBEEST ROLE OF HONOUR

Clive Hirshorn – *Sunday Express*
Christopher Hope – writer
Ronald Harwood – playwright
Donald & Wendy Woods – exiles and bores
David Protter – Psion Computers
John Craven – Chairman, Morgan Grenfell
Ross Devenish – TV director
Sydney Lipworth – head of Monopolies & Mergers Commission
Tiny Rowland – media magnate
Manfred Mann – pop star
Jack Klaff – actor
Alice Krige – actress
Peter Haine – SA's Bob Geldof
Stratford Johns – actor
Moira Lister – actress
Anthony Sher – actor

Capt de Klerk's Trekkies (clockwise from top): Richard E Grant, Anthony Sher, Nigel Hawthorne, Janet Suzman and Sir Michael Edwardes.

SIX PLACES SOUTH AFRICANS SAY THEY'RE FROM

Canada
Zimbabwe
Israel
Australia
New Zealand (North island)
New Zealand (South island)

"Let's face it – holy men are not what they were."

chapter 6

MR PUNCH   **ARBITER OF STYLE**

OUT COUTURE

Mustard tights, suede flares and platform boots are in fashion. So what on earth's out? TYM MANLEY consults the style magazine experts for the Punch Guide to Complete Unfashionability

IT'S BEEN fashion month on the catwalks of the western world. In Milan, Gianni Versace produced a floor-length red frock that plunged at the back and slashed at the side and let most of its owner's body play peek-a-boo in the middle. In London, Vivienne Westwood dressed her models in underwear made of carpeting, trimmed with baby-blue curtain fringes and teamed with a pair of marabou-fringed frou-frou platform boots.

This, it would seem, is the very height of contemporary style. And few serious trendies would dare show their face these days without first arranging their glossy panties *outside* their mustard tights in the manner of fashion designers Body Map. But if these are the latest modes to be IN, what on earth is OUT? Is it, indeed, possible to be OUT any more?

Reading the fashion pages over the past few weeks one might be forgiven for thinking that it's getting harder. It looks as though almost every decrepit style and sound is IN, all at the same time. You can wear zoot suits, listen to Jason Donovan and decorate the minimalist bidet with Nazi memorabilia and no one will blench (you see – even 'blench' is coming back).

Things weren't always like this. A couple of years ago you could get yourself accused of 'an arrogant contempt for other people's sensibilities', just by sporting a pair of suede bell-bottoms. (I did. It blew a free lunch but it was worth it.) Not now. Flares are back and so are hot pants – although cerise hot pants worn over orange bell-bottoms might still do the trick.

I say might. But we need to be certain. So I telephoned those self-appointed doyens of style, the staffers of the nation's glossiest magazines, to ask them what was now considered to be utterly, piquantly gross.

Dial styles

Mobile phones are definitely out. I'm not sure about melted phones, but that's what you get if you try and ring the Style Sybyls. Because it's IN to be OUT. These people are permanently at lunch, or at meetings discussing where to go for a working lunch to plan the afternoon's meetings about tomorrow's lunch. Also IN: promising to call back. OUT: calling back.

The trouble is that everything's moving so fast the doyens keep

getting desperately OUT, sometimes as they speak. For example, the up-to-the-second style-watchers at *GQ* tell me that boasting about how hard you work is OUT. But word obviously hasn't got around. A lot of High Fashion Priests still say: 'I'm simply far too busy to think.' I'm sure that's true, but imagine admitting it!

Others were very helpful. I put it all down to style. It has been OUT to waste time talking facetious nonsense with *Punch*. But this is now back IN. It's just that some people haven't caught up with the trends that's all.

Ins and outs

They're IN at *Elle*. Relaxed, amused with long vowels. Key word: o-kaaaay. No one person likes to dictate style on the fashion magazines. Glossy style is an open discussion with suggestions zooming in from all departments. Minor tiffs result:

'Michael Nyman is OUT.'

'No he's not, I rate him!' I hope he's IN, as I've only just learnt how to spell his name.

Elle's food tip

Ecstasy is not being eaten this year. The Fashion Director at Harvey Nichols is OUT but will ring back. Paul Smith is in Paris. Lisa Freedman, editor of the London *Evening Standard*'s ES Magazine, tells me she is looking for a photographer, but doesn't say if this is IN or OUT of fashion. They're IN at *GQ*. Again the group discussion style, but with a difference, because they're mostly men and when men are asked what's out of fashion they insist on describing the ensemble of the guy across the room.

GQ's talk tip

Male sensitivity is right OUT as a topic of conversation. (*Elle* think it's in, but they're mostly women). The young street-style mags (men again) *know* it's out. What is it? 'Oh, you know: "I've got a dick and I can cry about it".' I conclude this is IN for women and OUT for men. That can't be right.

Emma Soames is OUT. Helpful attenuated vowels at *The Tatler*. Key word: Ya. (Yes, despite everything.)

Short vowels on *The Face*. They really don't have time to discuss

THE LOATHES SHOW

SEEN HERE modelling the latest OUT looks for *Punch* are those charming BBC *Clothes Show* presenters, Jeff Banks and Selina Scott.

Casting aside his distressingly tasteful suit, jokey Jeff has picked an elegant leatherette blouson which is just right for market stalls and football terraces everywhere. He's teamed it with a white poly-cotton nudette executive shirt, set off by a Slim Jim leather tie and macho forearm tattoo. His blue marblewash jeans and thick white nylon towelling socks complete the ensemble, which is bottomed off with a pair of grey plastic causal slip-ons. Grooming enthusiasts might care to note that Jeff's unfashionable 'bogbrush' haircut, with its Malibu blonde highlights, was created by Chantelle at Hair-We-Go of Hornchurch, Essex. Nothing could make him prouder, of course, than to walk into his local theme pub, Plonkers, with sexy Selina on his arm. Our lovely lady of the air has abandoned designer labels. Now she looks modestly understated in her hot pink bubbleweave boob tube, with a matching skirt whose flirty ra-ra flounce comes in a high-contrast tropical print. Her legs, suntanned at Porky's Spa in Dagenham Heathway, Essex under ultra-violet light, are longer than ever in their high-heeled white cowgirl boots, complete with that essential fringe. And that sno-pearl Littlewoods handbag lets the world know she's an ambitious girl — she wants to be an air hostess.

Selina's beauty routine never varies: turquoise Benidorm eye-shadow; yummy pink Ibiza lipstick and perfume by Lanzarote de Lanzarote. A butterfly-clip restrains her hair, which is wittily styled by Beverly at Choppers in Romford, Essex and tinted by Sun-In at Boots.

We think you'll agree, they make a corking couple.

ILLUSTRATION BY MARTIN WELCH

147

OUT COUTURE

this jocular trivia. They're sure I'll understand. I do – *The Face* takes style far too seriously.

Peter York, consultant, pollster and Sloane Ranger guru, isn't available for this sort of thing. *i-D* magazine is. The street-cred word is that style is OUT – 'the word and all its associations'. All the doyens agree, but you don't find them taking up places on government retraining schemes. Odd.

i-D's clothes tip
If it can't take ten hours of wild dancing it's OUT.

Nicholas Coleridge, editorial director of Condé Nast, will try and think of something. The fashion director of Harrods won't. The telephonic bouncer at the Joseph Emporium insists on putting me through to the press office! Aaaagh, No! I won't go.

Bouncer's style tip
OUT – this sort of article. Emma Soames can only think of mobile phones. Hmmm. Nicholas Coleridge has thought of something. Almost everything's IN but he's certain about: Kiwi fruit, Dai Llewellyn, macaroons, Eddie Shah and *mille feuilles*. Surely a thousand leaves can't be wrong?

Arena is IN. The men's fashion mags are all short vowels and cynical humour. Key word: Yeah. Very quick with a list of the really appalling here from editor Dylan Jones:

Arena's clothes tip
Matt-black Gucci loafers, excruciating blue socks, black polo shirt, Prince of Wales Armani suit, large Rolex and a BMW and a Porsche parked outside. OUT, OUT, OUT!

It's what their ad manager, Rod Sopp (Odd Sock?), is wearing.

Arena is sure that male sensitivity is OUT. I'm going to try this one on *Men Only*.

The editor is at lunch – what do I expect if I ring at 4.30? At five he's IN. 'Do you mean male sensitivity as in "oops, sorry"?' No, as in crying over one's sexual organ. He thinks all men do this but they don't talk about it. And what's really out of fashion?

'Nothing is more out of fashion than men's magazines – except *Punch*.' Phew. ∎

WHAT'S REALLY OUT

Elle
For men: Grandad shirts, thin ties (especially leather); smart 'n' slimy leather jackets.
For women: White stilettos, ra-ra skirts (knee-length A-line skirts are really gross) boob tubes, blue eye-shadow and little white handbags with thin straps.
Decor: Black leather and chrome.
Food: Ecstasy and hamburgers.
Topics of conversation: Style, fashion designers, *Batman* and the ozone layer.
Music: Bros, Jason Donovan, Jive Bunny and Vivaldi.

i-D
For men: Doc Martens and clutch bags. Anything that won't take wild dancing.
For women: That goes for women too.
Decor: Minimalism – black and white contrasts and as little as possible. (Colour, clutter and junk are back.)
Food: McDonald's. Japanese and Thai food (it's too ordinary, exotic means Ethiopian at least).
Topics of conversation: Aids, global warming, the Summer of Love, Liverpool Football Club, sex.
Music: House music, heavy metal, Jason Donovan.

Gentleman's Quarterly (GQ)
For men: Galoshes or moon boots, motif sweaters.
For women: Ra-ra skirts and boxer shorts.
Decor: Anything in black and white.
Food: Anything that's good for you.
Topics of conversation: Masculine sensitivity, how late you work, CDs, the property market.
Music: Paul Anka and Billy Joel.

Arena
For men: Timberland boots or Doc Martens, white socks, boxer shorts, white Levis (no, they're IN), Ray-Bans Wayfarers and any sort of jewellery.
For women: Ra-ra skirts, minimalist busts.
Decor: Black and white wardrobes.
Food: Real ale, anything cholesterol-free.
Topics of conversation: Style, male sensitivity.
Music: House music.

TRY THESE APPALLING STYLES

Extrovert male
With moonboots and white socks setting off your ra-ra skirt, a thin leather tie emphasising your collarless grandad shirt and Ray-Bans Wayfarers giving a mean look to your slimy leather jacket, you serve Thai hamburgers off a black and white wardrobe to the sound of Jive Bunny while talking sincerely about male sensitivity.

Conservative male
In your Doc Martens, a sweater with little antelopes on it under your Armani suit and an anorak slung carelessly over the shoulders you serve Ecstasy in a stripped room and hold forth on style to the familiar strains of Vivaldi on CD.

Exhibitionist female
Whirling your knee-length A-line skirt to show your boxer shorts and supporting your gold lamé top to prevent your minimalist bust breaking a strap, you serve blue eye shadow in chrome 'n' leather chairs while yelling about sex over sickeningly loud House music.

Conservative female
Clad in white Levis and boob tube you totter around in white stilettos serving thin steamed handbag straps to the sound of Billy Joel, while discoursing lightly about Aids.

"Well, Mr Mackenzie, it says nothing in your CV about ponytails."

THE JOY OF BEARD

MARCUS BERKMANN
combs the issue of facial growth
and what is says about a man.
Or woman

AS NEW ORDER once so presciently put it, 'Everything's Gone Green'. Although nothing has actually been *done* to save the world just yet, ecological awareness is the dictum of the moment. Dinner parties across the nation resound to the tones of well-meaning eco-chatter, while for all of us additive-free petrol and unleaded food have become part of daily life. Even the fashion world is cottoning on. Real fur (the sort that was once lived in) is slightly less cool than leprosy, and it can be but a matter of time before anoraks and sturdy footwear return in triumph to the cat-walks of Paris and Milan.

What clinches it, though, is the return to public favour of perhaps the most controversial of all ecological fashion state-ments – the beard. Long associated with television naturalists, shipwrecked mariners and woolly rebels of all kinds, it has re-emerged as the most tangible (and itchy) symbol yet of the Green movement. As flamboyantly bespectacled ivory tinkling popster Elton John very nearly sang in 1974, 'The Beard is Back'.

To confirm this disturbing prognosis, take a look at any of our hallowed universities – or even one of the less hallowed ones. Stu-dents have always, of course, been at the very forefront of beard research – the discovery that they can actually grow one often proves a vital turning point – but suddenly they're all in on the act. Where once freshly-shaven cheeks gleamed purposefully, local-ised outbreaks of wispy bumfluff are now the order of the day. Everyone's trying to grow one – even the girls.

The spirit of the age has even extended to the mean streets of the metropolis. In London, leading trendsetters, pop stars and men with bow ties from design consultancies are binning their Bics, although many are buying infinitely more expensive equip-ment with which to keep their new growths under control. Social attitudes are adjusting with creditable speed. In the past, anyone sporting excess facial hair would naturally be assumed to be a fan of chunky knitwear and open-toed sandals, with a keen interest in murky sock-flavoured ales and only a passing acquaintance with anti-perspirant. Now, exactly the same is assumed, but instead of being reviled and ridiculed, beardies suddenly find themselves invited to fashionable dinner parties and surrounded by luscious young lovelies keen to discuss CFCs and acid rain over a pint of Thruxton's XXX 'Old Physicist'.

So should *you* be thinking of growing one? Aren't you worried about being left behind in the great race to look like Sir Ranulph Fiennes? There are certainly many advantages to owning your own beard. The job market, for instance, is suddenly thrown wide open – assuming, of course, that you want to be an old seadog, a trad jazz musician or Rolf Harris. And a beard is absolutely essen-tial should you be thinking of starting up your own religion or design consultancy.

Growing a beard, though, is no mean feat, as any beardie will tell you (usually at considerable length). Indeed, climbing Everest or painting the Sistine Chapel are mere bagatelles by comparison. From day one, you encounter hazards that have tested the mettle of the abnormally hirsute for generations. Will it grow evenly, or merely sprout in pathetic patches on random areas of your face? If it does grow, will it itch madly? And, most worrying of all, will it play host to unimaginable numbers of bacteria, insect larvae and rotting fragments of long-forgotten meals?

Beards can also limit you in other ways. Kissing babies, drink-ing soup and sitting too near an electric fan all present insoluble problems for the beardie. And for the woman in his life (if any), the difficulties are no less acute. Do beards moult in the bath? Is sex with a beardie an exhilarating and deeply satisfying experi-ence, or is it just a bit hairier than usual? How do you treat beard rash? And can a beard ever be truly hygienic?

The answer to the last question is, of course, No. According to a report in *New Scientist* magazine in 1985, beard owners actually breathe in air that is less fresh than everybody else's. The carbon dioxide they exhale is partially trapped in their beards, and floats up to be breathed in again. In addition (although the article pointedly failed to mention this) the human beard can support a remarkable range of wildlife, as long as it is kept suitably damp and well-nourished. Anything from lethal killer viruses to, in extremis, small nesting furry animals will happily settle down there and propagate.

What types of beard, then, are there to choose from? Not sur-prisingly, there's an almost bewildering array of different styles, from the Bee Gee (for Seventies pop stars and directors of design consultancies) to the Full Black Bogbrush (as worn by born-again chief constables and Muslim fundamentalists). Here, though, are some of my personal favourites:

David Bellamy: years of cultivation

Sir Peter Hall: nothing gets his goatee

Trevor Nunn: to beard or not to beard

David 'A' Stewart: the beard as chin substitute

Mike Gatting: badly needs extra cover

The subsidised theatre director

Could Sir Peter Hall and Trevor Nunn ever have got where they are today without strategic beard growth? It seems unlikely. Both beards, you'll notice, are well trained and skilfully manicured, and reveal a lot about their owners: to wit, a certain passing interest in the theatre combined with particular fondness for enormous cheques, not to mention a close physiognomic likeness to the Bearded Bard, Shakespeare himself.

The Jeremy Beardle

Some beards can claim a uniqueness of sorts, and Jeremy Beadle's bizarre topiary is a perfect example. Although irrefutably resembling a beard in the central area, the growth on the side of the face has been reduced to little more than a line – the world's first 'pencil beard'. Such a growth clearly serves no useful purpose at all, which, by coincidence, could also be said of Mr Beadle.

The international terrorist

How many Muslim fundamentalists have their beards frisked by security guards at airports? Caches of Semtex, illegal drugs, even small machine guns can be concealed in a well-developed set of whiskers. The Radio 1 DJ Dave Lee Travis modelled his own beard on international terrorist look – don't be fooled by his 'Hairy Cornflake' nickname.

Where's the chin?

One of the cruellest things you can say about a beardie is that he has grown it to hide a weak chin. Nevertheless this is often true, as in the case of Dave Stewart of the Eurythmics, who in pre-beard photographs is revealed to have no chin at all. Beards can also conceal huge jutting chins, as for example in the case of cricketer Mike Gatting, or football pundit Jimmy Hill. What you can always be certain of is that underneath the average beard lies a very funny face indeed.

It's a tough choice, as in the end your beard can speak volumes for you – sometimes literally, if you happen to have a pair of parakeets nesting in it. The religious symbolism of the beard, for instance, is worthy of a treatise all of its own. Notice that God, in his traditional European manifestation, boasts a large friendly white beard, while the Devil's is remarkably like Mr Beadle's.

What's beyond argument is that the Beard is here to stay. The clean-shaven style warrior of the Eighties with his portable phone, sharp suit and slicked-back hair has been consigned to history. The beardie, with his woollen socks, limited sense of smell and gigantic beermat collection, is the coming man. Attitudes will have to change. Beards are back, and no amount of congealed tomato soup is going to stop them this time. ■

Below left: Khomeini and Dave Lee Travis. Right: the beard as religious statement, Angel Gabriel lookalike Barry Gibb; Far right: in God's image?

Ten amazing facts you didn't know about beards (all guaranteed true)

1) Ostend's Chief Of Police has forbidden his constables to sport beards in case criminals set fire to them.
2) Egyptian pharaohs were forced to wear false beards from an early age.
3) Tsar Peter the Great of Russia imposed a tax on beards in 1698, although he later decreed that offenders would be shaved with a blunt razor or plucked clean, one whisker at a time, with pincers.
4) There are 13,000 hairs on the average beard.
5) Pogonophobia is a recognised psychiatric complaint, meaning 'fear of beards'.
6) The only non-bearded member of the pop group ZZ Top is called Mr Beard.
7) Such is Mrs Thatcher's dislike of beards that she refuses to appoint anyone with one to a Government post.
8) The children's game Beaver consists of shouting 'Beaver' at men with beards, pointing, laughing and running away.
9) M Beard scored one goal for Birmingham City in the 1969-70 season.
10) The owner of the longest beard in history, Hans Steininger, fell to his death in 1567 when he tripped over it.

'Flares are back, I see.'

'Help! Help! I can't move! Suction!'

McLACHLAN

A New
Year,
A New
WAISTLINE!

THE PUNCH DIET

After all that festive food, you're feeling full, fat and ghastly. You are not alone. According to the tabloids, Elizabeth Taylor's ninth husband-to-be has told her to slim down or stay single. But why should she worry? *Punch* says FAT IS FUN! Inside every beanpole is a glutton trying to get stout.
MITCHELL SYMONS, plump and proud of it, presents the P-Plan Diet, or How to Gain Girth and Influence People.

It happened during episode six of *Tutti Frutti*. I was sitting in my armchair working through a can of Coca-Cola and 100 grams of Payne's Chocolate Peanuts and Raisins and fancying Emma Thompson like crazy. I popped out of the room for a few seconds to fetch a few mini Aero bars, and when I got back she was in bed with Robbie Coltrane. I was amazed. For once, the fat man had got the girl.

For closet fatties everywhere, this was a red letter day: as if Sidney Greenstreet had walked off with Ingrid Bergman in *Casablanca*. The feeling of exultation at seeing the corpulent Robbie Coltrane entwined with lithe Emma Thompson was so great that I vowed then and there to come out as a fatty. No more dark clothing, no more holding my breath. I was free.

Being fat is more than just eating a lot and avoiding exercise: it's a whole attitude of mind, a way of life. In order to become fat, you have to develop a fat person's mentality. Never run when you can walk; never walk when you can ride. You must never strain yourself: if God had meant you to leave your armchair, he would never have invented the telephone, and certianly not the remote control television. As a general rule: if in doubt, do nothing.

I once saw Bernard Manning in nothing but underpants. He is a man who transcends words like plump, fat, and obese. Mr Manning could benefit from a prolonged stay in a health farm — life imprisonment perhaps. Our meeting came during research for a television programme ▶

ROLL MODEL
First Access, now Ikea furniture: flexible friend Sir Cyril Smith proves that large is lucrative

PLEASANTLY PLUMP

PAUL GASCOIGNE
ALISON MOYET
ROY HATTERSLEY
TIM RICE
VICTORIA WOOD
JENNIFER SAUNDERS
IAN BOTHAM
ERIC BRISTOW
DUKE HUSSEY
BILL BEAUMONT
TERRY WOGAN
DUCHESS OF YORK
GEORGE MICHAEL
EDWARD HEATH
CLIVE JAMES
STEPHEN STILLS
ASTERIX

Please note: being pleasantly plump doesn't confer pleasantness upon the person thus described. Example: Terry Wogan is 'pleasantly plump' but that doesn't mean that one would want to spend *any* time with him (unless one had a major book or film which required selling). Ditto Bernie Winters (without the unless).

SOMEWHAT PLUMPER

SIR CYRIL SMITH
CLAIR RAYNER
RUSSELL GRANT
ERIC HEFFER
ROSEANNE BARR
DAWN FRENCH
MARLON BRANDO
MOST DARTS PLAYERS
ROBERT MAXWELL
BIG DADDY
BERNARD MANNING
BERTICE REDDING
VAN MORRISON
REV. IAN PAISLEY
MEATLOAF
DAVID CROSBY
OBELIX

Above: Roseanne Barr and her chubby TV hubby. *Below:* Mr Loaf says nothing is a patch on his heavy rock

10 PEOPLE WHO MAKE YOU FEEL GOOD ABOUT BEING FAT

KYLIE MINOGUE
MANDY SMITH
LENA ZAVARONI
PHILLIP SCHOFIELD
NANCY REAGAN
BARRY McGUIGAN
MAUREEN LIPMAN
COLIN MOYNIHAN
JOAN RIVERS
KEITH RICHARDS

JUST YOU WAIT … (People who might one day be very fat indeed)

SYLVESTER STALLONE
ANNABEL CROFT
PRINCE ANDREW
ARNOLD SCHWARZENEGGER
GABRIELLA SABATINI
RUTGER HAUER
GEOFF CAPES
FRANK BRUNO
DONNA HARTLEY
ELIZABETH TAYLOR
LIZA MINNELLI
SIMON LE BON
BOY GEORGE

"Your father and I feel you are now old enough to know the truth. There is no such person as Tarzan ..."

Haughty couture

Mud-spattered JANE MULVAGH reports from the increasingly unseemly Paris Collections

Fashion's cheerleaders flew into Paris last week to witness the prize fight: a slug out between the champ, LVMH, (Louis Vuitton-Moet Hennessey, whose heavyweight line up includes Dior, Lacroix and Givenchy), and the flyweight challenger, Claude Montana, in the Lanvin colours, a hefty 34% of which is owned by the Midland Bank. Though the doom-merchants were keening over Fashion's demise – she'd apparently been cudgeled to death by the caring New Age 'Green' Giant – she defiantly rose like a flashy phoenix, through the wet grey Paris skies, for a last-ditch stand.

Bernard Arnaud, owner of LVMH, is determined to assemble the most lucrative luxury goods conglomerate in the world; Lanvin appointed the stripling lightweight Montana (a ready-to-wear not an *alta moda* designer), to challenge the monopoly with a couture clout. Odds were on the bruiser LVMH.

True to form, the Chambre Syndicale de la Couture had issued hysteria-inducing designer invitations to the international press; mega department-store buyers; the super-rich, long-distance shoppers, such as Nan Kempner, Judith Taubman and La Princesse de Beauvau-Craon; and the business elite. The front line was also peppered with French ministers, like Jack Lang, and rock stars, like Grace Jones and Elton John. But forget the frocks. We all knew that this was a fight over scent and stocking rights.

158

The *Punch* guide to the arts, entertainment, media and more ...

The international caravan of invitees was put into training on Sunday. Limbering up commenced *chez* Lacroix who showed another confection of unwearable, lip-smacking furbelows: a haphazard bouillabaise of lingerie lace, raffia, polka dots, diamanté, chiné feathers, fringes and crystal. His resurrected Lolita sent the front row into a *nostalgie de l'ingénue*. But who was going to wear these abbreviated soupçons? Even Lacroix admitted that he had no interest in designing for the reality of the street, preferring the unbridled fantasy of the grand opera or theatre.

The pace quickened at Dior. The audience's alertness was tested with a series of iconoclastic references, such as Lily of the Valley posies and lace handkerchiefs tucked into bodices and hat-bands. All these were supposed to register that Ferre, the newly-appointed house designer, had swotted up on a few of the old maestro's signatures. The strict but feminine day-wear was masterfully cut in shades of dove through charcoal grey, but by night the grand folly unravelled. *Ancien régime* princesses unwound themselves from ten-foot-long stoles, to reveal full-length, bouffant ball dresses of the most sumptuous silks. Lucy Clayton deportment lessons will surely be included in the price (a mere £25,000) so that the incumbent can be tutored not only in how to get into them but also how to feign lightfootedness with 50 pounds of silk slung across the body like festoon curtains. One is reminded of the Baronesse de Rothschild's solution to mobility in such constructions in the 1950s: she was chauffeured to balls in a horse box because none of her husband's limousines could accommodate the folds without unsightly creasing.

Kaiser Lagerfeld's seasonal dictate for the aspiring *mondaine* at Chanel aroused a deafening chorus of wolf whistles from the bank of lusty male photographers whose blood was up. Lagerfeld's sugared-almond sweetie will be hitting the boulevards in a curve-clinging tweed jacket weighted down with a few kilos of *passementerie* and boater worn coyly on the back of her head. Whisps of bias-cut chiffon were ambitiously described as a 'skirt' in the programme but such a *petit rien* was abbreviated so high up the *derrière* that pundits predict the most prominent label to be sported this summer will be that of Marks & Spencer.

The front row of uniformed Chanel clones was squirming with *démodé* guilt. Why? The Führer had declared that fool's gold was out. And what a bunch of half-wits sat in those hallowed seats weighted down like convicts in gilt chains!

This trashing of gilt was reiterated at the Lanvin show that evening, by the beautiful exile Ines de la Fressange who sat in proud defiance of commerce – there was not a label, gilt insignia or printed silk logo on her. She has recently been acclaimed the moral victor of a cat fight with her former employer, Lagerfeld, who disapproved of her modelling as the French symbol of womanhood, Marianne. He dismissed this national figurehead as a sentimental icon of the bourgeoisie. But France is made up of proud burghers and they stood by their new Marianne, suspecting that in fact the commercial Kaiser simply wanted to replace the skeletal Innes – an unfashionable silhouette – with the voluptuous neo-Bardot of the catwalk, Claudia Schifer.

The venue for the prize fight of the week was a marquee on the Left Bank. It was hardly an exclusive occasion in that over 2,000 attended. Suspicions were aroused that Montana was out of his depth since he had failed to understand that 'haute' luxury should always be a strictly gilded Right Bank affair unveiled under a golden, chandeliered dome, not a calicoed aerodrome.

Along either side of the quarter-mile-long white upholstered catwalk sat La Mode's muscle: the Editors in Chief of all the *Vogue*s, not to mention the pinchbeck glossies, a squadron of big financiers, half the French cabinet and a scattering of rock stars. All had donned their Sunday Best, bettered by meticulous manicures and coiffures. But who was that mud-bespattered changeling two down from the American *Vogue* contingent?

It was the critic of a prominent British magazine. Despite the prestige of the publication, the disorganised Lanvin press office had failed to issue a stiffy on time. In desperation, having faxed London, Lanvin and the President of the Chambre Syndicale, the critic had to take her chances. She completed an assault course through several hundred impatient photographers and arrived at the door of the marquee two hours before the show to explain the oversight. Despite brandishing a fist full of official cards, she was turned away by the brattish bouncer – there's nothing like French bloody-mindedness. Ever felt like a camel getting through the eye of a needle?

Well, sod French red tape. Our intrepid reporter emerged once again into the pouring rain, scaled a wall, climbed over an ornamental stone bridge which dropped 15 feet into a pool of mud, and scanned the vacuum-sealed tarpaulin for a point of entry. At last, she found a tiny black door open to admit a roll of lighting cable and slipped in. She threaded her way through the backstage labyrinth, into the white lights of the auditorium which was filled with 300 black-suited youths, the ushers. Spotting the interloper, they moved towards her with determined pugnacity and were about to bounce her into the night when the errant press officer recognised her, grovelled with apology and led her to the front row. A chorus of cheers went up from the bureaucracy-weary photographers.

All this for a few frocks worn by fewer women at greater and greater cost. The epitaph to the week was in fact written by the King of Couture, Saint Laurent, who sent down the catwalk a resumé of his best looks – nobody does it better – over the last 30 years. A final tribute to a dying art? Sadly, despite the scent and stockings, one guesses so. ■

Jane Mulvagh is a fashion historian and the author of The Vogue History of 20th Century Fashion.

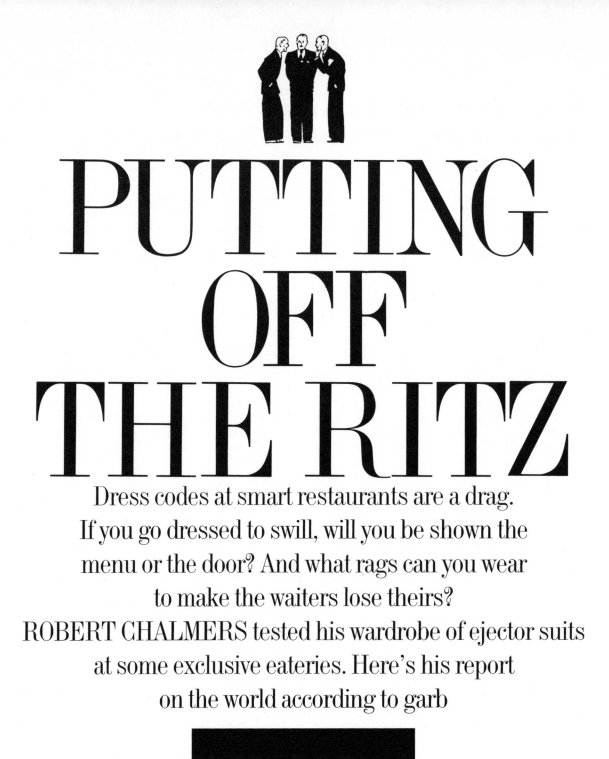

PUTTING OFF THE RITZ

Dress codes at smart restaurants are a drag.
If you go dressed to swill, will you be shown the
menu or the door? And what rags can you wear
to make the waiters lose theirs?
ROBERT CHALMERS tested his wardrobe of ejector suits
at some exclusive eateries. Here's his report
on the world according to garb

'**A** man of sense,' Lord Chesterfield wrote to his son, 'carefully avoids any particular character in his dress; he dresses as well, and in the same manner, as the people of sense and fashion of the place where he is.'

Anyone who has attempted the long walk from Tottenham Hotspur's stadium to the Seven Sisters underground station whilst wearing a red and white scarf will know what Lord Chesterfield was getting at. The idea of public propriety in dress depends less on fashion *per se* than on the style favoured by one's immediate neighbours. Some establishments still feel the need to encourage or formalise our natural tendency to conform; though the punishment for disobedience, admittedly, usually falls short of the kind of penalities imposed on the Tottenham High Road.

The strictest dress codes tend to be 'enforced' with the consent of members of private clubs: White's Gentlemen's Club in St James's, for instance, still requires a dress suit, collar and tie. Blazer and trousers 'may occasionally be admitted'. (Blazer and trousers do better than women in this respect. Ladies have been allowed in, White's told me, "about twice this century".)

The extension of a dress code to business premises with public access, like restaurants and hotels, is more bemusing in that it breaks the eleventh business commandment – the one relating to the wilful turning away, while being of sound mind, of a would-be paying customer. I visited some establishments in London and Manchester, to try to discover what on earth ▶

No Soiled Clothes: Robert 'the Charmer' Chalmers sports the grey two-piece suit, fashion accessoried with ketchup, mustard and relish. Always welcome at El Vino's

'Well, there goes the neighbourhood!'

possesses then to enforce their arcane complex set of dress requirements.

The Jacket and Tie

Where formal dress requirements for men are concerned, certainly in the more traditional establishment, all outfits aspire to the condition of black tie. These days, however, few British hotels or restaurants insist on dinner dress, except for special functions (though some, like The Savoy, encourage it on Saturdays). A jacket and tie, however, is still *de rigueur* in most of the public areas of the more exclusive hotels. I found this out during my two abortive attempts to gain admission to **Claridge's Tea Room** (*Jacket and Tie for Men; No Jeans*), finally I was allowed in with a three-piece suit.

Most male guests in the room were also wearing the modern 'sack suit', which remains, in many ways, the ideal leveller. Its rectangular shape and limited colour range offer the anonymity of a military uniform; at the same time the sack suit conceals sagging middle-aged flesh and is highly unflattering to the figure of a 'bronze Adonis'. I was reflecting on this when the combination of the heat and the *Eau de Nile* decor became too much. I slipped off my tie.

Taking your tie off in Claridge's has the effect of removing a more intimate garment in another place. The hotel tea-room has maintained its dress-code since 1814, but the embarrassment, even in 1989, is acute and immediate, though it *is* a good way of getting a waiter quickly. I had mine by my side in eighteen seconds, giving me the kind of look you see on the faces of regulars at the local in Dracula films when travellers stop and ask for a lift to the castle. The last of the three waiters who spoke to me argued precedent. "It's always been that way in Claridge's. It's been that way for – I don't know for how long – a hundred years or so." Finally, after heroic tact on his part, I got the red card, which in Claridge's takes the form of having your table cleared against your will. The classier establishments' desire to avoid an unseemly fracas has given rise to a 'hidden etiquette' of genteel alternatives to the Hollywood 'heave-ho' into the gutter. I found an interesting variation at **Brown's Hotel** (*Jacket and Tie; No Jeans*) where my 'expulsion' took the form of being asked to remove myself to the writing-room, taking, as Oliver Hardy once said when playing a butler, "Yer eats with you".

Terry Holmes of **The Ritz** (*Jacket and Tie; No Jeans*) told me that the rule is imposed "so that nobody will be embarrassed by turning up incorrectly dressed", though whether being cold-shouldered in the busy foyer is less embarrassing than getting outside of a Ritz tea *sans cravate* was, my companion pointed out, a matter of opinion. The idea of taking an informal tea would probably not have distressed the man from Birmingham whom I passed on my premature exit from the Ritz. "That," he told his friends in a stage whisper, "is the most expensive cup of tea I've ever had."

I rejoined my companion, who had bolted during the closing stages of play at the Ritz, and we set off for the **Savoy American Bar** (*Jacket and Tie; No Jeans*). Again I went in a suit and took my jacket off. After a couple of public ▶

Fearful of boosting my already considerable expenses beyond the tolerance of my commissioning editor, I decided on an early exit from Maxim's de Paris

ILLUSTRATION BY GRAHAM HIGGINS

161

warnings the senior waiter, a man of saint-like patience, opened the window for me, and stood by it. Seeing no reaction, he adopted the posture favoured by bathers on nineteenth-century posters advertising northern coastal towns, inhaling deeply and smiling to demonstrate the beneficial effect of the ozone ("Can you feel the fresh air coming?"). On the way out I asked him what his next move would have been if I hadn't left ("A punch"). Peter Crome of the Savoy group, which also owns Claridge's, put in a 'time and motion' plea: "If you went to The Savoy specially dressed and saw people in T-shirts, you would ask yourself why you had gone to all that trouble. It should," he added, "be the experience of a lifetime." (It certainly was for me…)

Fearful of boosting my already considerable expenses beyond the tolerance of my commissioning editor, I decided on an early exit from **Maxim's de Paris** (*Upstairs restaurant: Jacket and Tie; No Jeans*). I was a little surprised to be served at the bar, but then the waiter made his move: "Once you go into the restaurant you have to put your jacket and tie on." Following Alex Higgins, patron saint of the tieless, I pleaded fear of constriction around the throat during activities where huge amounts of cash were at stake. "In that case, sir, I am obliged…" – familiar by now with the valetudinal tone, I reached for my bag – "to make an exception in your case." The waiter looked genuinely surprised at our reaction; he was probably confused by the contrast between my look of horror as I fumbled for a credit card and the expression of undisguised glee on the face of my companion, who told me that the level of humiliation by association was making her feel a little like Lord Godiva.

Maxim's dress restriction is typical for a restaurant of its type. Most of the 'top' London establishments require jacket and tie for men, at least for dinner, and may dither over whether or not to serve ladies in jeans. Silvano Giraldin of **La Gavroche** argued exclusivity as his rationale. "La Gavroche is not a restaurant on the corner. We don't want or expect people to come everyday. It's an occasion to remember. And we ask them to dress up."

No Jeans

Jeans were in their heyday as code-breakers in the late Sixties and early Seventies, when events like the Isle of Wight pop festival inspired 'No Hippies' and 'No Denim' notices all over the country. Seventies football fans, too, got denim a bad name by viewing it as an acceptable 'second strip' when their Oxford bags were in the wash. Presumably they were attracted by the handy riveted pockets ("Ideal," says Sharon Rosenberg, in her book, *Denim*, "for carrying heavy ore samples"). Thirty-five years after *The Wild One*, I expected, as I set out in full denim rig-out, to have a relatively trouble-free evening.

I had not expected to be *persona grata* in **Annabel's** (*Smart Dress; Dark Suit or Black Tie for Men*), or **Stringfellows** (*Smart Casual; No Jeans or Training Shoes*); but I also got the thumbs-down at a number of mainstream clubs including **The Hippodrome** (*No Jeans; No Training Shoes*). One or two pubs felt that they

could do without me; notably **The Ship** in Lime Street, EC3, which continues to display a rather quaint 'No Jeans' sign.

Things started hotting up once I went outside London. On a Saturday night in Manchester I was turned away from most of the bars and clubs in the Piccadilly area, including **Yates's Wine Lodge** (*No Jeans Saturday Night*) in High Street. Yates's has rocketed up market over the last few years and has, like many pubs I visited, adopted a 'tight' door policy at the weekend. A lady from the company expained that "denim is associated with the kind of trade we would not want". This, she told me, meant "people likely to be undesirable in some way." Later that evening, when I returned to Yates's in a jacket and tie, I was rather taken aback to see one of my fellow revellers (not, admittedly, wearing jeans), comatose and spread-eagled in a pool of vomit in the Gents (the wall of which was decorated with the slogan 'Burnley Suicide Squad kick to kill'). But then it all depends, as Lord Chesterfield would no doubt have reflected, on what you mean by 'undesirable'.

Denim, being the only unambiguous uniform to have maintained its challenge to the sack suit, has become a kind of shorthand for the proscribable. The 'No Jeans' regulation is especially handy in places with no established practice and little faith in the ability of their door staff to judge character. With the most ferocious football supporters now wearing tweeds, and a Liberty denim jacket and standard designer jeans together costing well over £100, the received attitude towards denim has clearly been overtaken by events. But as Terry Holmes had told me at the Ritz: "You can't tell people that they can wear jeans as long as they're designer jeans."

No Working Clothes

The restriction of 'No Working Clothes' is probably the most puzzling of all to the philosophically-minded punter, who might argue that 'working clothes' could range – depending on your occupation – from top hat and tails to no clothes at all. (In the establishments where I tried to develop the argument, this train of thought turned out to be an express route to the exit.)

I 'teamed' a brand new boiler suit – laundered and pressed so that I would not be ejected on a 'bum rap' of soiled clothing – with a blue woolly hat, tool bag and polished army boots, and headed for the City. The area has a healthy mixture of construction workers and stockbrokers (so healthy that one pub, **The Viaduct** near Bart's Hospital, was displaying – with scant respect for the hands that made it – a 'No Builders' sign). I was served here, and at nine other of the fifteen pubs I visited. Interestingly, intimidating signs referring to working clothes seemed to offer little clue as to the establishment's attitude. Several of the places which refused me (like the **Three Compasses** in Cowcross Street) displayed no warning.

At **The City Pipe** (*Only Those Customers Respectably Attired will be Served*), near St Paul's, I got past the doorman easily enough. Combined with a purposeful look, overalls – especially with a name stencilled on the back –

command as much authority as any other dark blue uniform. Here I was turned away for being as Peter might have put it, in the 'condition' of boiler suit. The barman, who refused to serve me, told me that the sign meant 'suit and tie'; the doorman dutifully explained that "it means no jeans".

After a chat with a spokesman for Davy's, who own the pub, I was able to establish that my entry for the establishment should read: The City Pipe (*No Jeans, Boiler Suits Or Training Shoes. Jacket and Tie Essential Unless You Go In With a Group Who Are Appropriately Dressed and Keep Your Head Down*).

No Soiled Clothes

For my visits to City pubs displaying a 'No Soiled Clothes' sign, I chose a suit and tie with tomato ketchup and half a can of vegetable soup emptied down the front. As I'd had some difficulty in persuading a taxi driver to take me, I was surprised to be served in all the places I visited, including **The Jamaica Wine House** (*No Soiled Clothes or Dirty Footwear*). It was service with a smile this time at The Three Compasses. Even The City Pipe served me, after an old-fashioned look from the barman.

In desperation I set out for El Vino's. The Fleet Street bar/restaurant has long been in the van – or, depending on your point of view, the rear – guard of sartorial restriction. Here again I was served at the bar; I had lasted less than a minute in my denim outfit. It is as hard to be

The extension of a dress code breaks the eleventh business commandment – the wilful turning away, while being of sound mind, of a would-be paying customer

ejected from establishments like El Vino's 'suitably' attired as it is impossible to get in if you are not wearing a jacket and tie. *Any* jacket and tie. (On another occasion I tried a pair of 28-inch flared Terylene check trousers, an ill-fitting Seventies disco jacket with a floral shirt and kipper tie. I had only gone twenty yards on the way to the taxi in Crouch End before I was being loudly mocked by a group of teenage girls. El Vino's, however, was happy to serve me, though as I was leaving the barman called out "let me know when it comes back into fashion".

Mr Mitchell, director of El Vino's, explained the rationale behind the code at his establishment. "For gentlemen, we require jacket and tie. For ladies, a skirt or dress. Trousers are *not* suitable attire. In our humble opinion. If you do allow trousers," Mr Mitchell continued, "then you get awful scruffy old women in jeans and God knows what else and it's just not good enough." Mr Mitchell did, however, tell me that the bar would try to supply a spare tie "if a gentleman comes in with some chap from up north who hasn't got one"; news which should be of some comfort to the Burnley Suicide Squad.

Smart Casual

Dress codes are especially bewildering when experienced in rapid succession. You cannot get into most bars at The Savoy without a tie, but until recently at The Intrepid Fox in Wardour Street (now *No Restrictions*) they wouldn't serve you if you did have one. Older night people in suits reported difficulties in gaining admission to trendier clubs like The Hacienda in Manchester, established by pop entrepreneur Tony Wilson (39). Claridge's grudgingly allowed me to wear my 'Waialae Country Club' Hawaian baseball hat in their tea-room, The Chicago Pizza Pie Factory wouldn't have any item of headgear at all. Leather outfits won't get past the doorman in many West End clubs, but at Skin Two (at Zeeta's in Putney) they won't let you in without one.

Restrictions are overwhelmingly aimed at male guests. Silvano Giraldin at La Gavroche cracked a joke that I heard several times during my research, explaining that the code at his restaurant was "Men – jacket and tie; women naked". ("If a woman goes out with a man in a nice suit she knows very well that she cannot wear jeans.")

Apart from fretting about the soft furnishings, explanations of dress codes boiled down to three: The School Uniform (everybody does it, it stops people feeling embarrassed); Weddings and Funerals (it's a special occasion, you dress up); and Tradition (it's been like this since 1814). I found this last more convincing in the case of Claridge's than at the Manchester hotel/club **Sacha's** ("We've done it ever since we opened – last December.") Sacha's is a temple to roaring kitsch. The decor includes a model of a hammerhead shark, a stuffed polar bear and a teal. The effect is the more horrific when you realise that you are sitting in what used to be the children's shoe department at C&A.

I asked Mr Mitchell whether El Vino's would ever relax its code to admit what Sir Richard Maitland called "newfangleness of geir". "Relax? Never. We might even get tourists." ∎

URBAN LEGENDS
by Allen

'Jones, you're in no position to tell me what to do!'

'Hello, is that the Police Complaints Authority?'

Forget *boeuf en croûte* or *canard à l'orange*, the most successful recipe of all time is the Big Mac. Now, for the first time ever, former chef HUGH WHITTINGSTALL shows you how to make a completely authentic Big Mac in the comfort of your own kitchen

MAC ATTACK

THE ANALYSIS

Apart from being the longest word in the English language 'TWOALLBEEFPATTIESS-PECIALSAUCELETTUCECHEESEPICKLE-SANDONIONSALLINASESAMESEED-BUN' describes perhaps the most remarkable food phenomenon of our time. In common parlance, you know it as the Big Mac.

My assignment: to probe the very essence of its being, and discover its secret. What goes into it? Why do millions buy it? Why do many of the millions actually eat it?

The final challenge: to recreate in an ordinary kitchen, using no industrial machinery of any kind, the precise taste and texture, and unique appearance, of the McDonald's Big Mac.

There are a number of ways of looking at a Big Mac. (With an oblique sideways glance from a distance of at least ten feet has always been my personal favourite.) But never being one to resist the easy option, I decided to ring McDonald's and ask them straight, 'How do you make a Big Mac?'

'Why do you want to know?' replied the head of PR for McDonald's UK, displaying her verbal fencing skills.

'Well, I'm a freelance food journalist and I want to do a piece on how to make a Big Mac in your own kitchen.'

'Where's the interest in that?'

'I think it would be interesting to see if it could be done.'

'So, what exactly do you want to know?'

'Well, anything. Quantities of ingredients, preparation procedures, cooking times. Everything really. To start with, what are the exact dimensions and weight of the uncooked patties in a Big Mac?'

'I can't tell you that…we won't give that sort of information…we don't get involved in this sort of thing…' and, with a final flourish, 'What I am saying here is that I'm afraid your request falls into the category of being of the kind that we are unable to assist.' Apparently, what she was saying there was that she was afraid that my request fell into the category of being of the kind that they were unable to assist. She had, however, in the course of our conversation, alluded to certain factsheets, available in all the branches of McDonald's, which might tell me more of the things I wanted to know.

In the Chiswick High Road branch of McDonald's I found no such sources of information. 'You mean McFact Cards? We ran out of them weeks ago.' My disappointment was partially offset when I was given an invitation to McHappy Day – until I noticed the date on the invitation: McHappy Day had been and gone, three days earlier.

I finally tracked down some McFact Cards, but they did not exactly tell me how to make a Big Mac. McFact Card No. 1 informed me that 'Nowhere in the world does McDonald's use of beef threaten or remotely involve the Tropical Rainforests.' McFact Card No. 2 reassured me that McDonald's packaging is ozone-friendly. Finally McFact Card No. 3 insisted that 'ONLY prime cuts of lean forequarter and flank are used for our 100% pure beef hamburgers.' Here, at least, was some information I could use.

However, there was something about the way McDonald's were putting themselves across that was beginning to get me down. It was all in that little word *Mc*. McFact, McHappy, McNugget; what the McBloody Hell did it mean? What is a McFact, anyway? Clearly not the same thing at all as an ordinary fact. With this disturbing thought in mind, I decided a more scientific approach was called for.

The next day at 0900 hours precisely, I visited a McDonald's drive-in, the exact location of which I am unable to reveal. Suffice it to say that this particular establishment is situated not half-a-mile away from an independent food analysis consultancy, whose identity – for reasons of professional etiquette – must also remain secret.

At the drive-in I pulled up, as instructed by the notices, next to a metal grille, which broke the ice by addressing me thus: 'Good morning, we would like to welcome you to McDonald's drive-in.' 'Go on, then,' I thought. But the voice simply asked me for my order. 'Three Big Macs please.'

'Thank you. Please drive to the first window. Enjoy your meal, and have a nice day.'

I paid at the first window, drove to the second, where a spotty youth explained, 'Your Big Macs are just being prepared, Sir. There'll be a slight delay of a minute-and-a-half.' I received my parcel 86 seconds later.

At 0914 I was handing over my purchase to a man in a white coat. 'They don't smell very nice, do they?' he said, as he removed the first Big Mac from its ozone-friendly container. (This struck me as being a rather unscientific observation, but it was pleasing to have an official confirmation of my own amateur opinion.) The first Big Mac was to be analysed for nutritional content; the components of the second were to be individually weighed to give me my exact recipe; the third was for my breakfast.

My friend in the white coat began the analysis by placing an entire Big Mac into a Magimix, and flicking the switch. In a surprisingly short time, the item was transformed into a smooth and even purée. This substance was remarkably similar in colour, but perhaps marginally thicker in consistency, to a McDonald's chocolate milkshake. Hey McPresto – a Big Mac Shake.

Once the state of the Big Mac had been so radically altered, everything became impressively scientific. Small blobs of the purée were carefully weighed, and placed in test-tubes. While one such blob was being mixed with sand, I enquired as to its ultimate fate. 'We burn it overnight at a temperature of 550°C. This gives us the ash content.'

'I should think it does,' I said.

Another blob was to be broken down in a 'Kjeldetherm digester'. A third piece of purée would spend the afternoon inside a hydrolytic thimble, followed by a whole night in a Soxhlit ▶

PHOTOGRAPHS: JAN ABRAMS

MAC ATTACK

Galloping Hugh shapes the meat after (top) assembling the Big Mac imitation kit. Remember: sharp knives cut fingers

▶extractor. Oh, the wonders of modern science.

As all these exciting events were taking place, I turned my attention to the third Big Mac. I had rather lost my appetite. Nevertheless, I felt a tasting at this stage was important, for the sake of experimental propriety. I duly took a (not insubstantial) bite. My teeth fell easily through the layers, apparently untroubled by resistance from any meat-like substance. I was grateful for a small piece of gherkin which got stuck in my teeth. It actually tasted of something.

The following day I received the results of the analysis. A note at the beginning informed me that 'The values obtained were, nutritionally, as expected for this type of product, viz a good selection of meat cereal and vegetable protein which could provide the essential Amino acids required for growth.' Surely all those horrendous processes to which my Big Mac had been subjected would reveal something more controversial than this? I was consoled by the results of the itemised weighing. At least I now know that a Big Mac comprises 79.4g of bun, 63.6g of beefburgers, 13.2g of cheese, 34.1g of relish and shredded lettuce (a note explained the two were inseparable) and 6.2g of gherkin. It was time to go shopping.

THE SHOPPING

First stop, the butcher's, in search of beef-related substances for the patty. In the absence of hard evidence to the contrary, I decided to accept McDonald's specification of 'only prime cuts of lean forequarter and flank.' The butcher had an interesting alternative nomenclature:

'Forequarter? Well, we call it "chuck".'

'Sounds encouraging. I'm looking for about a 20 per cent fat content overall.'

'You'll get that with your flank – that's to say, ribs. Very fatty.'

The sundry garnishes, so vital to the final product, might have eluded a less resourceful shopper. Your average processed cheese squares in your average high street supermarket are sadly lacking that science-fiction fluorescent orange glow that characterises the Big Mac curd factor. I finally tracked down a close approximation in a tiny 24-hour grocer's in the Uxbridge Road. My selection was based on colour-match alone, on the grounds that if the artificial colouring was correct, the artificial taste would naturally (or unnaturally) follow.

I had to visit five delicatessens before I found gherkins of adequate dimensions, ie not less that 2.5cm in diameter. For the special sauce I purchased two different types of mayonnaise, two of salad cream, an inferior brand of tomato ketchup, and a small carton of UHT long-life milk, which I felt might be an appropriate thin-ner. I chose a good firm onion, and a crisp fresh iceberg lettuce, bearing in mind that it was not their initial state, but the processes to which I would later subject them, that would determine their suitability for inclusion in the end product.

The final shopping challenge was the bun. A particularly tough one to imitate, since McDonald's buns have not two tiers but three, and a distribution of sesame seeds so regular, so mathematical, that I can only imagine they employ cheap foreign labour to stick them on one by one, by hand. Or perhaps, robots. I eventually plumped for Safeway's 'sesame seeded burger buns' whose sesame pattern and density was relatively uniform, and whose size and colour seemed an excellent match.

Back in my kitchen, I began the patty-simulation phase. This meant throwing my meat into the Magimix and flicking the switch. I watched, transfixed, as the rough hunks of meat slowly transformed, via an intermediate stage of white and rose, into a homogeneous paste of pale coral pink. At this point I formed a little of the mixture into a sort of proto-patty, for a taste test. The resulting mini-burger was disappointing in two important ways: too much texture, and too much taste.

I returned my mincemeat to the Magimix and gave it another two minutes. In the resulting patty I felt I had achieved a close approximation to the original in terms of texture but I still had an excess of flavour on my hands. How do they do it? I wondered. Perhaps McDonald's buy their meat from Bovril, after the beefy flavour has been extracted. I could only hope that 24 hours at minus 16°C would help to chill out some of the remaining flavour.

Although the patty dimensions, cooking procedure and precise recipe for a Big Mac are proprietary information, I had managed to discover, by talking in a childlike manner to a junior member of the McDonald's PR staff, that the precooked weight of each patty was precisely 1.6 oz. For those of you at home who lack accurate weighing equipment, it is worth noting that this amount of minced beef will fit very neatly into a standard-size matchbox. As you might imagine, a matchbox of mince spread over an area the size of a burger bun comes out pretty thin. Four mm thin, to be precise.

The final dimensions of my hand-moulded imitation Big Mac patties can therefore be revealed (with apologies for mixture of imperial and metric measurements):

Diameter: 11cm (allowing for a 10 per cent shrinkage factor)

Thickness: 4mm

Weight: 1.6 oz *(See p. 40 for results)*

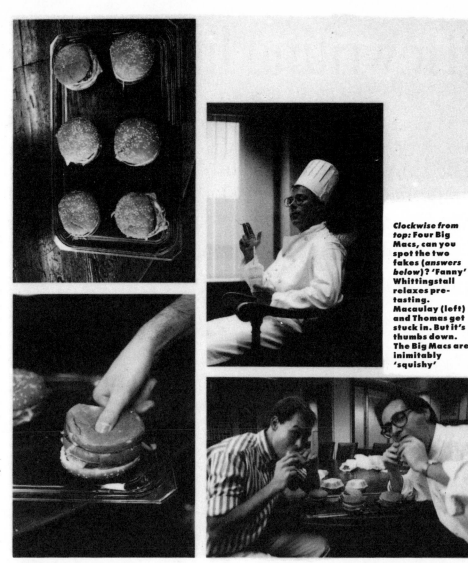

The following is your very own easy-to-follow-cut-out-and-keep-step-by-step *Punch guide to cooking a Big Mac at home.*

Components

1) The Bun: take your chosen brand of bun and slice it carefully in half. Take a second bun and slice off the top and the bottom, leaving a crustless segment about 8mm in thickness. This will serve as your middle tier. Toast both sides of this tier, and the insides only of the top and bottom tiers, lightly under a hot grill.

2) The Patties: cook your patties from frozen under a maximum hot grill for two minutes on the first side and a minute on the second. You should be aiming for a uniform dark grey/brown colour, both inside and out.

3) The Onions: these should be chopped as finely as possible, approx 1mm x 2mm, and steamed or boiled for at least 15 minutes. They may be kept warm indefinitely.

4) The Lettuce: chop this into shreds of about 3mm in width and 2cm in length. Don't be alarmed if the shredded lettuce is still crisp and crunchy at the time of burger assembly. The heat and moisture of the other ingredients should rapidly achieve the customary degree of flaccidity.

5) The Special Sauce: mix the mayonnaise, UHT milk and ketchup in a 3:2:1 teaspoonsful ratio.

6) The Pickle: you will need two slices of a large gherkin, approximately 1.5mm thick.

7) The Cheese: unwrap one 10cm x 10cm square of processed cheese, ensuring it is the correct Day-Glo orange.

Assembly

1) On the bottom layer of toasted bun, scatter a sprinkling of lettuce, a level teaspoon of onions, and a dab of sauce.

2) On top of this, place your cheese square, making sure the four corners peek cheekily over the side of the bun.

3) Place one hot patty on to the cheese, and press lightly, thereby gently encouraging the cheese to melt.

4) Arrange the middle tier carefully over the first patty and repeat stage 1.

5) Add the two slices of gherkin to this pile, and then mount the second patty on top.

6) Crown lovingly with the bun-cap.

7) The burger should be wrapped tightly in paper and left to 'settle' in a warm tray for at least an hour. (NB This final stage is crucial for authentic results. The ingredients have to coalesce. Subsidence is the key.)

Clockwise from top: Four Big Macs, can you spot the two fakes (answers below)? 'Fanny' Whittingstall relaxes pre-tasting. Macaulay (left) and Thomas get stuck in. But it's thumbs down. The Big Macs are inimitably 'squishy'

THE McTASTE TEST

The two-man tasting team that gathered around the famous Punch Table consisted of David Thomas, Editor of *Punch*, and Sean Macaulay, the magazine's lovelorn restaurant critic. Both men were fast food devotees and felt confident that they could distinguish the real McCoy from the McPhoneys.

The two home-made Macs were placed on a tray on which four genuine articles had also been placed. The imitations were remarkably lifelike, but, even so, were soon spotted by the eagle-eyed testers. The give-away was the distribution of sesame seeds; nothing can quite equal the precision with which the Big Mac's seeds are spread around the bun.

On biting into the burgers, Macaulay came over all pretentious: 'The imitation is like a chord – you can taste all the different notes, but they harmonise well together. The real Big Mac is just one great splurge. You can't de-structure it in terms of taste. You can't say, "Oh, there's the cheesy bit".'

For Thomas, the differences were tactile. 'The fake is too solid. I can feel the flour on the bun. There's too much to bite into. A real Big Mac is squishy. If you put your thumb on the bottom it sinks into the bun. If you take your thumb away, the bun reseals itself. The fake is too real, if you see what I mean. It's a real bun.'

Tastewise, the fake came out way ahead. It was a genuinely delicious burger. Having said that, however, both testers admitted that there was something about the acrid, pickle-y tang of a Mac Big Mac that was, well, McAddictive. There was one other crucial difference: the fake did not produce an afternoon's worth of McFlatulence. ∎

The Big Mac aftermath. The two fakes are top left and bottom right. The sesame seeds give them away

Rewriting literature, the Prince Charles way!

The Prince of Wales recently rewrote Hamlet's soliloquy in magnificently shoddy modern English. We were so impressed, we did the same to some more classic quotations. The new versions are printed below. But what were the originals?

THE MODERN CLASSICS...

1) It stands to reason. If a bloke's got a few bob and he's still not hitched, he's bound to be wanting a missus.

2) At this moment in time, the cold front which has been causing stress and depression is giving way to prolonged sunny spells thanks to Prince Andrew's favourite newspaper.

3) Was anyone naffed off? The squaddies were clued up, some berk had cocked it. Wasn't down to them to argue. They couldn't be bothered to work it out. They just had to get on with the job and snuff it. They went down the Valley on their bikes. About 600 of 'em.

4) The project began as an essentially ground-up construction. It was a greenfield site and visibility was far from satisfactory, as a result of which a number of memos were sent down from the top floor. The Chairman wanted instant action on the lighting front and he got it.

5) The acquisition of single-parent family status, Mr Worthing, may categorise you as a deprived child; complete de-parentage appears to constitute wilful self-neglect.

6) Globally-speaking, we're in a theatre situation.

7) If you make a pony every year and you spend twenty-four, ninety-five pee, you're well chuffed. But if you make a pony and you spend pony-and-a-half, you're gutted.

8) I walked about a bit on my own. Then I went to the garden centre.

THE ORIGINALS

1) It is a truth universally acknowledged, that a single man in possession of a good fortune must be in want of a wife. *Jane Austen – Pride and Prejudice*

2) Now is the winter of our discontent made glorious summer by this sun of York. *William Shakespeare – Richard III*

3) Was there a man dismayed?/Not tho' the soldier knew/Some one had blundered:/Their's not to make reply,/There's not to reason why,/Their's but to do and die:/Into the valley of Death/Rode the six hundred. *Tennyson – The Charge of the Light Brigade*

4) In the beginning God created the heaven and the earth. And the earth was without form, and void; and darkness was on the face of the deep. And the Spirit of God moved upon the face of the waters. And God said, let there be light: and there was light. *The Bible*

5) To lose one parent, Mr Worthing, may be regarded as a misfortune; to lose both looks like carelessness. *Oscar Wilde – The Importance of Being Earnest*

6) All the world's a stage. *William Shakespeare – As You Like It.*

7) Annual income twenty pounds, annual expenditure nineteen nineteen six, result happiness. Annual income twenty pounds, annual expenditure twenty pounds ought and six, result misery. *Charles Dickens – David Copperfield.* (We allowed for inflation.)

8) I wandered lonely as a cloud/That floats on high o'er vales and hills,/When all at once I saw a crowd,/A host of golden daffodils. *Wordsworth*

hey lighten up... come on... I'm up for that... Do me a favour Didn't you get my EM? Give me a bell.. Let's rap.. crucial Go for it... more than my job's worth.. You're dead meat.. Who you kidding... Your round.. Get them in... Cool it... You know.. No problem..

chapter

7

THE CRITICS

Song of ages

BILL MATTHEWS unearths an unsung historical source – the pop lyric

In the times before paper, history was passed on through songs sung round the fireside. It is only now that people are realising that the most reliable means of passing on history has not changed, even if the fireside has been replaced by a Bang and Olufsen. It is to the popular song that we must look to find out about our shared past.

Let us take the American War Of Independence as our first example. For two hundred years historians pondered the true consequences of the Boston Tea Party on the USA and Great Britain – the independence of the former colony leading to its emergence as a superpower and the concomitant decline of its oppressor. Yet it took The Alex Harvey Band to pinpoint the most far-reaching effects:

*The King says he's gonna put a tax on tea
And that's the reason y'all Americans drink coffee.*

They go on to pose a question that has puzzled, baffled and perplexed those same historians:

*Are you going to the party
Going to the Boston Tea Party?*

It is a question that may never be answered.

Harvey is not the only British historian to place a new and important perspective on American history. Nicky Chinn and Mike Chapman in their well-researched opus, 'Wig-Wam Bam', have revolutionised contemporary thinking about the Ojibway Indian legend, Hiawatha. It took the bespandexed Seventies popsters Sweet to carry the message forth to a grateful public hungry for knowledge.

Hiawatha didn't bother too much
About Minnie Ha Ha and her tender touch,
Till she took him to the silver stream
There she whispered words like he'd never heard
That made him all shudder inside.

And what were those words that perhaps changed the course of North American history? We now know.

Wig Wam Bam, gonna make you my man
Wig Wam Bam, gonna get you if I can.

If any sceptics should doubt Chinn and Chapman's definitive study, surely the authenticity of 'Wam bam bam bam sham a lam' removes any misgivings.

No historians before Chinn and Chapman satisfactorily explained why Alexander Graham Bell invented the telephone? Why on earth did he bother? In their biography, 'Alexander Graham Bell', they give an early clue to the unlocking of the connunication mystery:

Two thousand miles away she waits there
A young man thinking by a window
How would she know how much he cared?

He could write her a letter. Or send a telegram. Or blame it on the pony express. But this wasn't good enough for someone like A. G. Bell. The scene is set:

The sun rises early in the morning
Millions of people still unaware
What would be discovered without warning
So he could show a girl just how much he cared.

This is a motive for invention previously, and scandalously, ignored by historians. Why did it take until 1971 for the true facts to come out? Chinn and Chapman set the record straight once and for all:

Alexander Graham Bell,
Well he knew darn well
That he could find the only way
To talk across the USA
Telephone, telephone
Never be on your own
Many many years ago, he started something
With his first hello – hello.

It is on the subject of war that songs have filled a gap left by the inadequacies of scholars. As such a noted authority as Edwin Starr has pointed out:

War – hoo! – wo wo wo – what is it good for?
Absolutely nothing. Say it again.

The writings of Paper Lace reveal what few historians dare to show: the human face of suffering. Certainly, the members of 'the Lace' displayed a firm grasp of the requirements of Seventies academic life – horrendous flares, virulent tweeds and long dark hair dangling over bugger's grips. As social historians they are unsurpassed. 'Billy Don't Be A Hero' movingly evokes the dilemmas of war. Should you 'keep your pretty head low' or allow it to be blown to bits? In the end, Billy's 'young and lovely fiancée' learns of his death. Curiously, the cry of anguish sounded by the authors seems less for the wasteful destruction of human life than ▶

Above: Boney M from boa war to Rasputin. Below: Stubble-chinned tunesmith Mike Chapman, the pen behind 'Wig-wam Bam'

for the wasteful destruction of primary historical sources:

The letter said that he was a hero
She should be proud he died that way
I heard she threw the letter away.

Paper Lace's seminal 'The Night Chicago Died' displays painstaking attention to detail…

Back in the USA,
Back in the bad old days.
In the heat of the summer night,
In the land of the dollar bill
When the town of Chicago died,
And they talk about it still,
When a man named Al Capone
Tried to make that town his own.

…combined with shrewd, in-depth analysis…

Brother what a night it really was
Brother what a fight it really was

Joan of Arc sought to rid France of the English until she was betrayed by the Burgundians. Petty detail when seen against Orchestral Manoeuvres In The Dark's controversial and very personal study of her life and death:

She should have known better than to give her heart,
She should have known better than to ever part without me.
I gave her everything that I ever owned
I think she understood though she never spoke.

Unfortunately, they are unable to back up the claims that they were present 550 years ago with any documentary evidence. But they do proffer an interesting potential solution to her plight as she lay burning on the cross:

Listen Joan of Arc, all you gotta do,
Is say the right words
And I'll be coming through
Hold you in my arms and take you right away.

If those right words had occurred to Joan before she got burned to a cinder, how different might history have been.

War between people as well as war between nations is the concern of B. A. Robertson's wide-ranging and strongly-argued 'Bang Bang', based around the theme, 'Bang bang the mighty fall, bang bang when lovers call.' He uses as evidence the volatile affair of Lord Nelson and Lady Hamilton, and Cleopatra's dalliance with both Mark Anthony and Julius Caesar:

But Caesar had squeezed her in Rome
On his quilt for a day – hey hey
Now Anthony got really angry
About old Caesar's hanky panky.

But it is in his account of the relationship between Samson and Delilah that he leaves other historians standing.

When the temples started to crumble
Sammy for his comb did fumble
Life was in a ruin
She loved Johnny Frewin
Fell in love and threw him away.

The question is begging. Who *is* Johnny Frewin? And why has no mention been made of him before? One might suspect a conspiracy of conventional historians, plotting round the fireside to keep Frewin out of the history books, until one realises that only a historian of Robertson's calibre could uncover such facts.

Our final example of the reliability of the sung word over the printed word comes from the masters of the genre (Boney M). They begin their master work – with a quiz.

There lived a certain man in Russia long ago,
He was big and strong and his eyes would plainly glow…

Who could it possibly be? Tolstoy? Gogol? Czar Nicholas I? Catherine the Great, perhaps. They go on:

Lurex-clad recording artists Sweet, their song challenged the traditional interpretation of the Hiawatha legend

Most people look at him with terror and with fear.
But to Moscow chiefs he was such a lovely dear.

There are still a few million to choose from. But when we are finally told, we learn much more than the man's name.

Ra-ra-Rasputin – lover of the Russian Queen
There was a cat that really was gone
Ra-ra-Rasputin, Russia's greatest love machine,
It was a shame how he carried on.

Oh, the judgment of history! Tell us the story, tell us the story!

In all affairs of state, he was the man to please
But he was real brave when he had a girl to squeeze…
Hey hey hey hey hey hey hey hey hey hey hey
The man's just got to go, declared his enemies
But the ladies begged, don't you try to do it please.

The tale is told with startling economy. 'Some men of higher standing' sent him an invitation, 'and he really came'.

Ra-ra-Rasputin – lover of the Russian Queen
They put some poison into his wine
Ra-ra-Rasputin, Russia's greatest love machine,
He drank it all and said, 'I feel fine'
Ra-ra-Rasputin – lover of the Russian Queen
(a useful reminder in case we'd forgotten)
They didn't quit, they wanted his head
Ra-ra-Rasputin, Russia's greatest love machine,
And so they shot him till he was dead.

The final judgment, in three pregnant words, comes fittingly, at the end: 'Oh those Russians!'

One more question perhaps needs to be asked, and even answered. When one can learn more facts and get clearer analysis from a 3½-minute pop song about Rasputin, is there anyone who would prefer to read a 1,500-page book on the subject than listen to a record by Boney M? Or, more pertinently, is there anyone who wouldn't? ■

Bill Matthews' last article for Punch *was an in-depth technical study of pop producers Stock Aitken Waterman.*

Watership down under

DILYS POWELL on a rabbity tale from Australia

Trailing clouds of glory: isn't it about time for a return to Wordsworth's reverence for the angelic beginnings of the human child? **Celia** is welcome. It comes from Australia; it is the first feature film by Ann Turner, who both wrote and directed. It has been spoken of as a tale of innocence corrupted, but look again at the young creatures on the screen, children from the suburbs of Melbourne in the Fifties. Are they corrupted? You might say they begin as potential murderers.

Deep down the film has political significance; for the cinema audience, though, the psychology of the child is more obvious. Celia, rightly played without sweetness by 12-year-old Rebecca Smart, is nine; she has a pet rabbit. It is the period of an attempt to wipe out the rabbit, which once threatened Australia's agriculture, by the controlled introduction of myxomatosis. In Melbourne, it seems, pet rabbits were officially rounded up and taken to the zoo; later, under pressure, the scheme was dropped, and Celia in the film is among the owners who search vainly for their beloved animals.

One can sympathise with her devotion to her pet Murgatroyd; one can also feel thankful for the reassurance given that her rabbit was not hurt in the making of the story. But while defending this plump creature, she collects enemies. The policeman becomes an enemy, so does her father. She resorts to traditional black magic; she sticks pins into dolls which represent the enemy. On the screen she trails no clouds of glory, nor does the yelling gang of young boys and girls she leads in the countryside. Directing, Ann Turner apparently sees their actions, like the society in which they live, as bearing political significance; Celia thus becomes a justified activist. Perhaps she is.

But essentially *Celia* is a study of children faced with adult behaviour which to them can be inexplicable. This is really a film about failure in communication; and that is something which all children experience at some time or other. Miss Turner has tackled a difficult and important subject.

With **Weekend At Bernie's** we are back with Keystone Kops farce. Not that the film, directed by Ted Kotcheff, looks like it at first, it is later that you find the lunacy of chase which was so popular in the Mack Sennett days during the First World War. Action opens in the streets of New York, where two young employees of an insurance company set out for a day's quiet work in the office. They are played by Andrew McCarthy and Jonathan Silverman; they think they have discovered errors in a policy. They congratulate themselves, they hope for advancement, they hasten to inform their boss (brilliantly played by Terry Kiser). Their discovery is well founded. But they are reporting their triumph to the wrong quarters, for their boss knows all about the error. He has been making a good thing out of the company; he has been using the proceeds of his fraud to run a Long Island beach house. He asks the two young men to a Labour Day weekend there: ostensibly the invitation is a reward for vigilance. Actually the cautious Bernie intends to have the two of them killed by the Mafia.

But the Mafia have their own plans; they are tired of Bernie, and when the young men arrive for their weekend they find a dead body. Panic stricken, they think they will be accused of the murder; they pretend that the dead man is still alive and trundle the corpse throughout the festive crowd and drag it up and down the beach-house stairs. Then they learn the truth and recognise their own immediate danger; struggling to get rid of the body, they throw it overboard, and take off on a nightmare speed-boat trip. But their dead boss pursues them; and Terry Kiser is an actor good enough to make one sometimes forget the less palatable elements of black farce. He is almost as entertaining dead as alive.

I have to admit that I never enjoyed the Keystone Kops, and if it weren't for Mr Kiser *Weekend At Bernie's* would leave me as cold. Andrew McCarthy and Jonathan Silverman strike me as gifted, but they are given only one joke to play. The screenplay is by Robert Klane, who wrote an old favourite of mine, *Where's Poppy?*; but despite ingenious variations the dependence on corpse-comedy makes the piece tedious. Perhaps we ought to be thankful for promising players who are not over-familiar on British screens, and leave it at that.

There is a second film from Australia this week: **Encounter at Raven's Gate**, unlike *Celia*, is not much bothered with psychology. It is an encounter with special effects. Two investigators turn up at a house, or what is left of it, to make enquiries; one is a police sergeant, the other from the Special Branch; in cinema style they greet one another with firearms before they settle down to the job. A married pair used to live in the house, the farm-owner (Ritchie Singer) and his wife (Celine Griffin); they are joined by the farmer's younger brother (Steven Vidley) who is just out of prison on parole. The two men don't get on all that well, but the wife welcomes the newcomer and you can see why. Anyway it is the house which holds attention. That night it begins to flash and roar; everybody is affected, even the amiable dog, who bites one of the brothers. Walls crash on the cast, bodies fly; there is somebody saying helpfully that a spirit or poltergeist is around. I have failed to identify the spirit, but I am happy to name the directors of special effects, Jon Armstrong and Sue Richter. The general absurdity is directed by Rolf de Heer, who shared the writing of the screenplay with Marc Rosenberg. ∎

Snap judgement

ALISON BECKETT on an exhibition of photo-journalism

This is not for the squeamish. **In Our Time: The World as Seen by Magnum Photographers,** which opens at the Hayward Gallery this Thursday (8 March), is a catalogue of the great events of the past 50 years. But since bad is usually more newsworthy than good, the majority of the 300 or so shots are of death, deprivation, hardship and suffering. Even the occasional wedding photograph portrays the bride as victim.

Magnum, of course, is the photo-journalistic agency par excellence, the sort of elitist group of highly motivated, temperamental individuals that other photographers sneer at until asked to join. The tone was set by the four photographers who founded Magnum as a collective in 1947. All were war veterans. Robert – if the shot's no good, you're not near enough – Capa had begun dodging bullets in the Spanish Civil War; George Rodger had trekked hundreds of miles evading Japanese pursuers in Burma; Henri Cartier-Bresson, imprisoned by the Germans, had escaped to join the French Resistance; and Chim (David Seymour), having lost his parents to the Nazis, had received a medal for his work for US intelligence.

The aim of Magnum was to flout conventional journalistic practice of the day by insisting photographers retained the right to their own snaps, by curbing scissor-happy picture editors and by allowing photographers to devise their own projects instead of shooting images to fit someone else's story. Freedom of choice led to such notable whims as Burt Glinn's portrait of Nikita Krushchev in Washington in 1959, taken from behind as the Soviet leader faced the Lincoln Memorial. The other snappers there depicted Krushchev and Glinn.

Intuition, originality and energy were what Magnum demanded. Bruce Davidson's shots of the people of East Harlem, taken as if he were photographing gentry, are a prime example. So are Sebastião Salgado's pictures of the goldminers working like ants in Brazil; Jean Gaumy's black-cloaked Iranian women learning to shoot; and Chris Steele-Perkins' Uganda famine snaps. All he needed show were the legs. Any Magnum photographer who cannot mobilise opinion with his lens has failed.

Is Magnum's success all down to idealism? Well, not entirely, since its birth was timely – just as a host of picture magazines were starting up. Thanks to war experience, its first members had a remarkable number of languages and contacts between them; and Capa, the group's mainstay, reputedly had a nose for news 'like a truffle-hound' as well as an uncanny ability to be in the right place at the right time with the right people, drinking.

Capa's own most renowned snap of a Loyalist soldier in Spain depicted in the moment of death has since been called into question as a likely set-up. So much for his discourses on photographs as 'concentrated truths', one might say. Yet idealistically he could argue that the end justified the means. After all, one of the most famous portraits of Winston Churchill with defiant expression against Hitler was nothing to do with heroism. The grim expression was created by the photographer's surprise tactic of yanking the prime minister's cigar from between his teeth.

The dramatic effect of the Magnum shots is generally the greater for being in black and white, be it the nightmarish view inside a single women's centre in New York, a rain-sodden James Dean snapped without umbrella or a photograph of rather cannier Welsh sheep sheltering from a storm on an artillery range. Yet on occasion the use of colour is unsurpassable, not least with Michael Nichols' portrait of a Hutaboy in Rwanda.

Is it really art, though, if the purpose is mainly journalism or picture books? Is a portrait as good if it took a fraction of a second instead of months? On the whole, no. But Magnum is the exception which proves the rule, with most photographs worth a second, third and tenth look. ∎

'Face it, Dürer, nobody's going to believe us.'

Fifteen ounces

RHODA KOENIG finds Dustin Hoffman's Shylock too small

Clad in scruffy black, Dustin Hoffman's scrawny Shylock mutters and grumbles his way through the streets of Venice, a perambulating spitoon for any velvet-robed Christians who want to relieve themselves of phlegm and contempt. In the trial scene, the hated merchant in his power, Shylock returns the favour: wetting his knife and slapping it on his shoe, he tears Antonio's shirt from his back and spits full in his face, ready to carve out his pound of flesh.

Peter Hall's **Merchant of Venice** will not please professional guardians of niceness, but he is to be commended for not shirking the ugly aspects of the play. Visually, though, this *Merchant* is as handsome as its characters are reprehensible. Chris Dyer's set takes us from Venice to Belmont and back again in a twinkling, as the back wall of his colonnade dissolves into blue sky and returns to stone. Leigh Lawson's dark good looks lend authority to his mordant Antonio; the pretty Francesca Buller gives a warm, fluid portrayal of Jessica; and Nathaniel Parker is a sweet-natured, ingenuous, and decidedly fanciable Bassanio. Geraldine James's well-bred beauty makes her an elegant Portia, but she is

also a rather cold and skittish one – when she enters, complaining of weariness, one thinks, "Well, no wonder, if she's always throwing herself about".

Coldness – along with constriction – figures, as well, in Hoffman's Shylock. Asking, "Hath not a Jew eyes?" he does not thunder or extend a pleading hand to the two Venetians who have earlier ridiculed the accent of "the dog Jew". (Hoffman's tones do sound a good deal less reminiscent of the Mediterranean than of

Shylock does not seem so much tormented as crabby and grey

Atlantic Avenue.) Instead, he hugs his sides and sourly confirms his logic for loathing Christians, rather than waste his breath in an appeal. When the trial goes against him, he does not disintegrate in anguish but quietly submits, using his last reserves of strength to stop himself bawling before a hostile crowd that, as he leaves, surrounds him in a sickening little rush. Hoffman's performance is admirable in its refusal to beg for our sympathy – it's the collaborators in anti-semitism who ask for charity

rather than justice – but his stoniness cuts off our empathy as well. He does not seem so much tormented as crabby and grey, and we don't feel outraged, merely sad at his downfall, which is too low-key to impinge on the following scenes of moonlit Christian bliss.

Hall's treatment of some other characters is questionable at best. The Prince of Morocco is accompanied by some hokey pageantry (veiled, masked women bear Portia's caskets, and drums go boom-ba-ba-boom as he reads the scroll). The ancient, blind Gobbo rushes headlong into walls, repeatedly knocking himself out for the count. This may be historical comedy, but Shakespeare's treatment of the old and helpless is usually more humane. In any event, it got shrieks of laughter – as did, I was appalled to hear, the pathetic capering of a deaf and backward girl in *The Debutante Ball* the week before. In the face of behaviour that is so – as the short-sighted cliché has it – un-Christian, perhaps Hall's reading is the right one after all for our interesting times.

Paul Unwin's stylish **Misanthrope** (in Tony Harrison's brisk, racy translation) arrives soon after the RSC's *Plain Dealer*, another comedy about an ostentatiously honest man tripped up by his love for an unprincipled flirt. The play's trouble – damaging, but hardly critical – is in its leads. Edward Petherbridge zips through his lines in a manner that sacrifices passion to a simulation of intellectual brilliance and denies us the pathos that should underlie our amusement at his skirmishes with the society hypocrites. Sian Thomas is an overly theatrical Célimène, with showy gestures and eyebrows that creep into an inverted V suggesting aggrieved petulance rather than coquetry.

The other guests at this snazzy Gaullist-era soirée could hardly look or act better. As the reasonable, modest Philinte and Eliante, David Horovitch and Ingrid Craigie perfectly embody the immense charm of the second-rate. Donald Pickering, a rigid, handsome brute who has been speaking verse for 40 years and knows it, is a marvellous, orotund Oronte. Sheila Ballantine scrupulously resists the temptation to make herself sympathetic as the magisterially disingenuous Arsinoé. Seeing this brilliantly contemporary play and its English cousin (written ten years later) makes us consider afresh the questions they pose. Is criticism jealousy? Is virtue self-absorption? Does one love men more by loving what they might be, or loving them as they are, "monkeys in the zoo/doing what monkeys are supposed to do"? And is it better to be a fool among fools, or a fool alone? ■

THE MERCHANT OF VENICE –
PETER-HUGO DALY *as Lancelot Gobbo*
DUSTIN HOFFMAN *as Shylock*
GERALDINE JAMES *as Portia*

On the folk wagon

RICHARD COOK says hippy days are here again

"I whistle a happy tune," said Oscar Hammerstein. Maybe that's all there is to writing a good song. It's the worst kind of fogeydom to compare current pop tunesmiths with their Tin Pan Alley forebears, though. Not *everything* Gershwin and Kern and Porter (and Oscar) wrote was deathless stuff. George and Ira might have written 'Someone To Watch Over Me', but they also composed 'Blah Blah Blah', which doesn't have much of a track record on *Your Hundred Best Tunes*. What clapometer should we use for singer-songwriters who are too young to remember much, if anything, of the Sixties, even?

It was piquant timing to find the sombre young goddess of this scene, Tanita Tikaram, being followed onto London boards recently by Bob Dylan. Tikaram did three nights at Drury Lane, Dylan one at Wembley, but the choices of venue are misleading: she is selling many more records than the grouchy spokesman (retd) does these days. But Tikaram has pledged allegiance to the crusty old dignitaries of Dylan's generation in preference to most of her contemporaries. Maybe the haircuts in their audiences aren't so different after all.

Tanita has taken such an awful battering in the press of late that it's tempting to be a little chivalrous on her behalf. One waggish piece propped her up as the protest singer on behalf of young things who worry more about their mortgage repayments than the decline of the West. Pardon me, but hasn't it always been so? When the times they were a-changing, how many Dylanites actually took up the cudgels on behalf of, er, whatever it was he was on about? Maybe Tikaram's plight is that she hasn't yet got around to inventing a private language of metaphor that can be read either as orders to march on the palace or the ramblings of an eccentric strummer with a *Collected Blake* in the jacket pocket.

Ancient Heart (WEA), Tikaram's debut album, has racked up pretty vast sales all over the place, and she's recently returned from an American tour. If someone played you the record for the first time, you'd probably wonder what all the fuss is about. Tikaram sings with the good grace of someone accepting third prize in a school flower show, and the songs have a toffee-nosed sensitivity about them. What turns the trick is her very smart ear for what will work as a melody. 'Twist In My Sobriety' is a title even Bob Dylan would have struggled to work up, yet Tikaram's slinky, chilling delivery of the song makes it repeat in the mind. Aloof and unsmiling – I once saw Anne Diamond try and fail to jolly her along – Tikaram may yet do great things.

Bob Dylan must have stopped worrying about whether he does great things or not long ago. I can't say I've bothered to keep up with him these past few years. Actually, I don't know anyone who has. Try naming his last three albums. Give up? So did Bob, around the time of *Blood On The Tracks*, perhaps. And *that* was fifteen years ago. All right, he did some amusing tunes on the *Traveling Wilburys* LP last year, but it's hard to raise a cheer over that when we're considering the man who wrote something as beautiful and wasteless as '4th Time Around'. If that's the standard we're using, then Tanita Tikaram is as remote from Bob Dylan as she is from the nation's beloved Kylie Minogue. Remember, though, that Bob also started out with a routine set of old folk songs.

It's not the singleton acts that are running the song trade. I listened to the new record by The Feelies, *Only Life* (A&M), without much expectation. Wasn't this another has-been American new wave band from ten years back? But their patient, fatalistic music seems like more of a tonic each time I play it. Their tunes are grown out of very small ideas, and titles like these will give you the idea – 'Too Much', 'Away', 'For Awhile'. Each is played, folded, filed away. None of this appears to be the result of hours of pen-chewing. The Feelies use songwriting as a bridge into performance. Hand me that guitar – I think I feel a stanza coming on. ∎

Try naming Dylan's last three albums. Give up? So did Bob, around the time of *Blood On The Tracks*

WITH St**I**N**G** IN THE JUNGLE....

"Hark! I thought I heard distant applause."

High concepts

SEAN MACAULAY visits post-modern eateries Tall Orders and Bar Madrid

Tall Orders and Bar Madrid are two recently opened restaurants that swankily demonstrate a slight change in eating trends. The philosophy is quite straightforward: take an exotic style of food and make it palatable for a mainstream clientele. Previously, this entailed restaurants making a play for (inevitably) diluted authenticity, the English view of the foreign eating experience being rooted mainly in the peasant tradition. Only the French, the Japanese and to a lesser extent the Italians have tended to succeed over here with the supply of upmarket, urban, swish foreign food. The Greeks, Indians, Chinese, and Afro-Caribbeans, meanwhile, have had a plate-smashing field day at the other end of the scale. Gradually this Anglicised version of foreign cooking has become the norm. Curries and gold flock wallpaper are inextricably linked for the majority of people. Most people's idea of Nordic food is no doubt inseperable from the Ikea superstore's canteen special of Swedish meatballs. Even sphaghetti and chips has stopped sounding too unreasonable.

The new wrinkle that Tall Orders and Bar Madrid give the process is that neither one is bothering to feign authenticity. Both restaurants give the impression of being rigorously preplanned affairs. But the homesick expat owner throwing up a few postcards of Athens or a couple of bullfighting posters is not in evidence. Bar Madrid is a tapas bar, a designer tapas bar, to use a dreadfully Eighties epithet. The logo on all the paraphernalia — menus, books of matches etc — all feature the colour scheme. It is a large and long basement with stools, a bar in the middle and a restaurant section at the end. Design House 'created the interior' which gives the traditional Spanish elements a post-modern twist. But there's none of the just-like-home touches other tapas bars use. La Finca in Kennington has a couple of wagon wheels, and sawdust on the floor, for example, and Meson Don Felipe near Waterloo has cramped rustic style wooden booths. Bar Madrid is definitely London Latino chic.

Fortunately the food hasn't been neglected in all the design consciousness. The menu has been tinkered with since its opening in December. For a new restaurant finding its feet this is a good sign. Paellas have been introduced alongside the inauthentically large portions of tapas. The paellas ('made for 2 to 16 friends to enjoy') are hefty pans of good value grub. The Casa Paella Especial has a distinctly inauthentic seafood-rice ratio — far too much seafood, but that isn't a complaint — as well as chunks of pork, chicken and chorizo sausage. All this can be happily washed down with currently fashionable — catch them while they're still trendy — beers like San Miguel and Sol to a soundtrack of the Gypsy Kings and the odd lambada.

Tall Orders is a little more complicated. Not only is the interior post-modern, with Pompidou-style blue pipes visible on the ceiling, but the food is too. The restaurant's novelty — which will no doubt be adopted by a few other places soon — is the use of … Actually the press release describes it in incomparably evocative terms: 'Tall Orders breaks all the rules of the traditional restaurant, heralding a new decade with a totally unique concept in dining.' Oh you lucky people, not a partially unique concept, but a totally unique concept. The concept is 'the novel mode of service whereby a range of dishes is delivered to the table in a dramatic tower of stacked baskets.'

Despite the dim sum baskets, the food is a mix of Mediterranean dishes with Moroccan and Italian flourishes. You can order by the tower or pick your own selection. The Emerald Tower is the vegetarian option and the Fairy Storey is for — oh come on, behave — kids. Real gluttons can scale the Pudding Tower — pure desserts. The savoury dishes include salmon carpaccio, spiced meatballs with puntaletta, Cotechino sausage with lentils and peppers, and spinach tagliatelli with a sliver of salmon and some cream and lemon. These are all fairly tasty with nothing too jarring. The decor actually promises more than the food delivers, but then the food is very fairly priced. It is reminiscent of a dependable place like a Pizza Express, a decent place where you're not going to buckle your flexible friend.

There is a drawback with the dim sum basket towers. If they are placed on the table they have an odd effect on the speed of your eating. You feel obliged to guzzle through each tier just to get the tower out the way and on with the more sociable aspects of the meal. Like seeing the person you're speaking to. Some tables have a smaller table pulled alongside to store the obtrusive towers, which should come as standard really. The other odd design drawback is the toilets. According to Martin Amis, fearless post-modern fiction writers should cross the taboo threshold into these rooms quite happily. Food writers as well, presumably. If you're a female at Tall Orders you won't actually need to enter the Gents to see what it's like. The mirror opposite the door is so unfortunately angled that it unblinkingly reveals the vista of urinals, not to say users. Then again this may just be the extensive application of the post-modern architecture aesthetic. You know, having all the pipes visible. ∎

Bar Madrid, 4 Winsley Street, London W1 (436 4650). £30 for two. Tall Orders, 676 Fulham Road, SW6 (371 9673). £40 for two.

'We'd better wash it first.'

The pleasures of not-quite-great music

Give your ears a holiday. ROBERT HARTFORD has some suggestions

Fed up with Masterpieces? Bored by Great Music? As daunted as I am by the prospect of yet another soul-searing encounter with the Immortal? Never fear, for there is a vast reservoir of second- and third-rate music that will provide many a happy hour's listening with no challenge to your sanity or way of life. I am thinking of stuff from the likes of Glazunov, Saint-Saëns, and all those sons of J. S. Bach – stylish, well-crafted music that may be no more memorable than its duration but which is pleasing enough while it lasts.

Now, you are unlikely to come across the sort of music I have in mind in the concert hall because there self-important promoters and proud orchestras deal only in Imperishable Masterpieces. No, if you wish to engage in a bit of musical slumming you will need to turn to Britain's independent record companies, small and enterprising outfits such as Hyperion, Chandos and Nimbus that thrive on widening musical horizons to a most welcome degree.

For a number of years now Chandos has braved the Celtic twilight to seek an end to the late-Romantic outpourings of Arnold Bax and concludes its cycle with his Symphony No. 7, played for all its indulgent worth by the London Philharmonic, conducted by Bryden Thomson (*CHAN 8628*) and, as if one foot in the bog was not enough, it moves on to the real Irish boyoh himself, Charles Villiers Stanford, whose Symphony No 6, coupled with Irish Rhapsody No 1, recorded by the Ulster Orchestra under Vernon Handley (*CHAN 8627*) falls into place here most fittingly; engagingly lyrical and troubling not a jot.

Stanford and his fellow-academic, Hubert Parry (the one ran the Academy, the other the College) meet up on one of Hyperion's cunningly-conceived discs where Capricorn plays each of their Nonets (*CDA 66291*); Stanford goes for wind and strings, Parry for wind alone, and both embrace an eighteenth-century serenade style that tempers ambition with due modesty. Also from Hyperion, always a label worth watching, a collection of the urbane Francis Poulenc's Sinfonietta, and Aubade, plus Reynaldo Hahn's *Le Bal de Beatrice d'Este*, with Ronald Corp's New London Orchestra catching Gallic spirit for these witty excursions

into the Beau Monde (*CDA 66347*).

Mendelssohn's 12 String Symphonies, played on three Nimbus CDs (*5141-43*) by the English String Orchestra, conducted by William Boughton, show just how ingratiating a precocious fifteen-year-old can be without once getting out of his – or anybody else's – depth. But

For musical slumming, turn to Britain's independent record companies

another Nimbus disc (*5174*), some fourteen songs by Carl Michael Bellman, is a real corker. Bellman, a Swedish contemporary of Mozart, wrote dozens of wayward, sardonic numbers on the life of a drunken watchmaker called Fredman and his circle of dissolutes; sung here in English by Martin Best, who accompanies himself as did Bellman on cyster and guitar, they are indeed diverting to a degree.

I would be as remiss if I gave the impression

these independents dealt solely in trifles as if I suggested the big boys never touch them. For here is Decca, ranging splendidly from Bizet's *Jeux d'enfants* to Ibert's sly *Divertissement*, by way of Satie's *Gymnopedies* and all the hits of Chabrier, Saint-Saëns and Dukas played by Charles Dutoit and the world's best French orchestra: the one from Montreal (*421 527-2*). And Philips, with Antonio de Almeida conducting Ballet Music from the operas of Rossini (*422 843-2*) and Verdi (*422 846-2*) if you run to a spot of hoofing in *Otello* or *Macbeth*.

From EMI the five hair-raising Piano Concertos of Prokofiev, dashed off brilliantly by Michel Beroff and the Leipzig Gewandhaus Orchestra, conducted by Kurt Masur (*CMS 762542-2*) are a skittish, brittle foil to the post-Wagnerian luxuriance of Alberic Magnard's Symphony No. 3 in a glowing account by Michel Plasson and the Toulouse Orchestra (*CDC 749080-2*), and the descriptive works of Frank Bridge conducted by Charles Groves (*CDM 769870-2*) although one of these, his suite *The Sea*, comes very close to being what I set out to avoid – a true masterpiece.

But when I arrive at the Capriccios, Sinfonies and Hypochondries of Jan Dismas Zelenka, a Bohemian living at the time of Bach and Handel, I am at a loss. This quirky, odd-ball music given by Camerata Bern on DG Archiv (*423 703-2*) intrigues me as much as the Archimboldo painting on the box. The booklet tells of an enigma. I ask: is he being serious? ∎

"It's your fault for insisting we make love on the beach!"

179

Travelling rough

KATE ADIE looks at the coarsening tone of modern guidebooks

R ule One regarding a guidebook: it must not disintegrate easily. Having invested seven shillings and sixpence in *A Guide to Modern Berlin*, I was disappointed to see its back cover fall off after a trampling by an East German soldier. The front cover disappeared a few days later in a small, but intense, riot outside my university lecture room. The remaining pages were abandoned in an incoherent flight from an East Berlin bar, caused by an American fellow-student growing hysterical at his first-ever sight of real live Russians.

Admittedly, that was a Sixties guidebook, having to cope with Sixties problems. Had it survived, it would have faced even worse today: it ignored East Berlin, refused to mention the Wall, and pretended that politics and realism were not the stuff of a well-bred guide.

Many dignified tomes have trodden a similar path: full of Cultural Interests and Historical Facts, tactfully gliding round the problems of travelling in a country run by a crazed administration, crawling with secret police, and unable to display railway timetables – this being 'classified information'. The only hint that another kind of guide existed was the rumoured great American dollar book; tales were told of cunning students from Milwaukee and Idaho, who whizzed about the world on five dollars a day. They apparently carried a subversive manual which concentrated on living cheaply, rather than travelling as a piece of cultural blotting-paper.

Years later, the subversive has gently triumphed: travellers can get their paws on publications which concentrate on essentials; like survival. Rather than burden the reader with chapters of topographical notes, they have handy tips on Getting There.

But before you invest considerably more than seven and sixpence, perhaps you should question whether you really need a guidebook at all. Millions achieve satisfying holidays in foreign parts with no more than a routemap to Luton airport, or the ability to recognise that Gatwick *is* an airport and not a shopping centre. Why should you feel any guilt at having hand-baggage which contains a tacky potboiler novel, instead of a travel bible? Is there any need for you to digest the historical facts and cultural heritage of your destination, when you have never spent a moment considering these matters before a trip to Birmingham or Anglesey? Do you really wish to spend two expensive weeks studying a country? Come off it. Staring at it, yes. Swatting it up, no.

Not that ignorance and incuriosity should be part of your luggage, it's just that a charter-flight or a Channel crossing have rarely been known to *induce* intellectual thirst or academic craving. Certainly, there's no excuse for remaining indifferent to the architectural or artistic glories which litter the traveller's path; but it's much more interesting to chat up the locals, or point and mime 'What's that?', than to wait while a bookworm digs through old cheese rolls, mosquito

Kate Adie is Chief News Correspondent for BBC Television. She consulted: The Rough Guide To Eastern Europe (*Harrap, £7.95*) Eastern Europe On A Shoestring (*Lonely Planet £9.95*) Let's Go – Budget Guide To Europe, Let's Go – Budget Guide To Israel & Egypt (*Pan, £11.99, £10.99*) Official Guide Book of China (*£10.95*)

repellant, and spare socks to regale you with information from page 143, delivered with scholarly tedium.

So you may not need a guidebook. You're definitely unlikely to need it for the 'handy phrases' at the back. I have yet to encounter one which translates: 'Do not point that gun at me,' or 'Do we eat this or kill flies with it?' And by the time you've mastered 'When is the train leaving?' in any language, it will have left, been cancelled, or – in the Soviet Union – ceased to exist. This kind of information now appears in the ever-growing number of guides coyly self-described as Rough, Budget or On A Shoestring. The economic aspect is not the point. They are basically blunt, honest, and occasionally rude; their handy phrase chapters include 'What's up?' in Bulgarian, and 'There is none' in Polish. The *Rough Guide to Eastern Europe* even provides the lowdown on downtown Hungarian bars, adding that you won't need to learn *ne fogdoss* – 'keep your hands to yourself.'

The kind of information which comes in these guides acknowledges that life is not perfect. A small army of contributors gratefully saluted in an incomprehensible foreward testifies to having slogged through every conceivable travel mishap, and comes up with jolly, sympathetic observations: the *Let's Go Budget Guide to Europe* reports: 'buying train tickets in Romania will make you feel like you're being punished by God.' These modern guides don't avoid realities: war, riots, sneaky security people, unmentionable diseases, black-market money changers. So discard any dog-eared, sniffy book that fails, for example, to mention the subject of alternative currency. Virtually any economy that has a problem, has a way round it involving tourists. Failure to mention this indicates that the guidebook has been issued by the state tourist bureau, or written by someone whose research journey was paid for entirely by someone else.

Spotting a government guide is simple: merely look up the potted description under 'Our Nation Today'; if it's lavishly favourable, then the rest of the information will be equally out of focus. For instance, 'democratic accountability' figures large in the *Official Guidebook to China*. You have been warned. Also, official publications everywhere rarely suggest that there is anything other than unruffled peace throughout the land. And it is true that tourists have sometimes seen warfare as merely another dratted thing that the brochure omitted to mention: tales emerged from the last bust-up in Cyprus, of angry tourists asserting that as their country wasn't taking part in the surrounding hostilities, they were fully entitled to remain immune, on the beach, watching things go bang. However, realistic guides from non-government sources, should not, and do not mince words. *Let's Go to Israel and Egypt*, having printed an official statement advising against travel to the West Bank, immediately assumes that its readers will go there anyway; so it grabs the prickly cactus of traveller mid *intifada*, and gives practical advice. It also imparts an elementary Arabic phrase for use throughout the Middle East when someone attempts to overcharge you: *mish mumkin* – 'impossible'. The guide suggests you never say this. You shout it.

'Twas ever thus: early Baedeker in Italy recommends that 'importunate beggars should be dismissed with *niente* or by a gesture of negation'. One suspects the modern, rougher guide would describe the gesture. So if you feel you need to travel with book in hand, choose one with a sense of reality, and a sense of humour: travel consists of two states – movement and waiting. You will need the guide for the waiting bits. And never use a guidebook in a riot; *The Times Atlas* gives more protection. ■

Dulled wine
Crate bores of today

THERE IS NO shortage of contenders for the title of Most Boring Wine in the World. If we meet the Most Boring Person in the World at a party, we excuse ourselves to go and chat to the wall; so the most boring wines send us scuttling for a glass of water, however contaminated it may be.

In my experience, whites are more boring than reds. Imagine being stuck with Lutomar Laski Riesling or Liebfraumilch all evening: worse than a month watching paint dry. Yet they are comparatively interesting. The ones that would really have me bouncing off the walls of my padded cell come from Spanish co-operatives. Like those in La Mancha.

The grape variety is their big handicap. You must have come across the question, probably from that chap at the party: 'Which is the world's most widely planted grape variety?' You are expected to reel off Chardonnay, Cabernet Sauvignon, Muller-Thurgau and so forth, and then, if you're not already deep in conversation with the wall, he tosses out 'Airén,' with a triumphant smirk. At that point most people slope off for more water, but there is always one who says 'Airén? How fascinating.'

The next two hours are taken up with an explanation that this vast plain near Madrid produces nearly half of all Spanish wine; that the DO is bigger than any French AC or Italian DOC, but that even this accounts for only a fraction of the total wine produced in the La Mancha region, and so on. Be warned: the wine that Airén makes is even less interesting than the statistics.

I mention all this because of a recent change of heart. I had previously considered the Chenin Blanc grape to be among the world's worst raw material for wine, since it makes some of the Loire's most mundane dry whites. Now I am not so sure. For one thing, it makes glorious sweet wines in Vouvray, and in Coteaux du Layon, particularly Bonnezeaux and Quarts de Chaume. These honeyed, apricotty delights are fabulous, if you have the patience to wait 25 years for a good vintage to mature. For another, it makes pippin-fresh sparkling Saumur, crisp as a new fiver, which is one of France's best non-Champagne fizzes.

Both these take advantage of Chenin's most distinctive characteristic, its searing wipe-the-smile-off-your-face acidity. This apple-tart freshness balances the slightly cloying sweetness of Coteaux du Layon wines, and exposes the raw, jingly-jangly nerves of sparkling Saumur.

But when barely-ripened, over-cropped Chenin is just made into an ordinary, still dry wine, when there is no skin contact during fermentation and hence no flavour to speak of, then it is dull in the extreme. Taking the edge off with a little sweetness, making it medium-dry, is no solution at all. The top dry Chenins – Coulée de Serrant and La Roche Aux Moines, or Vouvrays from Huet, Brédif and Poniatowski – are very good but not cheap. If I want a daily dry white from the Loire, I would take a Sauvignon Blanc every time.

What is more, I had previously thought that wherever Chenin cropped up in the rest of the world it fared no better. But now Thresher is selling one from South Australia's McLaren Vale. The 1988 Tatachilla Hill (£3.99), made at the Southern Vales Winery, is all that a two year-old Chenin should be. Pungently apple-fresh, with a slightly nutty, quince-like flavour reminiscent of some of Italy's best whites, it is as pure an example of the young, off-dry style as we are likely to taste. If it seems excessively, clincially clean from its cool fermentation, then perhaps we can excuse the Aussie obsession in return for such a bright and lively new perspective on the grape.

I am not saying it is everybody's cup of tea – although it does come half-way to meet us by having the sharp edges knocked off to give it as much easy, rounded drinkability as is consistent with Chenin's spiky temperament – but it lifts it way out of the boring category. You could almost have fun with this at a party. ■
JAMES AINSWORTH

Muir the merrier

MILES KINGTON puts Frank Muir's ultimate comic prose collection to the ultimate test – does it make you laugh?

The Oxford Book of Humorous Prose
Edited by Frank Muir (*OUP*, £17.50)

THERE ARE TWO ways of acquiring a university education in Britain. One is by going to university and acquiring it, after which you more or less stop learning anything new. The other is by learning nothing much until other people are actually leaving university and being so galvanised by the thought of never having been there that you start learning and never stop. I chose the first course. I studied French and German literature at Oxford, and I can honestly say that what I learnt there about the art of comic writing could be written on a gnat's backside.

I can remember the thing I learnt, actually; it was that Voltaire was a great comic writer and could time a gag better than anyone in the 18th century.

'Right, next week we go on to Rousseau,' said my Voltaire tutor.

'Couldn't we do one more week on Voltaire?', I asked, aghast at the thought of tackling a man who had no sense of humour and was furthermore said to have invented socialism.

'I think our coverage is quite adequate for exam purposes.'

It was at that point I conceived a triple hatred of exams, syllabuses and Rousseau. Had I but known it, I could have waited 30 years and bought this wonderful book by Frank Muir, which is an education in comic writing as full as anyone could receive. Rightly or wrongly, I see Muir as belonging rather to the second group, the chaps who evaded university and have spent their adult life giving themselves a degree course. If so, it's fitting that this book, which must have taken him about 500 years to do (the same period, by a coincidence, which he covers), was commissioned by the OUP. One can visualise the phone call.

'Oxford University Press here, Muir. For your next project we'd like you to do your essay on humorous prose. Lots of illustrations from the masters, some historical examples, a few puns of the day, that sort of thing. With your own linking commentary. OK?'

'Yes, all right. About how long?'

'Oh, 1,000 pages, give or take.'

'Jolly good. Give me 500 years, give or take.'

'No problem. Come round for a sherry when it's finished.'

And now, 500 years later, here it is. You can tell it took him a long time from the fact that he consulted P G Wodehouse personally about what bits he wanted in, and Wodehouse died in 1975. That's what I call research.

Anyway, I tried all known ways of testing an anthology. First of all, I set out to read it all the way through, and I can record that I smiled at the very first extract (from Caxton), had already laughed aloud by 1642 (p.16) and heard myself roaring briefly with laughter on page 23 at something from Aubrey's Brief Lives, even though I had encountered the joke before.

Then I gave up reading all the way through, which I realised would also take about 500 years, and decided to apply the tricky test of seeing if he had included any of the off-the-beaten-path stuff which I could condemn him for not including. This included:

Something from Brigadier Gerard, the Conan Doyle creation you can still turn to when you're tired of Holmes; a surrealist playlet by Ring Lardner; something by D B Wyndham Lewis, the apparently forgotten man who started Beachcomber and was Timothy Shy; anything by H L Mencken, Ambrose Bierce, Frank Sullivan or A J Liebling.

He had them all, except Liebling. I then examined it for boringly predictable chronology and geography. Not guilty, again. He likes to pursue an idea wherever it takes him – for instance, after an extract from (of course) *Three Men In A Boat* followed by (of course) Mr Pooter, where do you go next? Daisy Ashford? Too easy – in fact, he's off to Australia for a quick tour of contemporary humour down there. Similarly the segue from Tom Sawyer to Alice is exactly right, heralding a switch from a long American section into a long English section, even though there is not much in common between Twain and Carroll. His sequences of ideas have all the freshness of a good conversation.

I was a bit surprised, actually. Previous book and radio compilations by Frank Muir have tended to the over-twinkly and arch, where a joke or quote masks the lack of a real link. In this book, I don't think he attempts a single joke. Admittedly, he does attempt a few theories in the introduction, but the only one which opened my eyes was the thought that in the 18th century it was thought impolite, if not boorish, to laugh out loud.

Still, theories about humour are a waste of time; what is important is that Frank Muir's comments on individual writers are well thought out, often deeply impressive, as the thoughts of a craftsman on other craftsmen should be, and I learnt a lot. I met writers I'd never heard of, many of them, and lots that I'd only heard of and not met. Where things are not funny, they are usually highly interesting, and only seldom do you wonder why he has given something house room. (The Kipling short story, for example, goes on and on…)

I WAS GLAD to learn that Twain quotes a sort of early Franglais. I was intrigued to know that nobody understood an early *Punch* cartoon by Thackeray, so much so that another magazine ran a competition to have it explained, to which there was no winner. Actually, by this time I was adopting the only possible method of testing an anthology like this, which was sitting down and just enjoying it.

I fancy it may not be approved of in academic circles, both for the chatty tone of the links and the lack of scholarly apparatus, but any anthology of humour which is given academic respectability is not worth its weight in mouse turds. The Muir book is like a wonderful party at which everyone worthwhile has turned up, and you get to talk to all of them.

Well, not quite everyone. There are one or two empty areas. There's not many postwar American men – no Russell Baker, no Woody Allen, no J D Salinger, nor the man they're saying is the funniest in America today, and I think he is: Dave Barry. And not enough of today's women. On *Bookshelf* the other day, Jilly Cooper nominated Barbara Pym as her funniest writer of this century. Neither of them is in this book, nor are Katharine Whitehorn, Nora Ephron…

Otherwise no criticisms. This is a labour of love. Also of sweat, toil, pain, exclusion, agonising, rejection, reinclusion, doubt, reading, writing and madness. Luckily, Muir did all that for us, so we could get on and educate ourselves at his expense. Between 1477 and 1977, I can't imagine there being a better traveller's guide to humour's top spots. It's a great book. I look forward to finishing it. ∎

Protest and survive

NORMAN TEBBIT looks at the life of Russian rebel Boris Yeltsin

Against the Grain
Boris Yeltsin (*Jonathan Cape*, £12.95)

Boris Yeltsin's book is more a tirade of somewhat sanctimonious self-justification than an autobiography. It is a book to be read, not in the expectation of a great literary experience, but as a unique insight into the socialist system in the Soviet Union. The pity is that Yeltsin is so earnest and so determined to tell us how good he is that he comes over as a prig. I suspect this has something to do with his style which to western readers has a stilted and dated ring. His account of how he virtuously refused to accept the Communist Party payola of rich and easy living for *apparatchiks* is redolent of those 19th-century missionaries who retained their virtue despite being so sorely tempted by the loose-living native women of the Polynesian islands.

For all that it has some entertaining moments, not least the description of his christening when he was amongst the dozen babies to be baptised by a drunken peripatetic priest. Having immersed the young Yeltsin in the font the priest, distracted by an argument, forgot to take him out. Fortunately his mother realised that something had gone wrong and saved him from an early death by drowning in holy water.

> ## The dirty tricks Mr Yeltsin claims were used against him go far beyond those of Watergate

Born within a few weeks of each other, neither Yeltsin nor I had much luck in the circumstances of our births, but his story of poverty and misery amongst the peasantry in Sverdlousk leaves me doubting that I ever knew real hardship in my own childhood. The death of the family's horse and cow forced them to leave the land and join the urban poor, living in a single room of a communal hut allocated to the gang of construction labourers in which his father had found work. There Yeltsin tells us he slept on the floor huddled together in the Russian winter with his parents, brother and sister and the family goat. She was, he says, as warm as a stove and it was by her warmth and her milk that the ill-clad and poorly fed family survived (the goat, not the sister). It was, he observes, a 'fairly joyless time' during which the Yeltsins had only one aim – to survive.

By his own account Mr Yeltsin was a natural leader and his tales of mischief-making at school suggest there is more humour in the man than the book reveals. However, the energy, drive and reckless streak which were part of the schoolboy Yeltsin remained with him through a remarkably stormy career as a member of the ruling elite under Breznhev as well as Gorbachev.

Having graduated as a civil engineer Mr Yeltsin began his career as a technocrat, struggling against the baffling byzantine bureaucracy and endemic corruption riddling Russia's socialist system. Like any professional engineer he was frustrated by such inane demands that as manager of a construction enterprise he was required, at times, to attend as many as 22 separate meetings being held simultaneously in different places. But despite his antipathy to the system – pure bolshiness one might describe it in any other context – he was steadily promoted. Inevitably that took him out of direct management and into politics, to head the provincial committee of the Communist Party responsble for construction.

By 1986 Mr Yeltsin had arrived from his provincial origins and was head of the Moscow city committee of the Communist Party, in effect the chief executive of the city. He paints a vivid picture of the incompetence and corruption which he found. Despite all Mr Yeltsin's energy and his purges (two-thirds of his district secretaries were replaced, 800 people were convicted of corruption), he confesses that he could never touch the big operators of a black economy which accounted for approximately 15% of retail trade, nor the top 'mafia' criminals linked to senior political figures.

He was rewarded with his appointment as a candidate member of the Politburo, but his abrasive style led to conflict with Mr Gorbachev and a sideways move from the sensitive Moscow secretaryship. His vigorous boat rocking was too much for the more gradualist Mr Gorbachev and no doubt Mr Yeltsin's refusal to accept the staggering privileges of his rank must have embarrassed his colleagues. If Westminster were Moscow, Sir Geoffrey Howe would have had no cause to moan about his official residence! Mr Yeltsin was entitled not only to his dacha, but his Moscow domestic staff included three cooks, three waitresses, a housemaid, a gardener and a team of under-gardeners as well. This was apart from his driver and the KGB bodyguard who fixed supplies of exclusive food and drink, medical treatment, holidays and every aspect of queue-jumping in a queue-ridden society. For the upper classes in this classless society every traffic light is turned to green both literally and metaphorically.

Much of Mr Yeltsin's story is about his election campaign to become a Soviet parliamentarian of the new style. The dirty tricks operation which he claims was mounted against him by the Communist establishment goes far beyond the wildest allegations in the Watergate affair.

But what does the book tell us of Mr Yeltsin, Mr Gorbachev or contemporary Russia? Well, Russia comes out as a hell-hole of incompetence, corruption and poverty ruled by the greediest and most power-drunk politicians outside the third world, but somehow struggling to the realisation that things must change if the Soviet Union is to be saved from disintegration.

Readers will be left wondering if Mr Gorbachev has fought for power to reform the system or has used the need for reform to ride to power within the system, as Mr Yeltsin seems to suggest. And Mr Yeltsin? His book leaves him an unconvincing two-dimensional figure. Is that the limitation of his literary style or simply the nature of his personality? I am left wanting to meet this man to talk to him and see if he is real. But the book itself is more than a small good deed in a naughty world. It is a brave act of real virtue in a society so wicked as that built by Stalin and his heirs. ∎

The Rt Hon. Norman Tebbit is the Conservative Member of Parliament for Chingford. He is a recent Punch *cover star (9 February 1990), and his autobiography,* Upwardly Mobile, *was published last year. It is not known whether Mr Yeltsin has had time to read it yet.*

Hardly annuals

CRAIG BROWN on the 1989 news annual

Chronicle of the Year 1989 (*Longman Chronicle, £5.95*)

Alexander Dubček gets four mentions, Sonia Sutcliffe, Austria and Eduard Shevardnadze three, Rajiv Gandhi, the Queen, Mark Thatcher, Syria and Kylie Minogue two, Diane Thatcher and Colonel Gadaffi one, and The Duke and Duchess of York both get no mentions at all.

1989 was that kind of year: rather mixed, like so many of the previous years. I myself had little direct contact with the events chronicled so dutifully and pithily in **Chronicle of the Year 1989**, though I was there to hear Pavarotti sing at the London Arena on 18 June (incidentally sitting next to Jimmy Tarbuck who said 'Thanks, love' when I lent him my Biro to sign a Pavarotti programme for a fan), and a day or two before Ken Dodd was cleared of his tax charges on 21 July, I was walking past two workmen in Holborn when one of them pointed at me and whispered loudly to his mate, 'Oi, that's Doddy, innit?'. I spent the rest of the day trying to brush down my hair and not open my mouth.

But, aside from these two meagre points of contact, I had little sway over the events of 1989. Reading this book, it doesn't seem to matter. An endless succession of events which might have encouraged the reader to believe in an unstoppable world conspiracy of earthquakes, train crashes, governments overthrown and nuclear threats is turned by the *Chronicle* into something sweet and cosy. The distress of the innocent bystander soon dissolves into the mawkish fascination of the gawping onlooker, and any worries about being a small pawn are soon forgotten.

One way the *Chronicle* series achieves this snugness is by reporting everything week by week in the present tense. Paradoxically (a word with which every journalist worth his salt who wrote a decade article in late December kicked off at least one sentence) this has the effect of making even recent events seem all the more distant and pre-ordained. Reading the *Chronicle* is like watching repeats of a soap opera six months later: where once one felt excitement and apprehension, one now feels a sense of inevitability. This is aided by the neat repetitiveness of the lay-out and the ubiquitous paciness of the prose: everything fits into place, and everything sounds roughly like everything else, and the space on page 104 seems as if it must have been reserved years ago for the picture of the dead Ceaucescu.

The main soaps running through this book are the will they/won't they question on the release of Nelson Mandela, the swift spin of elation into misery at Tiananmen Square and the non-stop tale of Salman Rushdie, which now seems doomed to be a perpetual cliff-hanger. As in soap opera, the conclusion of a particular storyline is often hard to discern because other storylines have already rushed into take its place. Hence the story of the rise and fall of John Moore MP through 1987, when he was widely tipped as the next Conservative leader, through his splutterings and blunders of 1988, in real life reached its sorry end in 1989 with his dismissal from the Cabinet. But by then everyone had forgotten who he was, so that his one and only entry in *Chronicle of the Year 1989* is on 11 May, when, still as Secretary of State for Social Security, he says that his critics are politically motivated people who would 'find poverty in paradise'. After that, not a blip or a glimmer: he simply disappears.

Every year has its copycat stories from all the years that have gone before, though for some reason there was a dearth of tug-of-love-baby-dramas in the second half of the last decade. Nevertheless, 1989 found its loony Californian mass-murderer, its (albeit Japanese) politician caught with his pants down, its water shortage in the West Country, its top-level investigation into police corruption, its fresh health scares, its loopy pronouncement from the Bishop of Durham and its Row Over Royal Portrait all delivered safe and sound. If there is a fault in the design of *Chronicle of the Year* it lies in its inability to give due space to the constant story or personality which never quite boils over into hard news. The absence of the Duchess of York, for instance, seems to me to have rather less to do with chronicling and rather more to do with wishful thinking. The Princess of Wales is mentioned just once, when someone lunges at her. Jeffrey Archer, the thinking man's Duchess of York, merits only two mentions, once as a best-selling author of the year, and a second time only as a precedent-setter for the Sonia Sutcliffe libel award, yet for me his grinning presence seemed to permeate every week of the year. On an even more personal level, I have found that every newspaper and television programme for the last three or four years has featured items about Sally Burton, widow of Richard, either coming to terms with her grief or modelling a new line of clothes, or sometimes both at the same time. Sally Burton this, Sally Burton that: obviously, in terms of the Berlin Wall, she is not as historic or even as divisive, but she seems to be built of tougher stuff, and her continued presence in public life would have found a small space in any truly omniscient chronicle of our times.

Any writing which eschews the coat of drabness is bound, from time to time, to flash its bias. 'Brave Backbencher Stands Against PM' is the headline given to Sir Anthony Meyer's challenge for the Conservative leadership on 23 November. A touch of jealousy can also be detected from time to time: at the end of the little obituary given to Georges Simenon: 'He also claimed to have slept with 10,000 women, an unlikely figure'. Unlikely maybe, but not impossible: Tony Blackburn claims to have slept with 500 women, and for Georges Simenon to claim that he is 20 times more attractive than Tony Blackburn does not strike me as remotely far-fetched. Other snippets of idiosyncratic writing are just plain odd. A mini-profile of Sir Alan Walters, to tie in with the Lawson resignation debacle, begins, over-yobbishly 'And who is Sir Alan Walters anyway?' and ends, cryptically, 'Whatever she thinks about Mr Lawson, she is sorry to lose Sir Alan. Her father kept a grocer's shop. He once tried a grocery business – and failed'. Eh?

The editors of this book should be commended for fighting off the temptation to express an 'overview' of the year, relating the end of the Berlin Wall to the return of the polo-neck to the appointment of Mrs Esteve-Coll to the emergence of Acid House, and so on. Instead, the reporting is commendably straight, commendably unconnected, commendably meaningless.

Queen's evidence

CHAPMAN PINCHER on the leaky craft of double agent Tom Driberg

Tom Driberg – His Life and Indiscretions *Francis Wheen* (Chatto and Windus £18)

NO SENSE OF EVIL would have been a more fitting title for this book because, as its contents confirm, its subject was not only an inveterate pouncing homosexual who corrupted youths and had been a male prostitute, but was incapable of filial affection, loyalty, honesty, gratitude, or grief. His only pleasant feature was charm, an essential qualification for the successful deceiver.

The author seems offended that when Tom Driberg, then Lord Bradwell, died in 1976, aged 71, *The Times* obituary mentioned that he had been a homosexual. It would have been dishonest otherwise, for his compulsive homosexual promiscuity dominated his life. Though it also dwelt on Driberg's journalistic, political and social life, it was incomplete because his role as an agent of MI5 and later of Soviet Bloc intelligence was then unknown.

The late Lord Rothschild once said to me, cryptically as usual, 'Driberg's life would repay study. I am not referring to his homosexuality.' Mr Wheen claims that when interviewing me for a magazine at my home I agreed that Driberg would make an interesting subject for a biography and that he set about it quickly for fear that I might do the job. Having read *Ruling Passions*, Driberg's own account of his sordid adventures with rough trade – mainly administering what Mr Wheen calls 'blow-jobs' – there was no way that I was prepared to descend into that cesspit. Presumably, after his service as a contributor to *Gay News*, Mr Wheen had no revulsion. Indeed he not only recycles the worst incidents with relish but introduces new ones which involve some distinguished people and may be untrue.

A look at the source-notes suggests that this book is in part a scissors job, a rip-off at £18, put together with paste and with venom for those, like myself, who despised Driberg, whom I knew, not only for his habits but his treacherous character. I am referred to as an 'official urinal' where high officers of MI5, MI6, Chiefs of Staff, politicians and others queue to leak. Since prime source leaks are the life-blood of investigative writing I take this as a compliment and appreciate that 'urinal' must readily have come to mind because Driberg – according to Mr Wheen – often spent several hours a day at such places looking for takers. Reliable sources can leak at this urinal any time and they still do.

Though Mr Wheen knows nothing about the intelligence world and would not be allowed near it, he gaily dismisses the information released to me about Driberg's secret service life by Peter Wright and other MI5 officers who were involved in his activities. In actual fact Driberg did penetrate the Communist Party on behalf of MI5 and later reported regularly on the Labour Party even while he was chairman in 1958. In 1969 he was exposed to MI5 as a paid agent of Czech intelligence and admitted it, claiming that he had only supplied internal information about the Labour Party and politicians. Driberg, who would do anything for money of which he was always short, was bribed back to MI5. He then operated as a double with the KGB which gave him two identical brief-cases, one for the reports, doctored by MI5, which he handed over to Russians in London, the other for the large payments in bank-notes, from which he abstracted 'expenses' before handing them in to MI5. The secret behind Driberg's notoriously blatant homosexual behaviour, at a time when it was a criminal offence, was the MI5 telephone number which he could trot out if caught in the act. Anthony Blunt enjoyed the same privilege.

Is Mr Wheen naive enough to swallow Driberg's claim that, in 1956, the KGB allowed Guy Burgess to give him material for a book about his defection and life in Moscow unsupervised? Or that Burgess was never a Soviet agent? Perhaps he is because he believes Driberg's story that Burgess, also a rapacious pouncer who had been in Moscow for nearly five years, had failed to find a homosexual partner until shown a urinal there by Driberg.

Because Driberg was playing both ends, as he so often did, the Burgess book was controlled by the KGB and MI5 for their different purposes. The difference between my account and Mr Wheen's is that I was there dealing with the security authorities and with Driberg himself.

The author is miffed that neither Lord Callaghan nor Lord Wyatt would deal with him. When he showed up at my house my wife urged me to get rid of him which we did as expeditiously as possible without giving the type of offence he enjoys handing out to others not of the same political persuasion.

Mr Wheen's researches show that, while Driberg fawned on violent criminals, he was unkind to his mother and unrelentingly sadistic towards the wife who married him believing that they could live in affectionate, if sexless, companionship. He was cravenly offensive to waiters and servants who could not retaliate. As Mr Wheen shows, his record as a politician representing other people's interests is grotesque. He was rarely on constituency duty, preferring foreign trips, and was bored stiff when he was. He left no political mark. According to Mr Wheen, Driberg regarded young men's semen as an elixir to be imbibed daily even

into his seventies, when he remained active in spite of various disabilities. Had he lived in the AIDS era he would not have survived so long. The elixir did not work. He died of a heart attack in a taxi he had hailed at Paddington probably after dropping in, hopefully, at the station urinal. ■

Chapman Pincher is the author of Their Trade Is Treachery.

I shall be staying in this time. The feast of St Valentine will pass me by. The nasty jangling little time-bombs of self-regard and betrayal can stay unpublished, nor will the greetings-card industry have any fiscal assistance from me. There is so little point in bothering.

I suppose this means that I have lost a grip on the *Zeitgeist* but who cares about the *Zeitgeist* anyway? The only interesting thing about it is that we don't have our own word for it, though oddly enough we seem more obsessed with it than any other nation on earth. I have had to read a number of women's magazines lately and they all seem obsessed with the notion that life is about being different today than you were yesterday.

They are wrong, of course. Life is all about deciding who you are and staying like it, even if you are wrong, but that won't do for the women's magazines. Oh no. You have to overturn your life, change your wardrobe, paint your face differently, shed your job, dump your man, lose unsightly fat, liberate yourself from the misery of painful periods, learn from others, share your experiences, face reality, take control of your relationships, buy a new car and learn how to show yards of slim, five-denier leg as you get out of it outside the Soho Brasserie to have dinner with a man in a slightly-dated black Armani suit who is, O my *gawd*, even wittier than John Sessions, never mind the sheer scrumptious mouth-watering, everythingelse-watering hunky *yumminess* of (*insert name of skilfully-marketed showbiz personality*) and a schlong like a stovepipe.

This is the Dream of the Nineties, and what you will do, girlies, is pair-bond. There's you with your reconstructed half-consciousness, and there's him with his subtly potent range of toiletries. I see (rubs crystal ball, peers in, sees reflection of grey, puffy 'face', recoils) you going back to His Place which of course is decorated in perfect taste. I see you smiling to yourself as you observe the wittily rococo decor. Pickled pitchpine, frescos, gilded gesso, bloody grapes and fruit everywhere. His spinet stands in a corner and apsley yards and yards of raw silk drape the Napoleonic daybed standing by the bonsai baobab from which Chatterton, a raven, taunts the two grey Persian cats circling beneath. A decanter of madeira – I was going to say mead, but I thought, fuck it – is decorously sipped from those nasty greenish glasses with the odd bubble in them because, frankly, they weren't much good at making glasses in those days. A little Orlando Lassus is … no, whoops, a little Monteverdi, the better class of Monteverdi, *Il Combattimento*, perhaps, is dispensed from the… no, what is dispensed from the gramophone (concealed behind a trompe l'oeil screen) is Handel. *The Triumph of Time and Truth*. The first version of 1703 if I'm not much mistaken, note the sublime sensuality and yet incorruptible purity of the bending trill on

the last aria, life is…delicate and fine and yet…yet…alone it all seems somehow so, so, oh I don't know, my sweet, it's just that when we met I simply realised that we pass through the world alone and our only chance of salvation is to make that … one might almost say that transcendent and miraculous *connection* with another human being, yes, yes, I speak of marriage, a celebration of our lives entwinéd, children running at one's feet, one does so see oneself as, oh, I don't know, one of those dickheads in a floppy hat out of a Flemish interior, say you will be mine my darling and, together, we will wave ta-ta to the tacky solipsism of the Eighties and welcome in a new era of black-and-white floor tiles, fidelity, and transcendent peace.

And now (*starts to rub ball again, remembers, stops*) I see a decorous but impassioned courtship take place. He bends over you: honeyed breath, eyes clear, something writhing in his irreproachable breeks like two frogs in a washcloth. Perhaps he bites into a ripe peach. You stretch langourously; he, overwhelmed by the promise of your acquiescence, carries you off to his bedroom. Who knows, the floor may even be strewn with rushes but they will be *nice* rushes, changed once a week by the nice young man from Justin de Blank … and he lays you down on the heavy linen sheets and gazes into your eyes and says: No…not now…not yet …I want it to be…*perfect*; when I make love to you I want it to be as man and wife, but, by the way, I have my own business, £150,000 a year and the house is paid for.

This is the Nineties. This is what it is going to be like. Elegant, civilised, monogamous. What a lucky little bimbette you are. Now you can leave that awful job. No need to elbow the men aside. No need to crush your feet into stilettos any longer. Throw away your Rifat Ozbek, pippit, and check into perpetual connubiality, your eyes full of babies. Happiness is striding up over the brow of the hill in its nice shoes and its velvet cloak, whistling *The Sun Has Got His Hat On* and you can stop *thinking*, stop *striving*, the heat is off, the pressure is off, all that self-obsessed status-definition is now just passé.

But who knows, really? Who are the people who *know the truth about what you are like and what it is like*? Yes: the people who do the advertisements. And have you looked at *those*? Have you noticed, darling, how, with your glossy hair and your slim figure, your control and equipoise, your GTi Turbo Convertible and your designer water…have you noticed, chickadee, that you are *alone*? with your cat? Sometimes with your bicycle or your hi-fi system, sometimes with your car, sometimes with your Rolleiflex, sometimes with your espresso, but always *alone*?

So it's going to be an interesting decade, an interesting year, and interesting week. Cut out the Valentines and keep them: next year may be very different: *Is there anyone out there who would like to be called Mister Toad? Luv, your Snugglebums.* ■

BARGEPOLE

From time to time I find myself in Clubs. Sometimes gentlemen's clubs, sometimes nightclubs. 'A victory for new Britain over old Britain'? Good God no. Both are definitely Old.

They are old because the men who go there are no longer young. Gentleman's clubs are full of men trying to make themselves feel younger than they are by pretending to be older than they are. Nightclubs are full of men trying to pull off the same trick by feeding cold champagne to cold young women in the hope of dancing with them, nuzzling them, then taking them off for a poke. Prolepsis made flesh.

Both are unsatisfactory but I suppose the primary difference is hope. Nightclub Man still clings to the hope that one day he will meet the one who will make it all worthwhile. It won't. The juicy baptism of a bimbo's loins cannot sanctify the unlovely struggle for power and money which has destroyed Nightclub Man. There's the vicious trap which springs too late: Nightclub Man wants the power and the money so that he can be part of the Nightclub set of men who are part of the Nightclub set because they've got the power and the money because *then … then* he can meet the sort of girls who go around with the sort of men who are part of the Nightclub set … No other reason. *These girls poke Eurotrash*: they will never, *ever* love him for himself.

But still he struts, he nuzzles, he settles the bill. His suit is Cerutti but his eyes are scared and when he tells her he loves her she thinks: sentimental: how I wish he would stop. He introduces her to his rich and influential friends: M&A specialists, shifty entrepreneurs, fringe-aristo lawyers, sallow poseurs with Bentleys and drivers because they know that Rolls-Royces and chauffeurs are common. She smiles and he thinks: which one will steal her?

Later, if there is a later, he wonders whether she will think less of him if he sucks in his little paunch or not. His platinum wristwatch scratches her buttock and her sighing and melting seems no different to him than all the other sighings and meltings he has pinned to the bed, but neither complains: two vampires, trained to the task: vampires stripped of the rumours of monstrosity are small and frail; their flight is clumsy; blind, they struggle in the dark and cry to find their way.

Failure after failure, ignominy after rejection after hateful revelation, they hope. The going limp. The going off with the chap he introduced her to (more money, bigger car, more power, more influence, bigger dining-room, smarter address). The going round to her flat and finding her in bed tangled up close with some 26-year-old *penniless* swine *actor* (more muscles, more hair, more soul, more *interesting* darling more in *common* darling you *do* understand darling it's been such *fun* but it couldn't *last* darling you must have known that darling but darling I'll *always* treasure the mink and the *lovely lovely lovely* emerald collar darling) when she never curled up with *him* but slept lightly on the far side of the bed.

Hope: the devil's gift: poor carrion hope that makes humanity contemptible. Hope: all they seek in the end is love: intimacy, commitment, preference. But to hell with them. They have career plans and dimmer switches, self-regard, dinner parties; tell lies, boast, spend and trample, wake up in the night crying for examples; their souls are barnacled like hobnail livers; frequently they have enlarged pores and precarious voices; the remote control for the CD lives under the pillow (mood is *so* important).

In the Gentlemen's Club, things are different. Hope? Good God no. So *striving*. No no. Decent food. Spot of Burgundy. Pictures on the wall. Look. That one's a Zoffany, rather good, don't you think? So they say. Personally, I know a lot about art but I don't know what I like. Ha! Ha! Comfortable here, under the stairs, by the fire. I remember the evening when old Father Tendentious from Farm Street set his soutane on fire, wonderful chap, did you know him? Died, of course. Have I seen who? Oh Yes. Rather unsuitable, I'd say, half his age, making a fool of himself, wife's frightfully nice and the soul of discretion but he's a bit of a laughing-stock. Terrible chap, turned up in new clothes with a Porsche … blackballed? Pure caviar, my dear fellow, not a glimmer of white to be seen when we looked in the box.

To be frank, I'd prefer to be Eurotrash, Nightclub Man: give me the big car, the hired man, the shifty occupation, the dodgy honorific, the Gold Card any day. Perhaps it seems odd to you. Being a member of neither sort of place nor ever likely to be; having no money, no power, no status; able to intimidate and boss nobody at all: why, surely I enjoy the greatest gift of all: knowing that I am loved for myself? Well, nuts. The fact is that nobody really gives a toss about me, just like nobody really gives a toss about you either. Trust? Intimacy? Bodies and souls merging as one? Pure fantasy. You might as well believe in Noddy, and while you're at it you might as well be rich and drink a lot and take cocaine and hang out with Nightclub Men and boff a lot of bright sparkling Azzedine Alaïa bimbos-on-the-make.

The only thing that bothers me about this entire strange episode is the prostitute stuff. Everybody seems anxious to prove that they hadn't a clue that Miss Bordes was a prostitute. Why? What is wrong with going around with prostitutes? I frequently go around with a prostitute and have done for years; I am extremely fond of her and she is a fund of excellent stories which I keep to myself; and if it was suggested by my enemies that I *knew* she was a prostitute, I would have to say: yes, one does need at least *one* honest friend.

Sue for damages? I wouldn't dream of it. Nor would that other chap. What was his name? Went around with a hooker; very fond of her; quite open about it. Oh, ages ago. Started a religion; you know the one I mean. ∎

Country Life

The Brontosaurus stamp is one of four dinosaurs in a series which was supposed to embody the business-like image of the now-privatised US Postal Service.

A. MELLIS (*The Guardian Weekly*)

Villagers ploughed their enthusiasm into digging up their best exhibits to go on show, particularly the children.

P. ROSS (*Selby Star*)

Telscombe Council's anti-nudist campaign is a success. New signposts have deterred naturists from baring their all on the seafront. And plain clothes police from Newhaven who are patrolling the area say the number of nudists has declined from more than a hundred to barely one.

J. M. SEGAR (*Brighton & Hove Leader*)

Mafia godmother Carmela Ferro dodged jail for 29 years – by constantly having children. Every time police closed in Ferro made use of an Italian law which rules that a pregnant woman cannot be arrested. But time ran out for Ferro, now 59, when she went through the change of life and last night the mother-of-eight was in a Genoa jail charged with running a Mafia drugs ring.

A. DRYSDALE (*Daily Express*)

'Beats me why newspapers want fuller coverage of TV programmes when there's sod all worth watching…'

Christmas carols were heard early at Stafford magistrates court yesterday when a solicitor's novelty underpants played *Jingle Bells*.

M. IVES-LACY (*The Daily Telegraph*)

We require additional sales people to join our rapidly expanding company. We offer: 1. 6 qualified appointments per day. 2. Basic wage. 3. Choice of company cat.

C. POTTER (*Bath and West Evening Chronicle*)

Maria Castro, an Italian schoolteacher, had no fewer than 12 men wanting to marry her. She decided that a man with a good memory would be an asset, so agreed to marry the first of her suitors who could recite word-perfect a 1,500-line extract from *Romeo and Juliet*. All made the attempt, but the first 11 failed to pass the test. The 12th completed the last few lines in a sleepy voice, then went sound asleep. He had sat up every night for a week learning his lines.

A. DRYSDALE (*Glasgow Evening Post*)

The famous cycling proficiency test is to be replaced by a new road safety scheme. The Rospa education officer, Mr John Richardson, said: 'The proficiency test has become rather pedestrian.'

C. LEWINGTON (*The Observer*)

Chief Inspector Laurie Fray, of Thames Valley police, said the 40,000 crowd at Reading Festival had been generally well behaved. Five hundred people went to the Samaritans' tent feeling lonely.

R. FORD (*The Daily Telegraph*)

A condom machine containing £200 worth of stock has been stolen from a hotel in Bath, Avon. A police spokesman said yesterday: 'We are looking for someone with a very full social diary.'

MISS V. JAMES (*Daily Mirror*)

Pope warns of mass defections.

MRS R. NESHAM (*The Daily Telegraph*)

Four tubby 10-year-old boys were revealed yesterday as the Plum Cake Gang of Sicily. They were caught trundling £500-worth of stolen cake through Trapani in a pram. The leader, called Fattie, confessed to 150 cake shop break-ins. Police found tuck worth £5,000 in their bedrooms.

A. DRYSDALE (*Daily Express*)

A doctor's group has asked the US army to stop paying for a study in which it said hundreds of cats had been shot in the head to help researchers figure out how to get wounded soldiers back to the front line quickly. The main conclusion was that cats stopped breathing as a result.

F. N. CROWDER (*Times Colonist*, British Columbia)